My Heart for His Glory

MY HEART FOR HIS GLORY

Celebrating His Presence

Foreword By
DON MOEN

INTEGRITY
HOUSE™

My Heart for His Glory

Published by Integrity House, a Division of Integrity Media, Inc.
660 Bakers Bridge, Suite 200, Franklin, Tennessee 37067

Devotions copyright © 2002 Integrity Publishers
Devotions written by Debbie Carsten, Greg Asimakoupoulos, and
Carol Chaffee Fielding.

ISBN 1-59145-485-9

06 07 08 09   TCP   6 5 4 3 2 1

Printed in Canada

Be cheerful no matter what; pray all the time; thank God no matter what happens. This is the way God wants you who belong to Christ Jesus to live.

1 THESSALONIANS 5:16-18, THE MESSAGE

Foreword

A New Thing in Your Life

I was on the plane flying to a funeral. My friends Craig and Susan had lost their eight-year-old son in a car accident. They had asked me to speak a few words at the service, but I had absolutely no idea what I as going to say. What can you say in a moment like that? My heart just ached and I looked out the window in silence.

Then the Holy Spirit gently nudged me toward a passage in my Bible where I read the words, "See, I am doing a new thing! Now it springs up; do you not perceive it? I am making a way in the desert and streams in the wasteland" (Isaiah 43:19).

I couldn't get away from a thought that kept echoing in my mind: *God will make a way...when there seems to be no way.* A melody joined the words. The Holy Spirit had written a song in my heart that day, especially for my friends in the midst of tragic loss, but for countless others who have sung those words together on a Sunday morning at church or in another worship setting.

That was one of my most profound moments of experiencing the Word and Spirit in writing a song. I was reminded of another passage from Isaiah where God says: "So will the words that come out of my mouth not come back empty-handed. They'll do the work I sent them to do, they'll complete the assignment I gave them" (55:11 *The Message*). God's words truly did go to work and fulfill their purpose during that funeral and beyond.

Every songwriter creates lyrics and music differently, but I believe the songs that truly speak and minister to people have one thing in common: They are "breathed" by the Holy Spirit. Something mysterious and miraculous happens. The same wonder, healing, deliverance, and call to action the songwriter encounters as he or she writes, is experienced by those who sing the song.

The following daily devotions are inspired by songs that have touched and changed the hearts and lives of millions upon millions of people. I pray that you, too, will experience a "new thing" in your life—a new healing, a new attitude, a new sense of joy, a new spirit of obedience, a new purpose and mission—as you open your heart to Him in praise and worship each day.

Don Moen

Mobile, Alabama

OPEN THE EYES OF MY HEART

Our vision may be twenty-twenty, but how well do we see with the "eyes of our hearts"? We cannot see Jesus with our physical eyes; it takes special eyes—the eyes of our hearts—to see Jesus, high and lifted up, shining in all of His glory and holiness. Such words well up from the bottom of our souls: Open the eyes of my heart Lord, I want to see You.

Jesus is at work; we just don't see it sometimes because His ways are so different from ours. Who would plan to birth the King of kings and Lord of lords in a stable, to a peasant girl? Alone and destitute, Mary could have doubted that she was seeing Jesus. Maybe it was her willingness to be so humbled and still believe that made her the best servant for the awesome task to which God called her.

You are seeing with the eyes of your heart when you hold on despite what your eyes can see. When God takes you through an all-time low, will you stay confident in His ability to still work through you?

I pray also that the eyes of your heart may be enlightened in order that you may know the hope to which he has called you, the riches of his glorious inheritance in the saints, and his incomparably great power for us who believe.

EPHESIANS 1:18-19

Prayer

Unless we remind ourselves of the truth, we slip into believing only what we can see. Confess what you believe about Jesus.
For example: "Jesus, I believe You are at work in my life.
I believe You have every situation under control.
I believe You want to work through me for Your glory."

CELEBRATE JESUS

The most exciting three words in the English language are "He is risen." The angel beside Jesus' open tomb spoke these words to the women who had come to anoint Jesus' dead body. The angel asked them why they were looking in a grave for someone who was alive. Jesus was no longer there! He is alive! He is risen! He lives forevermore.

Surely those three days while Jesus lay in the tomb were filled with darkness. Jesus had died, and along with Him seemed to go the dreams and hopes of so many. The women who came to anoint His body surely believed that the story was over. Perhaps a few of Jesus' followers remembered His words, "Three days later [I] will rise" (Mark 10:34). But most seem to have missed it somehow.

When Jesus arrived among His followers after His resurrection, they were filled with joy! Can you picture it? We serve a Savior who died and who rose again. Because He lives, we too will live forever. Join in the celebration! Come rejoice in the resurrection of our Lord!

He is not here; he has risen, just as he said. Come and see the place where he lay.

MATTHEW 28:6

Prayer

Meditate on the awesome promise of living forever
with Jesus. Talk to the Lord about how He wants
you to be prepared to be with Him forevermore.

THIS IS THE DAY

Scripture is always prompting us to embrace today. "Now is the day of salvation" (2 Corinthians 6:2); "Today, if you hear his voice, do not harden your hearts" (Hebrews 3:15). God knows we can only live in the present, and He encourages us to make good use of it.

This day is our gift from God. We can waste it with regrets over our past or worries about our future. We can squander it trying to outrun yesterday's miseries. We can ignore it, becoming lost in our wishful thinking. It's up to us to decide what to do with it. God would have us make the most of this day. What are you seeking for tomorrow? More opportunities? Better relationships? Personal growth? Embrace today. Learn the lessons the Lord requires of you today. Be faithful with the things God entrusts you with today. Let God's presence sustain you through this day's trials. Rejoice in the opportunities God brings to you today.

God has a future for you, but you have to live in today to get there. Step out in faith when God asks you to trust Him. This is the day that the Lord has made. Rejoice and be glad!

This is the day the Lord has made; let us rejoice and be glad in it.

PSALM 118:24

Prayer

Ask Jesus to help you trust the past and the future into
His hands. Affirm that He will lead you into His future
for you and prepare you for it, as you are faithful today.
Then listen to what He has called you to do today.

I WILL CELEBRATE

When God gets hold of us, He doesn't just give us a makeover on the outside. He changes us from the inside out. He makes us brand-new people. When Jesus comes into our lives, "the old has gone, the new has come" (2 Corinthians 5:17b).

So what is the "old" that God replaces with the "new"? Our hearts which once were cold and closed are replaced with new hearts that beat in tune with His—hearts that rejoice from within. Our minds which once were controlled by the lies and fears of Satan are transformed to think like Christ—minds that focus on God. Our hands that worked to please ourselves are transformed into instruments of worship—hands raised to heaven in praise through our work.

This gives us the "new song" we sing. Our new song comes from a rejoicing heart, a focused mind, and serving hands. With every fiber of our being, all that we are, we worship the Lord. Now that's a real celebration!

I will sprinkle clean water on you, and you will be clean; I will cleanse you from all your impurities and from all your idols. I will give you a new heart and put a new spirit in you; I will remove from you your heart of stone and give you a heart of flesh.

EZEKIEL 36:25-26

Prayer

As you pray, ask God to take His place at the very
center of your life. Ask the Lord to show you how to revolve
your heart, mind, and hands around Him and His plans.

HE IS EXALTED

These moving words remind us that God rules. He is exalted on high; forever His truth shall reign. Even as we rejoice, so heaven and earth rejoice with us in our King's holy name.

When life hands us situations we don't understand, we can remember that our King reigns. He is the Lord. When we sorrow over the shortness of life, we can remember that our King is forever. When we worry that lies surround us, we can remember that our King's truth shall reign. When we tremble at the evil in the world, we can remember that our King's name is holy.

Nothing that happens is beyond our King's control. Nothing surprises Him. Unlike any human king or leader, God is incorruptible, unchangeable, and eternal. He is worthy of our exaltation. He deserves our highest praise. Heaven and earth are rejoicing in His holy name. As Jesus said, even "if they keep quiet, the stones will cry out" (Luke 19:40). There's a chorus being sung in all of creation. We can sing along, exalting our King!

Yours, O Lord, is the greatness and the power and the glory and the majesty and the splendor, for everything in heaven and earth is yours. Yours, O Lord, is the kingdom; you are exalted as head over all.

1 CHRONICLES 29:11

Prayer

Spend some time just exalting and praising God.
Rejoice in His holy and eternal name.

BLESSED BE THE
LORD GOD ALMIGHTY

How often do we truly think of God's mighty works on our behalf? Do our friends and family know what God has done for us? When was the last time we declared His mighty works?

Psalm 106 describes how the Israelites repeatedly forgot about God's many kindnesses to them in the desert. When they stopped remembering God's greatness, however, they started relying on themselves. They rebelled against God. Life became all about their rules and plans and happiness—with devastating results.

We can learn from the Israelites. Declaring God's mighty works and praising Him every day will help keep our lives on track and inspire hope in the people who hear us. Join in the chorus of praise to our Lord God Almighty who reigns forevermore! When people see what God can do in an ordinary life, they just might open the window wider to God's possibilities for them. Maybe they will even see ways that God is already at work in their lives. Then they too can praise Him and declare His mighty works for all to hear!

> *Great is the Lord and most worthy of praise; his greatness no one can fathom. One generation will commend your works to another; they will tell of your mighty acts. They will speak of the glorious splendor of your majesty, and I will meditate on your wonderful works.*
>
> PSALM 145:3-5

Prayer

Reflect on the past twenty-four hours with a thankful heart.
Don't neglect the small things God has done. Sometimes
it's the little things that show us how lavishly we're loved.

LORD, I LIFT YOUR NAME ON HIGH

"God, I love telling You how wonderful You are!" What joyous words of adoration to our Lord. And He loves to hear us sing. He loves to hear our voices raised in praise as we thank Him for coming into our lives, for saving us.

The words to this song are the gospel in a nutshell. Jesus came from the glories of heaven down to this earth. The Bible tells us He left paradise to come to this tiny planet all because of His great love for us. We were lost, and He came to show us the way—the path to follow to find salvation. He came as a human so that He could die as a human on the cross and pay our debt—the death penalty our sins deserved. Through His death, we are set free from our sin and from eternal death. But Jesus did not stay dead. He rose again and returned to heaven with the promise that one day we will join Him there. He came, He died, He paid our debt, and He calls the whole world to come to Him.

No wonder we lift His name on high.

Therefore I will praise you among the nations, O Lord; I will sing praises to your name.

PSALM 18:49

Prayer

Thank the Lord for the awesome privilege to sing
His praises! Thank Him for giving you something to
sing about—His presence in your life, His salvation,
His payment of your debt in full.

I EXALT THEE

Something about beholding vast beauty draws us in. Whether it's an endless sky or a rolling ocean, our spirits are refreshed in the presence of greatness. We're wired to revel in it. We want to drink it in.

God knows how much we need this experience, so He invites us time and again to come to Him—the greatest One of all. His hands spread out the heavens. His authority set the stars in place. No beauty or majesty on earth can compare to His.

Yet often we miss it because the worries of life crowd God out. When the pressure is on, we are tempted to want everyone and everything to revolve around us—our tight schedule, many demands, and important agendas. It takes God-given willpower to make Him our focus. Yet when we do, our spirits are refreshed by His greatness. When we exalt our awesome God who is "high above all the earth," we place our focus where it belongs: on Him.

Praise the LORD, O my soul. O LORD my God, you are very great; you are clothed with splendor and majesty. He wraps himself in light as with a garment; he stretches out the heavens like a tent...He set the earth on its foundations; it can never be moved.

PSALM 104:1-2, 5

Prayer

Ask the God to reveal more of His beauty to you today.
Then look for the ways He will answer.

SHINE, JESUS, SHINE

As Christians who pray, "Your Kingdom come," we long to see our homes, neighborhoods, and workplaces filled with Jesus' light. When we sing this uplifting song, we explain how this can happen as we ask Jesus to fill our land—our lives—with the Father's glory.

The more time we spend in God's awesome presence, the more we become changed into His likeness. Every minute we spend gazing into His face, the more He will consume our darkness so that our faces can display His glory. Because we tend to become like those with whom we spend time, why not spend some time lingering in God's presence today? Imagine His perfect ways that can weave together a good plan for your life. Listen to His gracious and forgiving words as you confess your failures. Soak in His relentless tenderness as you give Him your burdens. Gaze on His kingly brightness so that your face can display His likeness. The more you spend time with Him, the more you will be changed. Then so will your world.

And we, who with unveiled faces all reflect the Lord's glory, are being transformed into his likeness with ever-increasing glory, which comes from the Lord, who is the Spirit.

2 CORINTHIANS 3:18

Prayer

Thank the Lord for allowing you into His awesome
presence. Ask Him to make your face display His
likeness. Ask that your life will tell His story—
the story of salvation through Him.

THERE IS A REDEEMER

God deserves our most heartfelt thanks. He desires to hear our expressions of profound gratitude for sending Jesus to us. He didn't have to. He could have let us live aimless, worthless lives, eventually dying far from Him. He didn't have to love us; He didn't have to save us. After all, our sin had hurt Him deeply and separated us from Him eternally. *Thank You, Father.*

God knew we were lost. He knew we were hopeless and that the only way to save us would be to do it Himself. So He did that, coming to earth in His Son. *Thank You for the gift of Your Son.*

Then, when Jesus returned to heaven, He gave us His Holy Spirit. Jesus called Him our "Counselor" who would be with us forever (John 14:16). God did not leave us to our own devices; He left us the Holy Spirit to walk with us and to guide us. *Thank You, Lord, for Your loving, guiding presence.*

The Holy Spirit empowers us to do Christ's work on earth—the work of serving, loving, sharing, and helping others enter the kingdom. One day God's work on earth will be done. On that day, we will rejoice at all that God has done in us and through us for His glory! *Thank You for working through us, O Lord.*

> *And I will ask the Father, and he will give you another Counselor to be with you forever—the Spirit of truth. The world cannot accept him, because it neither sees him nor knows him. But you know him, for he lives with you and will be in you.*
>
> —JOHN 14:16-17

Prayer

Thank God for giving His Son for you.
Thank Him for the presence of His Holy Spirit
in your life who helps you live for Him.

SHOUT TO THE LORD (1)

This song moves us because it combines the two essentials of great worship. First, it encourages our utmost abandonment. When we sing this song, we declare complete devotion—with every breath, with all that we are. Our hearts never truly engage in worship so long as we hold anything back.

Matthew 28:17 tells of Jesus appearing to His eleven disciples after His resurrection: "When they saw him, they worshiped him; but some doubted." Clearly two camps of people stood in Jesus' presence: the worshippers and the doubters. Maybe the doubters held back because they feared what Jesus might do. Just recently they had relied on Him, only to find their world shattered by a crucifixion. We are just as vulnerable to disappointment. Christians aren't spared from pain, sorrow, and trials. But we can know God's love as greater than our pain and so abandon ourselves into His care. When doubts hold us back, we miss the life-changing power of worship.

Second, this song inspires great worship because it raises Jesus to the highest place. All power and majesty belong to Him. Even inanimate objects have the good sense to bow at the sound of His name. Nothing exists that isn't subject to His authority. Yet, this same Jesus is so intimate and personal that we dare to call Him "my Jesus," "my Savior." Truly no one else is like Him.

My lips will shout for joy when I sing praise to you—I, whom you have redeemed.

—PSALM 71:23

Prayer

Ask God, who gave Himself completely for you,
to help you give yourself completely to Him.

SHOUT TO THE LORD (2)

The psalms are filled with exhortations to "shout" and "rejoice," to praise God enthusiastically. At times, however, we simply don't feel like praising God—certainly not aloud. Loss and pain push us from Him, causing us to focus on our hurts and tears. Doubt, fear, and defeat also become enemies of joy, bringing with them an almost suffocating cloud of depression.

At these times, we need to raise our heads and look again at who God is and what He has done for us. As this powerful song reminds us, He is our Savior, comfort, shelter, refuge, and strength. Surely no one compares to our powerful and loving God.

What is stealing your joy? Bring it to the Lord and then thank Him for being with you and working in you. Remember who He is, what He has done, and what He has promised. Your praise may start as a whisper, but keep praising. Soon you will be singing and shouting for joy! Nothing can compare to the promises we have in Him!

Rejoice in the Lord and be glad, you righteous; sing, all you who are upright in heart!

—PSALM 32:11

Prayer

Spend five minutes praising God in prayer.
Don't ask for anything; simply thank Him for who
He is and for His work in the world and in your life.

I COULD SING OF YOUR LOVE FOREVER

*L*ike a surging river, God's love flows into our lives. Over the difficulties and through the trials, it penetrates every part of our souls. Nothing can stop its flow. It is at once the most powerful force and the most intimate truth we will ever know.

The question is, will we receive it? Will we open our hearts and let the Healer in? Will we bare our souls to Him and be so bold as to rely on Him? Will we let Him wash away our sins and shame? The river of His love is always giving, always available.

Expectations of how life should go, feelings of unworthiness, and giving in to self-pity can block the love God wants us to know. When we relinquish our attempts to control how and when God's love should come to us, we open ourselves to a flood. Today, you can let God be God and do what He does best—love you! Open your heart to receive the river of His love—and be ready for a swim!

They feast on the abundance of your house; you give them drink from your river of delights.

—PSALM 36:8

Prayer

Personalize and pray Paul's prayer from Ephesians 3:17-19, "I pray that you, being rooted and established in love, may have power, together with all the saints, to grasp how wide and long and high and deep is the love of Christ, and to know this love that surpasses knowledge—that you may be filled to the measure of all the fullness of God."

THY WORD

How feeble we are at following Christ. We love Him so much, not for a moment forgetting His love for us, and yet our hearts forever are wandering. We need Jesus to guide us, to hold us close by His side, to keep us on the right path.

Where can we meet Jesus, our Guide? In the pages of His Word. His Word is a lamp, like a bright flashlight, for our feet, giving us enough light for the next step on the path. God's Word provides direction for our lives. We may not always get the clear answer we want, but as we read about men and women like us, we'll be encouraged at what God can do through ordinary people, and our faith in God's possibilities will grow. Plus, the Bible has a way of examining our motives so that we can see more clearly what is God's leading and what's just our own thinking.

We can take comfort in knowing that God desires to guide us and is actively seeking to teach us to follow Him. We overcome our fear to step out when we rely on God's ability to find us and bring us back if we lose our way. Our decisions are messy and imperfect at best, but His hold on us is infinitely reliable.

For the word of God is living and active. Sharper than any double-edge sword, it penetrates even to dividing soul and spirit, joints and marrow; it judges the thoughts and attitudes of the heart.

—HEBREWS 4:12

Prayer

Ask the Lord to use His Word to light up the
path ahead and show you the way you should go.

AWESOME GOD

Saying that God is "awesome" means that we recognize awe-inspiring He is, that thinking about Him causes us to stop in our tracks and forget everything else. His awesomeness would be frightening if we did not know of His great love for us. When we take the time to meditate on God, we cannot help but be changed. God is indeed awesome! Life is all about God. Everything was created by Him and for Him. He reigns from heaven over all of this earth. And His reign is perfect and perfectly just—He reigns with wisdom, power, and love.

We can get so caught up in our day-to-day lives that it's easy to forget that life isn't all about us. Even our prayer times can become frantic and self-centered as we list what we want God to change and jabber on with our requests. When this happens, we walk away empty and wonder why we don't see more of God in our lives.

This awesome God invites us to revolve our lives around Him. He calls us to live His purposes, to receive all we need from Him, and to share the concerns on His heart. Then His awesome presence will fill us and overflow to a needy world.

Who among the gods is like you, O Lord? Who is like you—majestic in holiness, awesome in glory, working wonders?

—EXODUS 15:11

Prayer

Amos 3:3 asks, "Do two walk together unless they have agreed to do so?" Have you agreed to let God be God? Is He "awesome" to you? Talk to Him about that.

WHAT A MIGHTY GOD WE SERVE

The book of Revelation tells us about a future party—one to which we are invited! Multitudes from every nation will rejoice before God's throne. Angels will fall before Him in worship. All of heaven and earth will celebrate God's ultimate victory. We can only imagine what it will be like to have no more tears or sorrow, all things made new, and a wedding feast prepared for us by God Himself.

God indeed is mighty. Do you believe it? Do you believe in His might to work on your behalf? Release your faith to believe in your mighty God. Then watch and see. You will soon find yourself joining Mary in exulting, "The Mighty One has done great things for me—holy is his name" (Luke 1:49).

But God has even more in store for us. Not only does God work mightily in our behalf, but He also works in and through us—even when we are weak, frail, and unsure of ourselves. His might, working through us, can accomplish anything. Ask God to go to work in and through you. Then you'll understand what the angel meant when he said, "Nothing is impossible with God" (Luke 1:37).

Therefore God exalted him to the highest place and gave him the name that is above every name, that at the name of Jesus every knee should bow, in heaven and on earth and under the earth.

—PHILIPPIANS 2:9-10

Prayer

Ask God to work mightily in your behalf. Then ask Him
to work mightily through you to help someone else.
Remember, with Him nothing is impossible.

MY LIFE IS IN YOU, LORD

My life, my strength, and my hope are in You, Lord. What encouraging words these are! If the source of our life or strength or hope were anything less than the Lord, we would be bound to fail.

Because our life is rooted in God, we are eternal. Our lives are given purpose and fulfillment when we acknowledge Him as our Source.

Because our strength comes from Him, we are unbeatable. We have strength to sustain us through times of pain, difficulty, and suffering. We are strong even when we feel weak. In fact, we are promised that God's strength is made perfect in our weakness (2 Corinthians 12:9).

And when our hope is in Him, we will never be disappointed. Is it a hope that promises to give us what we want? Hardly. Is it a hope that promises lives that are free of pain? No, it's better than either of these. It's a hope that one day we will be changed to be like Jesus. God's power, love, peace, and joy will fill us completely. Instead of just a taste of His life in us now and then, we'll know the eternal bliss of oneness with Him. The Holy Spirit that God gave us guarantees that our hope will be fulfilled.

In him was life, and that life was the light of men.

—JOHN 1:4

Prayer

Ask God to help you remember that everything
comes from His hand. Your life, your strength, and
your hope depend on Him and His grace toward you.

MIGHTY IS OUR GOD

These can be challenging words to believe: Our God is mighty. If God is so mighty, why do children stray from the truth? Why do our loved ones still suffer from cancer? Why are families broken apart by divorce? Surely the Creator has the power and authority to change these situations.

God rarely tells us the reasons why He allows suffering. But He does ask us to trust Him even when we don't have any answers. These times test our faith in God's character. Will we still believe He is mighty and good when He doesn't do what we want?

Every now and then, God's might brings healing and restoration to turn a hard situation around. At other times, if we are to see His power, we must stretch our faith to look outside our limited idea of what we think is best. Our mighty God may choose to sustain us through a trial or, perhaps, take a handful of dust from a bad situation and slowly create something good.

We will never be hopeless as long as we keep believing in the truth of God's character. When you can't see His mighty power at work, look to the cross and remember that what appears to be defeat may just be God preparing for an even bigger victory.

Mightier than the thunder of the great waters, mightier than the breakers of the sea—the Lord on high is mighty.

—PSALM 93:4

Prayer

Are you facing a challenge today? God is mighty; His power is great. Ask God to walk with you through the difficulty and to reveal Himself through it.

HE HAS MADE ME GLAD

Do you want to be glad? Some people don't. They think they're better off not believing that anything good will happen to them. Gladness, to them, is only foolishness. Their version of Christianity has all the appeal of lemonade without the sugar.

Other people don't know how to be glad. They've lived for so long feeling bad about themselves that they don't feel right unless something is wrong.

Gladness springs from a heart full of childlike faith in a loving Heavenly Father. Glad Christians know that they are precious to God. They believe God wants to bless them and lead them into good plans for their lives. When life sours, glad Christians pray, "Lord, You knew about this rough spot and have a plan to get through it. Show me Your way."

Being glad is up to you. You can choose to surrender your worries and lay down your burdens. A life of fear leads to despair, but faith leads to gladness. What will you choose?

The psalm writer knew about this choice. That's why so often we read words like "I will give thanks to the Lord...and will sing praise to the name of the Lord Most High" (Psalm 7:17). What will you choose today? Come to the Lord and let Him make you glad!

Surely you have granted him eternal blessings and made him glad with the joy of your presence.

—PSALM 21:6

Prayer

Revise Psalm 100:4-5 as your prayer: "Enter his gates with thanksgiving and his courts with praise; give thanks to him and praise his name. For the Lord is good and his love endures forever; his faithfulness continues through all generations."

I WILL CALL UPON THE LORD

*L*ife rarely goes as we've planned. If you're not living the life you thought you'd have, you have plenty of company. Life, it seems, is what happens when we had other things planned.

Such was the case with Asa, the ancient king of Judah. A vast army took up battle positions against him, leaving him little chance of survival—on his own strength. To his credit, Asa called on the Lord for help. Maybe he even sang a song like this one—for indeed it was the Lord who saved him from his enemies.

When a friend shares bad news, or a job promotion passes you by, or your kids act like they hate each other, where do you turn for help? Turn first to God's throne and call upon Him. Our Savior stands there, interceding for us. He is always asking His Father for the strength and courage we need to find victory.

Trusting the Lord requires that we stop focusing on our problems, trying to figure everything out, and thinking it's all up to us. When we call upon our God, He fights for us. He has the power to change circumstances, create new solutions, and sharpen our perspective. With our eyes off our problems, the battle is won. Then we can join the chorus and exalt the God of our salvation.

Then Asa called to the Lord his God and said, "Lord, there is no one like you to help the powerless against the mighty. Help us, O Lord our God, for we rely on you, and in your name we have come against this vast army. O Lord, you are our God; do not let man prevail against you.

—2 CHRONICLES 14:11

Prayer

Ask the Lord to help you call upon Him with your battles, your fears, and your worries. And trust Him for the victory.

PRAISE THE NAME OF JESUS

How we love to complicate life! We easily take on more commitments than we can handle and fill our calendars with more activities than we can fit in. Yet all the busyness leaves us empty. We long to find our place, where we belong. We want to know what we were made for and how we fit in to the big picture.

Our great God answers all of our questions and fills all of our emptiness. When we worship and praise Him, when we bow our hearts and knees before Him, we realize who He is and what He has done. He is our rock—solid, immovable. We can count on Him always to be there. He is our fortress—a place of refuge where we can run for safety, protection, and comfort. He is our deliverer—our help when all hope seems gone.

Jesus told his friend Martha, "You are worried and upset about many things, but only one thing is needed" (Luke 10:41-42). That one thing is Jesus Himself, and a willingness to sit at his feet and listen to Him. Will you slow down today and make Jesus your one thing? Instead of a full agenda, you'll find a full life.

He is the Rock, his works are perfect, and all his ways are just. A faithful God who does no wrong, upright and just is he.

—DEUTERONOMY 32:4

Prayer

Thank God for inviting you, again, to leave the swirling chaos of life and find your focus at His feet. Lay aside your pressures and burdens and give Him your full attention. Ask Him to fill your heart and mind with Himself.

ALL HAIL KING JESUS

We praise our Emmanuel, "God with us," for who He is and for what He has done for us. And we will sing throughout eternity, for we will reign with Him forever. As Paul wrote to Timothy, "Here is a trustworthy saying: If we died with him, we will also live with him; if we endure, we will also reign with him" (2 Timothy 2:11-12).

Imagine eternity with Christ! Our lives on this earth are merely a breath compared to eternity. The hardships we face here are a moment in time, preparing us to reign with our Lord forever.

Paul knew that those who endured hardships for the gospel would one day reign with Christ, and so he encouraged Timothy to persevere. As a prisoner, bound in chains, Paul could have resented his limitations. Not only did he endure the hardship, he refused to allow it to stop him from fulfilling what God had called him to do. Paul redirected his energies into mentoring Timothy, trusting that God's plan was bigger than his circumstances. His faith in God fueled his endurance.

We can have this same faith, a faith that lifts us above complaining about our lives and helps us embrace the opportunities in front of us. We can endure hardships when we remember that eternity is just around the corner, and we will be reigning with our Lord forever.

He has made everything beautiful in its time. He has also set eternity in the hearts of men; yet they cannot fathom what God has done from beginning to end.

—ECCLESIASTES 3:11

Prayer

Thank God for the promise of eternity. Ask Him to prepare you for the glorious future with Him.

MAJESTY (1)

Jesus has all authority in heaven and on earth. He is King of kings and Lord of lords. Worshiping his majesty means that we acknowledge His sovereign power and authority over us. His authority does not make us fearful; instead, it brings us peace because we know that He guides and protects us every step of our lives.

Jesus also gave authority to His followers, commissioning His disciples to go and change the world. They wouldn't be doing it in their own power! The good news of the gospel is that God can now live in us, giving us the power to do His work.

This power flows from Jesus' throne to us. When we acknowledge Jesus as our Lord, we can say, "the one who is in [us] is greater than the one who is in the world" (1 John 4:4). We have authority over darkness because the power of Jesus' light is in us. We have authority over lies because the Spirit of truth lives in us. We can have power over bitterness and resentment because the God of all mercies lives in us.

We have victory in Jesus if we'll just live out what we've been given. It's not a victory to live the way we want to, but to live the way God wants us to. When we do that, we show His majesty and power to the world.

To him who is able to keep you from falling and to present you before his glorious presence without fault and with great joy—to the only God our Savior be glory, majesty, power and authority, through Jesus Christ our Lord, before all ages, now and forevermore! Amen.

—JUDE 24-25

Prayer

Ask God how He might want to build His kingdom through you today. Believe that He will give you the power to do what He asks.

MAJESTY (2)

*A*mong its many components, worship includes an attentive and extended meditation on God's attributes, such as patience, love, holiness, and justice. We understand these characteristics because they have been described and demonstrated in God's Word and because we find them dimly echoed in ourselves.

The word "majesty" describes a reflected part of God's nature that emphasizes how different our Creator is from us. The Authorized Version uses the word twenty-seven times to convey words that can also be translated "excellence," "greatness," and "honor." Majesty is not a quality of God that we observe primarily with our senses, but with our spirit. Majesty helps narrow our attention from worship as a general attitude to worship as a specific awareness of one over-whelming fact about God—His divine, royal position.

Even if we can't define majesty, the setting in the chorus allows us to grasp the meaning. Words like "glory," "honor," "praise," "kingdom authority," and "glorify" all point to Jesus' exalted position and role. The word "majesty" remains part of our worship vocabulary because we worship the King of kings. Even, and perhaps especially, among people who no longer use royalty as their social order, majesty helps describe one of those qualities of God we are not charged to imitate, but to deeply appreciate.

> *The Lord reigns, he is robed in majesty; the Lord is robed in majesty and is armed with strength. The world is firmly established; it cannot be moved.*
>
> —PSALM 93:1

Prayer

Alter the text of "Majesty" to personalize the song and turn it into a first person expression of worship to Jesus. Experiment in prayer, using words related to royalty (like "throne," "crown," "scepter," "majesty," "kingdom") to highlight and think about the unique and overwhelming privilege to know and be loved by the King of kings.

COME, NOW IS THE
TIME TO WORSHIP

This invitation is for each person. Amazing as it seems, Jesus calls us to come to Him just as we are. How accepting! How welcoming! How hard to do, sometimes!

In God's presence, we never have to be anything more than who we are. Satan works hard to convince us that we have to be more. Who hasn't, at some time, shunned God because of feeling unworthy? Thankfully, it's not our own merit on which we come. We come into God's presence by invitation. The blood of Jesus has stained the red carpet rolled out to us from God's throne. The One who paid for us to be cleansed invites us to come give our hearts to Him.

Satan will always tempt us to hide our true selves from God. He tells us to keep our doubts secret or hide our shame. He knows that once we realize that God accepts us as we are, his plans to keep us from God can't succeed.

As we tell God honestly how we feel, whether we're anxious about a difficulty, ashamed over our behavior, or doubtful of His love, He strips away our pretense and self-delusions. Then we can rejoice in our true identity—as God's beloved children.

You have no reason to hide. God invites you to come. Come— just as you are—to God.

Come, let us bow down in worship, let us kneel before the Lord our Maker.

—PSALM 95:6

Prayer

Thank God for inviting you to come to Him
just as you are. And then come—in worship,
in praise—giving your whole heart to Him.

HOLY GROUND

When have you sensed God's presence? In a moment alone in prayer? As you held a newborn baby? As you watched a stunning sunset? During that moment, you felt something that touched you deeply. Like Moses so long ago, you sensed that "the place where you are standing is holy ground" (Exodus 3:5).

How about when you walk through the door of your place of worship? Do you sense the presence of God? Do you feel that this is a place where love abounds, a temple where Jehovah God lives?

Of course, the Holy Spirit lives in every believer, so we are in God's presence no matter where we are. Yet as we gather to worship, our love for God and for others should overflow. Jesus taught that "where two or three come together in my name, there am I with them" (Matthew 18:20).

To be in God's presence is to sense completeness, joy, and love. As we come into His presence to worship with fellow believers, let us come with a realization that we are on holy ground. May others who come discover that love abounds among believers, and may they want to join us!

You have made known to me the path of life; you will fill me with joy in your presence, with eternal pleasures at your right hand.

—PSALM 16:11

Prayer

Sit quietly and sense the Lord's presence.
Pray that your church will become a place where
God's presence is very real to all who enter there.

YOU ARE MY ALL IN ALL

We all need strength for our times of weakness. At times, when life overwhelms us, we feel that we can't go on. We need the One who can give us the strength to endure, to move ahead, to be victorious. Jesus can be our strength when we are weak.

Do you long for a love that never diminishes, regardless of how you act? What a treasure that would be! Would you like to live in a love so high and wide and deep and long that you never reach the end of it? Do you want to be so loved that you are pursued at any cost, even death? Many seek such love as though it were a precious jewel—a treasure beyond compare. This is the love Jesus offers.

Jesus can be our "all in all." He has enough strength for every difficulty. When we depend on Him, we are never disappointed. Tough times will come, and we may wonder how to get through another day. But, thankfully, we don't have to depend on ourselves or other people. With Jesus as our strength and our precious treasure, we can rest in knowing that He is always enough, today, tomorrow, and forever. He is our all in all.

The Lord is my strength and my shield; my heart trusts in him, and I am helped. My heart leaps for joy and I will give thanks to him in song.

—PSALM 28:7

Prayer

Ask God to remind you that He has all the strength you need.
Thank Him for being your precious treasure.

WE WILL GLORIFY

Thomas Aquinas taught that God is pure act. In other words, whatever God is, God does. It is impossible for God's acts to be inconsistent with His character. For example, we may be patient people but have impatient moments. Not God. The great "I Am" is consistent, always the same. So we glorify our King, our Lord, the Lamb, worshiping Him alone because we can rely on Him 100 percent of the time.

No burden or need exists that His character can't meet. He doesn't have days off or suddenly decide to treat us differently. In fact, He is able to do much more than we could ever think or ask.

When we need a loving parent, He is our "Abba" Father (Romans 8:15).

When we're feeling insecure, He is a "sure foundation" (Isaiah 28:16).

When we're thirsty, He is our "spring" of living water (John 4:14).

When we're vulnerable, He is able to "keep [us] from falling" (Jude 24).

When we're lost, He is our "light" and our "salvation" (Psalm 27:1).

We get into trouble when we try to meet our needs ourselves! When we focus on God's amazing sufficiency, we find more than enough. He wants to fill us to overflowing. Thank God for being your great "I Am." He alone deserves your worship.

Every good and perfect gift is from above, coming down from the Father of the heavenly lights, who does not change like shifting shadows.

—JAMES 1:17

Prayer

As you review your needs, ask God to reveal an aspect of His character to you. Believe that He wants to be this for you today. Don't forget to praise Him for being so consistent.

GLORIFY THY NAME

No matter how hard we seek to glorify God in our everyday lives, our pride puts up a good fight. When someone forgets to acknowledge our effort, we often feel slighted. If we're asked to serve behind the scenes, we may squirm. We may even struggle with doing something just because God asked, feeling tempted to do only that which brings us praise.

Thank God He knows how human we are! In His extreme grace, He uses us in spite of ourselves, even when our motives are less than pure.

As we ask Him to be glorified in our lives, little by little, He changes our desires. Instead of caring about what we look like, we begin to care about protecting God's image. We honor His name and give Him full credit because we know, what people think of us isn't nearly as important as what they think about God. When He is glorified, lives are changed.

My soul will boast in the Lord; let the afflicted hear and rejoice. Glorify the Lord with me; let us exalt his name together.

—PSALM 34:2-3

Prayer

Ask the Lord to make you willing to let go of
your own glory and to glorify Him instead.

CHANGE MY HEART, O GOD

Only the most courageous Christians sing this wholeheartedly. Like a potter working with clay, God will mold us if we yield to His touch. The touch of His hand transforms us, changing our hearts and making us more like Him. Sometimes God uses difficulties and trials in the shaping process. But all that we face is under the sovereign hand of the Potter.

When a difficulty strikes, we may wonder how to respond, which direction to turn. We may even devise a plan and take control. But God wants to use the situation to shape our hearts. God calls us to action, but He wants our hearts right first. When we focus on Him, we will do what is right.

As we yield to God's touch, we learn the lessons He wants to teach us: how to love those who may need it most, but deserve it least; how to believe the best of others instead of jumping to negative conclusions; how to see people's hurts instead of just the wounds they inflict.

This isn't easy! But as the Potter molds us, we become more and more like Christ. And we find joy.

Yet, O Lord, you are our Father. We are the clay, you are the potter; we are all the work of your hand.

—ISAIAH 64:8

Prayer

Ask God to help you yield to His hand, molding
and shaping your life. Ask Him to help you to see
His sovereign hand in whatever you are facing today.

HE WHO BEGAN A GOOD WORK

Sometimes we have a song in our hearts in the stillness of the night. We can sing with joy and thankfulness. Our hearts are full. We feel God's blessings.

At other times, we lose that song. The night turns to a starless void. Our struggle, where we once held out hope, has caused us to despair. We have been patient, so patient, but the process has been so long that we just can't sing anymore. The weight is too heavy to carry.

Our difficulty may cause us to question God's love and protection. We feel as though we have been forgotten, lost somewhere in the darkness. But God never abandons us. We are like priceless pearls to Him—His treasure.

God never forgets us, never gives up on us. Again and again he offers His fiery love to burn away impurities in our hearts and to draw us back to Himself. As we come to know and rely on God's love, we find our fears and doubts replaced with hope. Our struggles dim as we bask in His great love.

God never stops working, and He finds great pleasure in us. No matter how difficult the struggle seems today, remember that God has His hand on you—that means you are safe and secure, no matter how dark the night.

Being confident of this, that he who began a good work in you will carry it on to completion until the day of Christ Jesus.

—PHILIPPIANS 1:6

Prayer

Ask the Lord to give you a song in the night.
Pray that you will sense His hand of safety and security,
knowing that you are His greatest treasure.

SEEK YE FIRST

Seek first the kingdom of God, Scripture tells us. In other words, make the kingdom of God a priority. It sure would feel safer if Jesus had said to take care of our needs first and then to look for ways to build His kingdom. That's because we want to give out of our overflow, after we know we have taken care of our needs. But Jesus tells us to put Him first, seeking His kingdom and His righteousness, trusting that He will meet our needs.

We can share honestly everything about ourselves with Christ, knowing that He will purify our hearts. His love is strong enough to mold our desires and to remove any obstacles that keep us from wanting His kingdom first.

So He invites us to ask—to tell Him all our desires, not just the spiritually correct ones. We may never know what Jesus thinks about them until we do. He invites us to seek, for only in the seeking can we find what we truly need. He invites us to knock, expecting Him to answer. We can only do that when we realize how much God loves us. He only has our best interests in mind. He isn't stingy, nor does He rejoice when He sees us in need. Like a loving father, He delights in caring for us, and He wants us to know He can be trusted.

But seek first his kingdom and his righteousness, and all these things will be given to you as well.

—MATTHEW 6:33

Prayer

Ask, seek, knock. Talk with the Lord about how you can seek first His kingdom and His righteousness, today and every day.

HOLY AND ANOINTED ONE

What joy to sing the name of Jesus. His is a name above all names, a name so sweet it is like honey on our lips. The Bible promises that one day, "at the name of Jesus every knee should bow, in heaven and on earth and under the earth, and every tongue confess that Jesus Christ is Lord" (Philippians 2:10-11).

To say His name should remind us of His great love for us—a love so great that He came from heaven to become like us in order to die for us. He sends His Holy Spirit into our thirsty souls to revive them and make them strong. He gives His Word, the Bible, as a lamp to our feet, showing us just enough of the path ahead to step with confidence.

When the disciple Thomas believed after having seen and touched His risen Lord, Jesus said, "Blessed are those who have not seen and yet have believed" (John 20:29). We cannot see our Lord Jesus, and yet we believe in Him. Why? The sweetness of His name on our lips, the refreshment of the Spirit in our lives, the guidance of the Word on our steps all point us toward Him.

Yes, Lord, we love You.

I will praise you, O Lord my God, with all my heart; I will glorify your name forever.

—PSALM 86:12

Prayer

Meditate on the sweetness of Jesus' name. Thank Him
for the refreshment of his Holy Spirit. Praise Him
for His Word that provides a lamp to your feet.

MORE PRECIOUS THAN SILVER

Imagine being offered the world's greatest treasure, more precious than silver, more beautiful than diamonds. Imagine not having to do a thing to obtain this treasure because it had been bought by someone else. How thrilled would you be?

Actually, that's just what the gospel tells us has happened! God offers us the greatest treasure of all time: salvation. If you think salvation only means being guaranteed heaven and having your sins forgiven, you've barely scratched the surface of what is yours in Christ. Perhaps the greatest thrill of all is that Jesus gives us Himself.

The life-giver, dream-maker, soul-changer, wrong-righter comes to live in us. Out of Him flows a river of peace, an ocean of joy, a wellspring of hope. He promises to be our shepherd, our brother, our faithful friend, and our strong deliverer. Not only will He never fail us or forsake us, but He promises to call us, heal us, anoint us, bless us, cleanse us, prepare us, and fill us. He gives us His blood for holiness, His spirit for joy, and His mind for wisdom. The One who causes angels to fall prostrate before Him promises to reign over us, dwell in us, and walk beside us.

The more you go through with Jesus, the more valuable He becomes to you. What other treasure can compare with that?

Then the Almighty will be your gold, the choicest silver for you. Surely then you will find delight in the Almighty and will lift up your face to God.

—JOB 22:25-26

Prayer

Tell Jesus He is your greatest treasure. Nothing you desire can compare with what you have already been given by Him.

AS THE DEER

Our fantasies deceive us. They tell us that if everything went our way, we would be satisfied. High pay, a glamorous house, and an exotic vacation all seduce us as worthwhile pursuits. In reality, even if we had all those things, we would still feel empty. That's because quenching the soul's thirst with selfish pleasure is a lot like drinking salt water. The more we do it, the thirstier we become.

Jesus said, "Everyone who drinks this water will be thirsty again" (John 4:13). Only He can really quench our thirst. He knows that we are broken, thirsty, and needy, panting for refreshing water as a deer pants upon approaching a stream. So Jesus invites us to come and drink His love. When we worship Him, our cravings are met. By giving Him our praise and adoration, we find that our heart's desires are fulfilled.

Our worship need not end there. We can stay filled as we live each day by continually giving to God. Every time we yield to Him, we give Him more of ourselves and in turn experience more of His love. The world teaches that we feel fulfilled by giving in to ourselves. But only giving in to God brings soul-quenching satisfaction.

As the deer pants for streams of water, so my soul pants for you, O God.

—PSALM 42:1

Prayer

Ask Jesus to open your eyes when you begin to believe a lie about what will truly satisfy you. Thank Him for quenching your thirst.

COME INTO HIS PRESENCE

Often we treat thanksgiving as an extra in our time with God. We only praise Him if we have finished confessing our sins and laying out our requests and, then, have time left. As this song makes it clear, however, a thankful heart is the key to entering God's presence, the ticket to God's inner courts.

Everything God asks us to do is for our good and His glory. So when He tells us to praise Him, we can trust that He has our best interests in mind. As we reflect even on small events with a thankful heart, we're reminded that God is good, loving, faithful, and true. Soon our challenges will shrink in the light of who God is and what He has done for us. Sincere praise fans our small spark of faith into a blaze.

If we think of praise as a ticket, we will remember that we owe it to God. He is worthy of our constant admiration. If you can't see His hand at work in your situation, you can still praise Him for who He is and for what He will do in your life. God is always at work in you, drawing you to Himself. Even now, you only come because He initiated the relationship and because He gives you the strength to respond.

Thankful hearts aren't an option. As simple as this song seems, it's good advice!

I will praise God's name in song and glorify him with thanksgiving.

—PSALM 69:30

Prayer

Spend time in thankfulness and in praise
for all that your Lord has done for you.

IN THE PRESENCE

This powerful song teaches much about God. We get mere glimpses of God's holiness on this side of eternity, but we couldn't bear to see any more of it. Like Isaiah who had a vision of God's throne, our first response would be, "I am ruined!" (Isaiah 6:5).

Our God is completely holy. He is perfect in all His ways. God's holiness so reveals our utter sinfulness that we would shrink at His presence. Even the angels, who live in God's presence continually, covered their faces with their wings lest they would be overwhelmed and overcome (Isaiah 6:2). But only when we understand God's holiness can we really appreciate His grace toward us. As unclean as we are, He still invites us into His presence. Why? Because Jesus took all our sins upon Himself.

God's grace allows us to look honestly at our sinfulness in the light of unconditional acceptance and forgiveness. We don't have to fear letting God shine into the dark corners of our hearts. He knows who we are, and He knows who we will become with His help. As we come into the presence of our holy God, He examines our hearts, reaches into our lives, and takes hold of our motives. Then His truth changes us. No wonder we stand amazed.

Each of the four living creatures had six wings and was covered with eyes all around, even under his wings. Day and night they never stop saying: "Holy, holy, holy is the Lord God Almighty, who was, and is, and is to come."

—REVELATION 4:8

Prayer

Open your heart completely to God's holiness.
Show Him what is churning inside you and let Him
do what He needs to with it. You can trust Him.

GOD WILL MAKE A WAY

Have you ever become lost? Ever reached a dead end and felt trapped? Ever been in a situation from which there seemed to be no way out?

We have plenty of ability to get ourselves into trouble—and if we don't do it ourselves, others do it for us. But God specializes in making the impossible possible, the hopeless hopeful, and the end merely a new beginning.

"God will make a way," says the song, "where there seems to be no way." He can help us discover a pathway that moments before had been hidden. When we ask Him to be our guide and to keep us close, we will find that He has a way for us to walk. The path is not always guaranteed to be easy—in fact, sometimes it is fraught with dangers, falling rocks, or steep inclines. But always there is a way, and always He walks beside us. No matter how difficult the path, He provides the strength we need to get where we need to go. He clears the path and then takes our hand to guide us.

Let God make your way today, through that impossible, hopeless, difficult, dead-end situation. The path is there—you just haven't seen it yet. Ask Him to show it to you. He will.

I guide you in the way of wisdom and lead you along straight paths.

—PROVERBS 4:11

Prayer

Tell God that you need Him to show you His way.
Ask Him to guide you, make a way, and then walk
with you wherever the path may lead.

JESUS, NAME ABOVE ALL NAMES

How fitting that the name "Emmanuel" means "God with us." Jesus embodied what God's plan had been all along: to be with us. From the beginning of time, this has been God's desire. Genesis 3:8 tells of God walking with Adam and Eve in the Garden of Eden. Then sin separated this first man and woman from Him. Later, He told Moses to instruct His people, the Israelites, to "make a sanctuary for me, and I will dwell among them" (Exodus 25:8).

God wasn't content to be with just some of His people, however. So He sent his Son, Jesus, as the ultimate sacrifice for sin; then He sent His Holy Spirit, "the Spirit of truth" to live with us and be in us (John 14:17).

In addition, John reveals God's ultimate plan finally completed: "And I heard a loud voice from the throne saying, 'Now the dwelling of God is with men, and he will live with them'" (Revelation 21:3). Nothing can or ever will stop God from being with us.

God wants to share our lives and be invited into our hearts. He wants to laugh at our jokes and hang out in our homes. He enjoys our kids and understands our weaknesses. When others leave or reject us, He will stay. When we're angry with Him, He won't turn away. We go through nothing alone.

God is with us in our doubts, in our confusion, and even in our darkness. This has always been His plan. How do you respond to this message of love?

The virgin will be with child and will give birth to a son, and they will call him Immanuel—which means, "God with us."

—Matthew 1:23

Prayer

Thank God for His awesome plan never to leave you.
Even though you could never deserve so great a love, it has been
freely offered to you. Take time to sense "God with you" today.

I WORSHIP YOU, ALMIGHTY GOD

This song expresses a desire to worship God and give Him praise. Is that what you truly long to do—or are other activities a higher priority? What drives or motivates you? Most people can't answer that question. Sure, they can probably explain a specific decision based on available money and time. Beneath such obvious reasons, however, lie motivations we rarely acknowledge. Usually these hidden motives determine our actions. It could be the need to achieve, the desire to prove one's worth, the push of a guilty conscience, or the drive of an unhealthy appetite.

When we are driven by such motives, praise and worship don't even seem to fit anymore. In effect, we give in to little, lesser gods without even realizing it. Misguided motivations can easily lead us astray.

God longs to free us from that trap. He invites us to worship Him. Then, as we do, He pours His worth into us. As He brings our hidden motivations to light, we can choose to replace them with the desire to please only Him. And this frees us from our fears and from living self-protecting, self-promoting lives.

God sets us free to live the abundant life, free to worship Him.

Whom have I in heaven but you? And earth has nothing I desire besides you.

—PSALM 73:25

Prayer

Ask God to examine why you do what you do.
Be sure to listen to His answers. You'll be amazed at
how well He knows you and how much He loves you.

I LOVE YOU, LORD

How often do you say to Jesus, "I love You"? Amazingly, He receives joy when your soul rejoices. Your words are a sweet sound in His ear.

Jesus invites you to be His close friend. Do you dare accept such an invitation? He knows your personality, gifts, and circumstances so intimately that your relationship with Him won't be like any before or since. It is unique to you and Him. Other people can tell you about their experiences with God, but you can be sure that yours will differ. What He asks you to do will be especially designed for you. He speaks in a language you understand. He knows your needs and the desires of your heart.

What does He require of you in return? Oh, just everything— your total commitment, total devotion, total willingness to be lost in His love. His love goes two ways! He'll share His life with you if you'll ask Him what's on His heart and gladly carry it as your own, be willing to let your heart be broken by what breaks His, and make His glory your priority.

Jesus delights in your worship, even as you delight in His presence. So lift your voice in praise!

We love because he first loved us.

—1 JOHN 4:19

Prayer

Tell the Lord that you want to receive all the love that he
has to give you, and that you want to love him in return.
Worship and adore him; let your soul rejoice.

OH LORD, YOU'RE BEAUTIFUL

What hope keeps you going when life gets rough? This song tells us that we can seek the Lord's face and there, in His eyes, find the grace to go on.

Simeon sought the Lord's face. We read about him in Luke 2:25, shortly after the story of the birth of Jesus. Simeon had waited his whole life to see God's plan unfold. The Holy Spirit had promised Simeon that he would see the Messiah, and that promise had kept his hope alive. Imagine Simeon's joy when, after a lifetime of obedience and longing, he looked into the face of Jesus!

Like Simeon, we too will one day see Jesus. Revelation 22:4 promises that we "will see his face." What better hope to keep our spirits refreshed than knowing we will see God. This truth transforms the hard work of serving Him into the sweet anticipation of being with Him. The One who called us and equips us will one day welcome us home.

Yet even today, God promises that we can see His face. The psalmist wrote, "Let your face shine on your servant; save me in your unfailing love" (Psalm 31:16). When you seek God's face, you will find it—in prayer, in His Word, in the kind word of a friend. Look closely today. Ask God to reveal His face to you.

My heart says of you, "Seek his face!" Your face, Lord, I will seek.

—PSALM 27:8

Prayer

Ask the Lord to show you His face today.
Be ready for Him to reveal Himself in unexpected ways.

WHEN I LOOK INTO
YOUR HOLINESS

Do you want the joy of a close relationship with the Lord? That's easy enough to answer. The real question is, are you willing to do your part to get there? This song holds a key.

As we focus our hearts and our minds on worshiping God, we soon realize that nothing else is more important. Jesus affirmed that the most important commandment is "Love the Lord your God with all your heart and with all your soul and with all your mind and with all your strength" (Mark 12:30). Far from restricting us, loving the Lord this way meets our deepest needs. Deeper than our need for answers, deeper than our need for relief, and deeper than our need for a miracle is our need to love God. We were created to do that. It's easy to let difficulties consume us, taking our focus off our loving Father. Whenever we push worship to the side, however, we lose our way and feel empty. The more wrapped up in ourselves we become, the less satisfied we are. In contrast, when we unwrap and turn our focus to God, we discover real life. When we look into His holiness and gaze into His loveliness, everything else dims in comparison.

It's hard work to quiet all our other wants and just want God. But when we do, our lives are changed, our minds are renewed, and our spirits are refreshed. When we worship God, we find that He fulfills every need and every desire.

Come, let us bow down in worship, let us kneel before the Lord our Maker.

—PSALM 95:6

Prayer

Ask God to let His light shine so brightly into
your heart that everything else fades in comparison.
Ask Him to teach you how to truly worship Him.

OPEN OUR EYES

We would love to see Jesus—perhaps that is a longing in your heart. Just to see Him, to reach out and touch Him, to say that you love Him.

The people of Jesus' day got to walk and talk with Him. Many touched Him—jostling against Him in the crowd, perhaps giving a friendly hug, or tentatively hoping to be healed. Many were touched by Him—receiving from Him restored limbs, sight, and freedom from demonic oppression. Jesus was a real person. He got tired and slept in the back of a boat; He felt the heat of the sun and needed to sit by a well and get a drink; He enjoyed a good meal.

That's the point: Jesus walked here as one of us, as a live human being, a man. But He was also more than a man—He was God. The Bible tells us that Jesus returned to heaven and now sits at God's right hand. And you know what He does? He intercedes for us because He understands our weaknesses. He is intimately involved in our lives—He loves us, understands us, helps us.

Do you want to see Jesus, to reach out and touch Him? Go to His Word. Read His promises and claim them for your own. Do you want to tell Jesus you love Him? He's only a prayer away!

Therefore, since we have a great high priest who has gone through the heavens, Jesus the Son of God, let us hold firmly to the faith we profess. For we do not have a high priest who is unable to sympathize with our weaknesses, but we have one who has been tempted in every way, just as we are—yet was without sin. Let us then approach the throne of grace with confidence, so that we may receive mercy and find grace to help us in our time of need.

—HEBREWS 4:14-16

Prayer

Tell Jesus you love Him. Reach out and touch
Him through the pages of His Word.

SPIRIT OF THE LIVING GOD

Imagine being one of Jesus' disciples when He breathed on them and gave them the Holy Spirit (John 20:22). With Jesus' breath, the disciples received the power and authority to bring His life to the world. Christ has also given us that authority. Because "all Scripture is God-breathed" (2 Timothy 3:16), we encounter the living Word every time we open the Bible. And God's Spirit breathes into us as we receive His truth.

This truth, the truth about Jesus, is meant to set us free (John 8:32)! We become all God wants us to be as we let the Holy Spirit apply His Word to our lives. We break out of old patterns and ways of thinking and are given newness and freshness. The Holy Spirit knows how to use Scripture to melt us, mold us, and set us free.

Instead of being fearful about what God may do in us, we can be assured that He wants to bring us into new levels of freedom. He wants to melt our resistance to change, mold our desires to higher purposes, fill us with the power to live an abundant life, and use us beyond what we could imagine. All that and heaven too!

Look into God's Word and heed Jesus' words from John 20: "Receive the Holy Spirit."

Now the Lord is the Spirit, and where the Spirit of the Lord is, there is freedom.

—2 CORINTHIANS 3:17

Prayer

Ask God to remove any fear you might have of letting Him change you. Pray that His Holy Spirit will fall fresh on you, today and every day, bringing fresh newness to life.

WE WORSHIP AND ADORE THEE

*I*n order to truly worship and adore our God, in order to bow down before Him, we need complete humility. We need to acknowledge that we don't know it all or have it all. We need to recognize that He is in authority, and we need to be willing to obey.

"Obedience" and "authority" don't sound positive or enjoyable. Being rebellious and self-centered by nature, we want what we want when we want it. And what we want most is control. We don't naturally give in to letting God decide what's best for us. It seems that our way has to fail before we finally understand and then follow God's way. Only then do we realize that not only are we not in charge, but we're just a small part of a much bigger picture.

God should be our ultimate authority. Only He sees the end from the beginning. Only He has a good plan for our lives. Only He has the power to bring it about. When we bow before God, we submit ourselves to His control.

As difficult as it is to give up control, doing so brings great relief. Now we can give up trying to run our world. In addition, we don't have to know all the answers and aren't responsible for changing other people. We only need to trust and obey. Such simplicity makes life sweet!

Take your rightful place at God's feet and let your heart fill with praise.

All the ends of the earth will remember and turn to the Lord, and all the families of the nations will bow down before him.

—PSALM 22:27

Prayer

Acknowledge God alone as your authority.
Worship Him, thank Him, praise Him, and obey Him.

YES, WE ALL AGREE

For what clues do you look to determine whether the people you meet are believers? Key words? A church name? Christian jewelry?

The apostle John had much clearer criteria. John knew that all the peripheral issues aren't nearly as important as this: What do people think about Jesus? "If anyone acknowledges that Jesus is the Son of God, God lives in him and he in God" (1 John 4:15). When we know that someone acknowledges that Jesus is the Son of God, that is the only issue that really matters. Opinions may differ on a whole range of other issues, but Christians who agree on Jesus can sing with one voice "in the power and strength of unity."

Unity is powerful. Unified, the church can prevail; torn by division, it will fall (Luke 11:17). No wonder Jesus prayed so sincerely for His followers to be one. When we let our differences divide us, we forget who our real enemy is and start attacking each other.

How silly, when no one is perfect and perfectly correct. Praise God, we don't depend on that! The gospel is not about who is better or more correct, but about grace and about Jesus. God works for us and in us despite our faults and shortcomings, and, in His great mercy, He continues to work through us. Let us rejoice in our Savior, humbly joining with others who affirm Christ as Savior, with our whole hearts proclaiming Him worthy of our praise.

My prayer is not for them alone. I pray also for those who will believe in me through their message, that all of them may be one, Father, just as you are in me and I am in you. May they also be in us so that the world may believe that you have sent me. I have given them the glory that you gave me, that they may be one as we are one.

—JOHN 17:20-22

Prayer

Ask God to see your oneness in Christ with other believers.

JESUS, LOVER OF MY SOUL

What God did before, He still does today. Those who have had God pull them out of the "miry clay" know how much they need Him. It is a defining experience. Up to that point, they may have squeaked by knowing all the right answers or having a godly heritage. But when all of one's good efforts prove useless, real faith begins. Everything before this experience was self-reliance; after, it's all God-reliance.

God saves us when we are at our weakest so that we'll learn to rely on His love. We see that He is stronger than our sin and more real than our circumstances. Personal abilities, favorable circumstances, worldly success, and people's love will all let us down. If we depend on them, we'll be up when they're strong and down when they're weak.

Only total reliance on our soul's Lover can give us true stability. Once we have that, we have a source of strength that will endure. Trusting in God's unchanging love gives us the security we need. If your feet are planted on Him, your Rock, you can say with glad determination, "Come what may, I'll never let You go."

I will declare that your love stands firm forever, that you established your faithfulness in heaven itself.

—PSALM 89:2

Prayer

Do you feel mired in life? Ask God to help you remember the words of God to Paul: "My grace is sufficient for you, for my power is made perfect in weakness." Ask Him to give you a heart that responds, "Therefore I will boast all the more gladly about my weaknesses, so that Christ's power may rest on me" (2 Corinthians 12:9).

THERE IS NONE LIKE YOU

These words portray someone totally in love with Jesus. Do you sense the songwriter's longing to be with the one he loves? Such a close relationship doesn't happen quickly. It's nurtured through careful, deliberate time together.

How much time do you devote to listening to God? Do you feast on His Word? Not just quickly skimming the verses, but lingering and savoring them? Are you letting Scripture check your thoughts and attitudes? Have you allowed it to transform your priorities? Is God's Word your guide in determining decisions? Hopefully you are able to say with Moses, "They are not just idle words for you—they are your life" (Deuteronomy 32:47a).

The measure you use will be measured back to you. If you want Jesus to be your everything, then make Him more important than anything. When we give Him prime time (not leftover time), speak from the heart, and listen carefully for His answers, He will meet us and touch us.

Daily the riches of His glory await you. His Word can take you deeper and higher than you've ever been. Your time together will become the best part of every day. There is no one like Him.

Among the gods there is none like you, O Lord; no deeds can compare with yours.

—PSALM 86:8

Prayer

Ask God to develop your relationship with Him as you spend time in the Bible. Ask Him, "Is there something you want to teach me about this?" Wait and listen for His answer.

I WILL PRAISE YOUR NAME

Without a doubt, the most powerful word in the world is "Jesus." By calling on His name, we are saved (Romans 10:13). Trusting in it frees us from the strangleholds of legalism, shame, and pride. When we embrace it, we overcome our self-centeredness. No other name rules like Jesus.

The book of Acts records mighty deeds done in Jesus' name: casting out demons, healing the sick, and conquering sin. The power of Jesus' name threatened the authorities so much that they tortured, beat, and jailed the disciples in attempts to get them to stop using it.

Eventually, at the name of Jesus, Satan will be utterly defeated. Every knee in heaven and on earth and under the earth will bow and every tongue will confess that Jesus is Lord (Philippians 2:10), all because of the name, "Jesus."

This truth is so simple and yet so profound. No matter what comes against us, we have Jesus. No matter how hard the road or how dark the night, we have Jesus. He can't be put off by our sin or doused by our doubt. He won't be thwarted by injustice or defeated by Satan. He is eternal, unchanging, inexorable, and victorious.

Jesus! Praise His name. Come into agreement with all that He is. This is the heart of worship—not fancy music or lengthy prayers, but the name of God's precious Son on your lips. Lift Him up and bless His name.

Therefore I will praise you among the nations, O Lord; I will sing praises to your name.

—PSALM 18:49

Prayer

Tell Jesus that you want to know all the riches of His name: its power to delight, release, forgive, heal, and overcome. Ask Him to teach you to honor and revere His name above all else.

IN MOMENTS LIKE THESE

When is the best time to tell Jesus that we love Him? It may be in moments when we contemplate His great love for us. At these times, it's as if the screen between now and eternity is lifted and we get a glimpse of how Christ treasures us.

Think of Christ's love for you and sense His pleasure. Feel His desire to share His dreams with you and how He can't wait to show you heaven. Know that He wants to bless you and that He wishes you would hold still long enough for Him to give you all He desires. Imagine Him looking at your life and swelling with pride at all He's done. These are great moments to tell Jesus, "I love You, Lord!"

In contrast, our struggles present another great time to express our love for Christ. Everyone has unpleasant relationship issues, frustrating circumstances, and painful tragedies. That's when we should make a conscious choice to express our love for Jesus. Lifting our hands, like little children, we can say, "I love You, Lord." We experience freedom when we love Him even when life seems upside down.

Sometimes Jesus has you by the hand and you can sense His smile. Other times He has you in His arms, carrying you through difficulties. In moments like these, or anytime in between, tell Jesus you love Him. He is always with you. Sing out a song of love to your Lord.

I love you, O Lord, my strength.

—PSALM 18:1

Prayer

Let God examine your love for Him. He can show you why you have held back and help you overcome. The more you love the Lord, the easier it becomes. And the easier it becomes, the more you will love Him.

SURELY THE PRESENCE
OF THE LORD

The overwhelming awareness of God's power, the light "brush of angels' wings"—sensing God's presence brings unexplainable peace and joy.

Those who know God recognize His presence the best. We can quickly recognize the presence of our loved ones. They are close to us, crossing paths with us every day. We know the sound of the voice; we recognize the handwriting. We can pick out the laugh in a crowd or even the scent of perfume or aftershave.

God's personality has many subtleties as well. The more familiar you become with Him, especially His work in your life, the easier you will find it to recognize His work in others. Because He has pardoned your guilt, you will identify the look of someone at peace with God. Because He has restored your dignity, you will be able to see His glory in others. If He has delivered you from an abusive past, you know how a hardened face can be transformed by joy.

Do you want to sense more of God's presence in your life? Get to know Him better. You'll soon see the evidence of His power and grace everywhere you turn.

Blessed are those who have learned to acclaim you, who walk in the light of your presence, O Lord.

—PSALM 89:15

Prayer

Thank Jesus for giving you the ability to
recognize His voice, and confess anything that
may be blocking your ability to hear Him.

HERE IN YOUR PRESENCE

When we bow before God, everything is put into perspective. Certainly the way is not easy—something always threatens to put our lives on tilt. So we scramble to get back our balance, thinking if we could just get this one thing right, we'd be okay. If we let ourselves focus for too long on the frustrations, problems, fears, and worries, we soon would feel overwhelmed and anxious.

But we have a refuge, the Lord Himself. Focusing on God and His love for us brings us relief and peace. We stand in awe and wonder of who He is.

No one is like the Lord. As we respond to His great love—laughing with Him, crying out to Him, humbling ourselves before Him, being awed by Him—we realize that His presence changes everything. Worship awakens us to new truths and helps put our troubles in perspective. But most of all, we find joy in spending time with God. Nothing and no one is more exciting or more wonderful. No relationship is more intimate or faithful.

Don't wait for life to be perfect, for everything to fall into place. Find your peace and joy in God's presence.

You will show me the path of life; in Your presence is fullness of joy; at Your right hand are pleasures forevermore.

—PSALM 16:11 NKJV

Prayer

Thank God for the power of His presence. Enjoy being with Him. Stand before Him, loving and adoring Him.

FATHER, I ADORE YOU

How often do you truly lay your life before Jesus? Is your life an open book, revealing everything about you? Even if you choose not to do so—hoping to hide something back—Jesus already knows. He knows your sins; He knows you need His forgiveness; He knows your heart and your desires. Once you understand the breadth of Christ's knowledge and the depth of His love, you will love Him even more.

It's human nature to try and justify our questionable motives and to attribute our sins to mere quirkiness. But the Holy Spirit breaks our pride as He convicts us. We gain humility as we catch a glimpse of God's grace and forgiveness. Instead of rejecting us, He works with us. Instead of condemning our actions, He looks at our thoughts and motives and shows us what needs to change. How can we help but love a just, perfect, and holy God who binds Himself to sinners like us?

Instead of being afraid to let God find out what's wrong inside, we can lay our lives before Him with confidence. Then He will reveal even more reasons to love Him.

If we confess our sins, he is faithful and just and will forgive us our sins and purify us from all unrighteousness.

—1 JOHN 1:9

Prayer

Spend a few minutes adoring our loving
Heavenly Father and laying your life before Him.

I STAND IN AWE

Do questions like these percolate in the back of your mind: "What will I do if I lose my job?" "What can I look forward to this week?" "Can I afford to buy what I want?"

We desire security. We enjoy recreation. We want to possess beauty. God designed us to experience all this. It's part of our innate desire to live life to the fullest.

Unless we're careful, however, the drives meant to push us toward God can lead us into pursuing the world's counterfeits. The world tells us to put our reliance in a steady paycheck or plan the perfect event or buy another item we don't need. Even though we know these can't satisfy us, we fall for that line again and again.

Only God can live up to all our hopes. The more we enjoy Him, the freer we are to enjoy life's other pleasures for what they are—extras, not necessary for our satisfaction. Then, when the job falls through, the plans get cancelled, or the new gismo becomes outdated, we can still have joy. We don't need perfection from anything else when the Perfect One is satisfying us.

The next time you grasp for security, focus on God's majesty and awesomeness. When you long for good or goods, remind yourself of your wonderful Lord. And when you yearn for beauty, fix your eyes on the One who is beautiful beyond description. Stand in awe of Him. Let Him meet your deepest desires.

Dominion and awe belong to God; he establishes order in the heights of heaven.

—JOB 25:2

Prayer

Stand in awe of God. Meditate on His beauty,
wisdom, and love. Then praise Him.

COME LET US ADORE HIM /
THOU ART WORTHY

Singing, "O come let us adore Him," we usually think of Christmas. And we picture the Magi bowing to Jesus, laying their treasures of gold, frankincense, and myrrh before Him. We would never picture them stopping halfway to Bethlehem saying, "I'm too tired," "This is taking way too long," or "I have better things I could be doing."

We smile at how lame that would sound. If we were really honest, however, we would have to admit that we let similar excuses stop us from true worship. But all our excuses fade in light of the one reason to worship Him—because He's worthy!

As we honor God, we discover a great mystery of the Christian life: If we're willing to overcome the obstacles to worship (whether our schedule or problems that arise), God will take care of the things that had kept us from it. Will these statements be true for you? "I'm going to enjoy God whether or not I have all the answers to my problems." "I'm going to put Him first whether or not it means I get my stuff done today." "I'm going to take the next step whether or not I know where it will lead." That's living by faith! Come and adore Him!

You are worthy, our Lord and God, to receive glory and honor and power.

—REVELATION 4:11

Prayer

Spend time simply adoring Christ, your Lord.

OH, THE GLORY OF
YOUR PRESENCE

The Israelites had a day they would never forget. When the Ark of the Covenant was brought into Solomon's newly built temple, "the priests could not perform their service because of the cloud, for the glory of the Lord filled his temple" (1 Kings 8:11). They were so overwhelmed with God's presence that it knocked them off their feet!

As believers, we are God's temple, and He fills us with His glory through the Holy Spirit. Paul explained it this way: "Do you not know that your body is a temple of the Holy Spirit, who is in you, whom you have received from God? You are not your own; you were bought at a price. Therefore honor God with your body" (1 Corinthians 6:19-20).

We experience the glory of God's presence in our lives when we live His way. So before rushing in and asking Him to bless us again, we may need to ask ourselves some tough questions: "Am I involved with something (or someone) God wouldn't approve?" "Am I not doing something I should be doing?" "Is God pleased with the way I am acting?"

With obedience, there is no automatic pilot. It will take a constant dialogue between you and God to know what He wants and to carry it out. Then, as you live according to God's will, you'll experience life's greatest reward: the glory of His presence.

And in him you too are being built together to become a dwelling in which God lives by his Spirit.

—EPHESIANS 2:22

Prayer

Ask God to examine your actions, your thoughts, and your motives. Tell Him that as His holy temple, you want to live to glorify Him.

WE BOW DOWN

What kind of a king would insist on making you an heir to all he owns? What kind of a king invites his subjects not only into his palace but also into intimate fellowship with himself? What kind of a king would see everything his people lack and constantly say, "Here, take mine." What kind of a king says, "I'm here for you. Just call."

Only the King of kings! The One who keeps His subjects by His extreme kindness, overflowing tenderness, and unlimited compassion.

Why would we ever refuse to bow to such a king? So we could go back to striving to achieve our worth? So we could depend on ourselves and claw our way to the top? So we could relive the envy and anger we harbored against others? Oh, aren't you glad that you're saved! Aren't you relieved that instead of harsh pursuits, you know the joy of being blessed? Jonah 2:8 says it best: "Those who cling to worthless idols forfeit the grace that could be theirs."

Our God is a gracious King. You can stop striving and let Him give you what you need. You can come to Him and find rest from all your futile efforts. Grace is His to give. The King will do for you what you could never do for yourself. He will heal, bless, restore, and cleanse. What more could you want, but to bow down and thank Him for being your King?

For he has rescued us from the dominion of darkness and brought us into the kingdom of the Son he loves.

—COLOSSIANS 1:13

Prayer

As you bow before Jesus, ask Him for what you need.
His resources of strength, joy, and peace are endless.
Believe that He wants to share them with you.

BE EXALTED, O GOD

If you have ever been around someone who has recently fallen in love, you know that every other word out of the person's mouth seems to be about the new relationship. With starry-eyed enthusiasm, the person describes every detail, sometimes again and again!

That's a wonderful picture of how passionate God wants us to be about Him. All through Scripture, people just couldn't keep quiet about their love for God. David wrote psalms while his enemies were pursuing him. Paul encouraged the churches while he was imprisoned. Others were tortured and exiled, but they all focused on their love for the Lord. What could explain their commitment? Only a powerful love that had swept them away.

Every believer has a story to tell. What has God brought you through? How has He shown you His love? What unshakable quality of His nature do you rely on? Ponder these truths. Be thankful for them. Let them sink into your heart and delight you. Then, maybe the next time you feel like singing praises to God in public, or bringing up the "G" word in conversation, you won't stop. You'll be so in love with God that the world hears it—again and again. What better testimony could there be?

Your love, O Lord, reaches to the heavens, your faithfulness to the skies.

—PSALM 36:5

Prayer

Ask God to open your eyes to His love which
always surrounds you. As you go through your day,
acknowledge every reminder that He cares for you.
Thank Him and tell Him you love Him too.

BLESSED BE THE NAME
OF THE LORD

Worship is contagious. It just takes one person willing to be vulnerable to God and others to infect a whole group.

Throughout Scripture, the people who led worship had to take some risks. Moses broke out in song after crossing the Red Sea— a bold move for a reluctant leader with a stutter. David, overcome with joy, danced before the Lord, not caring whether or not it made him look foolish. Daniel openly worshiped God even though it meant putting his life on the line.

For each of these men, fears of what they might look like or how they might be labeled or what might become of them could not hold them back. As a result, whole nations were led into God's presence. Lives were saved, and people were directed back to God.

Have you ever stopped to consider the effect your worship might have on those around you? Your praise can help lift their spirit of heaviness or give them the hope they need for their future. You might make the difference between their pressing on or giving up.

God is looking for true worshipers who will bless His name. Will you be the one to shout out loud and not hold back? Could this be your song?

Blessed be the name of the Lord from this time forth and for evermore.

—PSALM 113:2 KJV

Prayer

What risks are you willing to take to worship God?
Let God examine what might hold you back and ask
Him to help make your worship pleasing to Him alone.

HE IS LORD

Sometimes we can feel like walking away from God. Sorrows threaten to break us. Grief sneaks up on us. Unfair treatment takes us by surprise. We want to protest, "This wasn't supposed to be so difficult!"

Jesus never promised that it would be easy. In fact, the first disciples soon discovered that following Him turned out to be tougher than anyone had expected. When disappointments overwhelm us, we may feel like we want a new god. But the fact remains that He is Lord whether we like it or not. Our only choices are to be angry and alienate our only source of help, or to bow to the mystery and follow Him as Lord.

By following Him through the tough times, you will discover this wonderful truth: Life may feel like a roller coaster, but the people who trust the safety belts enjoy the ride. Even through steep dives and dark tunnels, you need not fear. He is Lord over the things that threaten to destroy you, and He is Lord over anything that could separate you from His love.

Jesus didn't come to make our lives more difficult. He came to give us the security we need to live them with joy. You can abandon yourself to His plans, knowing that Jesus Christ is Lord.

They will make war against the Lamb, but the Lamb will overcome them because he is Lord of lords and King of kings—and with him will be his called, chosen and faithful followers.

—REVELATION 17:14

Prayer

Is life difficult today? Confess your frustration, confess your unbelief, and ask Jesus to take over and be Lord of your life. Then trust Him, and begin to enjoy the ride.

IN HIS TIME

What parent hasn't been asked by an anxious child in the back seat, "Are we there yet?" We understand our children's desire to arrive. Maybe that's why we, as God's children, ask Him, "When will this be over?" We want so badly to just get through the difficult times and reach the final destination.

God has His own timetable. His plan is established, and He's eager for us to get with it. Living in step with the Holy Spirit, we work in sync with Him. Every time we lay down our sense of timing and willingly take up God's, we move into a plan much greater than ourselves. Doors open. Needs are met. Even small details fall into place.

But this requires that we give up our desire to hurry events. God's plan isn't to rush us through our troubles. It's to take those troubles and use them to make something beautiful for us. Don't give up just short of God's time! It may be just a little while until you see God turn your anger into peace, your weariness into rest, your dread into hope, your loneliness into belonging, and your disgrace into honor. The Christian life isn't just about sorrow and suffering, but about God's ability to make all things beautiful in His time.

Will you give God the time to do that?

God has made everything beautiful for its own time. He has planted eternity in the human heart, but even so, people cannot see the whole scope of God's work from beginning to end.

—ECCLESIASTES 3:11 NLT

Prayer

While God may never answer our questions of when and why,
He will answer, "What do you want me to learn from this?"
If you're going through a difficult time, ask Him that today. Then
listen for the beauty He wants to bring in your life—in His time.

I WILL COME AND BOW DOWN

In Jesus' presence, we find joy. Not condemnation, not guilt, not fear—but joy! Think about it. Jesus wants us to enjoy our relationship with Him. He wants us to delight in Him as He delights in us. He plans for us to inherit every possible spiritual blessing!

Feeling blessed doesn't sit well with joyless friends. They are much more comfortable when we feel badly about our sinfulness. They live under condemnation, and they want our company in their misery. But they're missing out on the joy! In God's presence, we find that the price has been paid in full! Nothing is left for us to do but to confess our sin and then let it go, moving on to enjoying life in Christ.

When we bow before Jesus, we find that He more than makes up for all that we lack. We can face our unworthiness because we know the Grace Giver. We can acknowledge our brokenness because we know the Healer. We can deal with all that our sin has ruined because we know the One who makes all things new. All that we need is in Him.

So throw wide open the door to your heart and dance with Him, sing to Him, and rejoice in how He fills you. In His presence, find fullness of joy!

Surely you have granted him eternal blessings and made him glad with the joy of your presence.

—PSALM 21:6

Prayer

Jesus invites you to rejoice when you are weak because He is still strong, to rejoice when you're defeated because He is still victorious, and to rejoice when you feel lost because He still knows the way. Find the freedom, the relief, and the pleasure of worshiping at His feet.

COME LET US WORSHIP
AND BOW DOWN

Sheep depend on their shepherd. He leads them to food and shelter and protects them from enemy attacks. If it weren't for the shepherd's care, sheep would be hopeless and helpless. Maybe that's why the Bible so often refers to God's people as His sheep. We simply weren't designed to be self-sufficient.

Our Good Shepherd knows this. He doesn't expect us to live or even survive on our own. On the contrary, He expects us to ask for help. Our neediness never surprises Him, and our asking does not put Him off. But when sheep think they know better than the shepherd, they get into trouble. They wander off and get lost—or worse, become captured by a lion or a wolf. They fall into ravines; they drown in streams. When we think we know better than God, we experience the consequences.

Did you know your needs are God's problem? The Good Shepherd is waiting to help you. He will come to your aid. No request is too large or too small.

People who remember that they're God's sheep make their requests, then lie down in a green pasture and rest. That's the life God wants us to have. He wants to be our Good Shepherd. Find the comfort of being His precious lamb.

For he is our God; and we are the people of his pasture, and the sheep of his hand.

—PSALM 95:7 KJV

Prayer

What do you need today? Better treatment? Financial support?
Improved health? Tell your Good Shepherd about it.
Acknowledge that because you are one of His sheep,
it's His problem, and ask Him to do something about it.

ONLY BY GRACE

You have been summoned into God's presence. He has called you and drawn you, and you have come. God has put a longing in your heart to know Him better, and by His grace He allows you to come.

Grace is God's favor, offered as a gift. We cannot earn it or buy it. We could never deserve it no matter how hard we might try. We can only accept this gift freely and gratefully.

God pours out His grace so consistently that we sometimes take it for granted. By grace He overlooks our faults, extends undeserved kindness, and opens the door into His presence. Far from an automatic response, God chooses to be gracious to us countless times each day. What an enormous favor that is!

Our obedience goes up and down. We get on track and off. Yet God's grace never wavers. Grace is never reluctant, never absent, even for a moment. If it were, we would be utterly destroyed. Thankfully, God's treatment of us has nothing to do with who we are and everything to do with who He is: consistently good, unfailingly merciful, abounding in grace—grace that is always loving, always present, always faithful.

Come into His presence—you have been summoned there by your God of all grace.

For it is by grace you have been saved, through faith—and this not from yourselves, it is the gift of God.

—EPHESIANS 2:8

Prayer

Come into God's presence. Ask God to remind you
of His abundant grace toward you. Thank Him for
all He has done for you—all because of His grace.

YOU ARE MY HIDING PLACE

When life gets to be too much, when you are afraid, do you need a refuge? God can be your hiding place. When you are with Him, He fills you heart with joyful songs, replacing your fear with trust and peace.

Satan would like you to be afraid. He would like you to think that seeking a hiding place in God is cowardly. He wants you paralyzed by fear and afraid to turn to God for help. And he wants you to be ashamed of your fear.

But it's all right to feel afraid. God knows that having sweaty palms and racing hearts are part of being human and how He created us. God asks us to bring our fears to Him and to hide in Him.

In God's presence we find the strength to confront our fears. When we run to Him, He reveals the truth behind what frightens us. In the light of knowing His goodness and trusting His love, fears are revealed for what they are: mere balloons, inflated to appear much larger than reality. As God points out His truth, He pops each one.

What fears hold you back? God can get you through any difficulty if you'll trust in Him. Run to your hiding place. Trust in His truth.

You are my hiding place; you will protect me from trouble and surround me with songs of deliverance.

—PSALM 32:7

Prayer

The psalm writer often wrote of what he would do.
"I will trust in you" (Psalm 56:3). "I will sing to the Lord"
(Psalm 13:6). "I will sing praises to your name" (Psalm 18:49).
Ask God to show you what to do the next time you feel afraid.
Ask Him to be your hiding place and to show you His truth.

ISN'T HE

How can we be friends with this infinitely holy, always perfect God? Even on good days, we probably make someone angry. Without even trying, we disappoint people. Between the cracks of our intentional living, careless words slip out.

Then there's our Friend. Beautiful. Spotless. Capable. Wonderful. Able to always counsel us. Almighty. How can He want to be with us?

Our relationship only works because Jesus knows how to lovingly deal with our sinfulness. Over and over He treats us as His friends. When we are misled, make poor choices, or retreat into unbelief, Jesus still upholds our dignity. He is able to convict our behavior without assassinating our character. He never sacrifices being loving for the sake of being right.

How different this is from how Satan would treat us. Instead of giving us grace, he wishes to disgrace us. Satan's desire is for us to feel disapproved, disowned, and discarded.

But not our wonderful Friend, Jesus! No matter how marred or buried His image in us seems, Jesus still sees Himself in us. Underneath our woeful behavior, He sees beauty—beauty that He refuses to give up on until it is shined and polished and made perfect like He is.

Your perfect Friend believes in what He put in you. Such love is so far beyond words that all we can say is: "Isn't He wonderful?"

For to us a child is born, to us a son is given, and the government will be on his shoulders. And he will be called Wonderful Counselor, Mighty God, Everlasting Father, Prince of Peace.

—ISAIAH 9:6

Prayer

Express your gratitude for having a Savior who treats you with such dignity. Soak in His love for you until the image He sees becomes your vision, too.

BE GLORIFIED

God wants to prove His might in your life, especially when you feel weak. No kidding. So many people whom God used in Scripture were extraordinarily under-qualified. Abraham, King Saul, Gideon, and the disciples all could have asked, "Who, me?" God certainly didn't choose them for their greatness. No, He chose them to glorify Himself.

If you want God to be glorified in your life, you may as well know that it probably will happen through your emptiness, weakness, and inability. Whenever God wants to really impress people, He begins with an impossibility—like creating a world out of nothing, giving a virgin a child, or bringing a crucified man back to life. Those are His favorite projects!

God is looking for people who feel as though they have nothing great to bring to the table. His only qualification is for them to say yes to whatever He asks.

Do you believe in God's goodness and power? Do you believe He can use all your unanswered questions and limited resources to produce something wonderful? Then pray the prayer that God loves to answer: "Be glorified." When the impossible happens, people will know that God is at work again!

> *But he said to me, "My grace is sufficient for you, for my power is made perfect in weakness." Therefore I will boast all the more gladly about my weaknesses, so that Christ's power may rest on me.*
>
> —2 CORINTHIANS 12:9

Prayer

Don't just give Jesus all you have; give Him
all you lack too. Allow Him to use all you
can't do and all you don't have to glorify Him.

MORE OF YOUR GLORY

God has an interesting way of handling trouble. When life is most difficult, He reveals His glory. Often it is difficulty that causes a stirring in our souls, a stirring that causes us to know how much we need Him.

A week before the Transfiguration, Jesus had told His disciples clearly that He would be killed (Matthew 16:21-28). Imagine their heartache. All their hopes seemed lost. Then in one memorable moment, their suffering Savior changed into dazzling glory: "There he was transfigured before them. His face shone like the sun, and his clothes became as white as the light" (Matthew 17:2). All their doubts and fears crumbled into dust.

How we need God's glory in our troubled lives! How we need the stirring of our souls to cause us to cry out for more of His glory, more of His power, more of His Spirit in us.

God's glory provides all the hope, strength, and perspective we need to press on. His glory renews our assurance that God will be enough. It reminds us that one day our tragedies will be swallowed up in triumph. And it diminishes our present troubles as compared to the "eternal glory that far outweighs them all" (2 Corinthians 4:17).

Life is difficult, so ask God to speak to your heart, to change your life, to manifest Himself in you. He rewards such trust with a revelation of His glory.

His divine power has given us everything we need for life and godliness through our knowledge of him who called us by his own glory and goodness.

—2 PETER 1:3

Prayer

What do you need? More power? More love? More truth?
Fix your eyes on Jesus and ask Him to reveal that aspect of
His character to you. Then press on, believing He will.

SHOW ME YOUR WAYS

Have you ever stared at one of those jumbled images of colored dots long enough to see the three-dimensional picture underneath? What a parallel to life. We can become so busy that our days seem like fragmented dots. Unless we stop long enough to ask God to show us His ways, we miss the real picture. That takes time. It takes that unique blend of concentration and relaxation as we pray: "Show me Your ways."

God will answer by giving us a perspective that we otherwise would have missed. Instead of seeing an opportunity to get ahead, we will see a chance to treat others right. Instead of seeing an unreasonable person, we will see the deeper image of hurt and want. Instead of focusing on our rights, we will see a chance to dispel strife. Instead of looking for ways to impress others, we will see what we can learn from them.

What a difference God's perspective makes! Every time we choose His way over our own, not only do we find meaning and purpose, but we also find the joy of life with God. Walking with Him is the best reward of all.

God always has a way. You don't have to guess to figure it out. Step back from the fragmented pieces of your life and ask Him to show you. Soon you'll see it, too.

Show me your ways, O Lord, teach me your paths; guide me in your truth and teach me, for you are God my Savior, and my hope is in you all day long.

—PSALM 25:4-5

Prayer

Take a few minutes to consider your upcoming activities. Ask God to show you how He sees them. Open your heart to hearing His purposes and perspective, and cooperate with Him.

MEET US HERE

What makes a church service powerful? Is it the amount of planning and preparation? Is it the quality of the music or preaching? Is it the obedience of the listeners? While all of these items are important, they only add up to a pile of dead works if God doesn't show up. We can sing, pray, and lift our hands, but apart from God, we will just be making religious motions. Worship is meaningless without the Lord. Once we know how desperate we are without Him, we pray, "Meet us here!"

Christ's powerful presence cuts through our confusion and breaks our bondages. His Spirit overcomes our sinfulness and fills us with peace. He restores our souls. The Bible tells us that when we gather in His name, He is right there with us.

You can't make your heart right, but He can. You don't know what you'll need for the days ahead, but He does. You can't have victory over Satan's attacks, but He can. You don't know God's mind, but He does. The Lord meets you with arms full of everything you need. He so much wants to help you! His dream is to live with you, walk with you, be your God, and make you thoroughly His.

God can do it! Ask Him to meet you right where you are.

For where two or three come together in my name, there am I with them.

—MATTHEW 18:20

Prayer

Ask God to meet you. Pray for Him to answer
your every "I can't" with His "I can."

LORD, YOU HAVE MY HEART

*I*f God has ever gotten a hold on your heart, you know how desperately you want to keep Him close. Thoughts of breaking fellowship seem ridiculous. We'd rather give up our sin than endanger our intimacy. Such a heart-to-heart relationship with God is the only thing that empowers us to offer ourselves to Him as a living sacrifice.

One of the most difficult things to sacrifice is our desire for a pain-free life. We're all too aware that to love is to risk being injured. Yet Jesus risks this all the time. He loves and pursues us even though we regularly let Him down. He continues to be jealous of our affection even though we give it to many lesser gods. His heart breaks when we refuse to learn the lessons He has for us! Yet His love for us is unquenchable.

Could Christ really ask us to love each other this same way? It's uncomfortable to love those who criticize us, bless those who persecute us, and pray for those who hurt us. But compare it to the alternative: Either we suffer a little now as we die to ourselves and enjoy a pain-free eternity, or we live solely to enjoy this life and suffer a pain-filled eternity.

God lets us choose our pain! Our small sacrifices now will one day lead us into His everlasting arms. Together, forever, He will hold your heart. That makes it all worth it!

And so, dear brothers and sisters, I plead with you to give your bodies to God. Let them be a living and holy sacrifice—the kind he will accept. When you think of what he has done for you, is this too much to ask?

—ROMANS 12:1

Prayer

Don't let Jesus waste His love on you.
Open your heart to let Jesus heal and cleanse you.

COME INTO THE KING'S CHAMBERS

God has a plan for your life and it includes everything you're facing today. He knows what He's trying to work in you. He knows what He wants to do through you. Not a detail of your life has been left out. He plans to use it all for good.

Where do you learn this plan? In the king's chambers. The outer courts are where the crowds gather for praise, but in the inner room, lovers share their secrets. They express complete devotion, utter vulnerability, and genuine intimacy.

Your King wants to meet the requests you've been too afraid to even acknowledge. He wants to heal the wounds you've been too ashamed to mention. He wants to assure you that you cannot ask for too much of what is right and good and true. All the world's resources are His to share. Every opportunity comes from His divine arrangement. Your King is free to do as He sees best.

Are you discontent living in the outer courts? You would not long to go deeper if there wasn't something more. So quiet your heart. Learn to listen. Enter His chambers and let Him knit your soul together with His.

"For I know the plans I have for you," declares the Lord, "plans to prosper you and not to harm you, plans to give you hope and a future."

—JEREMIAH 29:11

Prayer

Ask God to look inside and show you what He sees.
As you tune into what He wants to do in your
own heart, you'll begin to follow His plans.

PSALM 5
(GIVE EAR TO MY WORDS)

Where would we be without our heavenly Friend to listen to us? When there's no one around to talk to, He hears. When no one else would understand, He will. When no one else cares, He does. Like the psalm writer, we can cry out to Him and know that He considers our silent meditations and hears the words that we cry.

Although any time is the right time to be with God, Psalm 5 mentions coming to God in the morning. It's a good time to evaluate the events of the previous day and to prepare for the new day. In the morning, our mind is fresh to process the thoughts God wants to give us. We might cry out for hope and let God build our expectation of His goodness. Or we might express our need for love and let God point out the obstacles we need to overcome, like how we long for an apology more than we long to forgive. Whatever our felt need, we can tell God about it and listen for His answer.

Living through a day without first receiving God's mercy is a lot like trying to make it until dinner without eating. We have to deal with the constant distraction of emptiness demanding to be filled. God's grace is ready to give us everything we need if we'll spend the time to receive it. He doesn't want us to run on empty for even a minute.

In the morning, O Lord, you hear my voice; in the morning I lay my requests before you and wait in expectation.

—PSALM 5:3

Prayer

How would you fill in this blank? "If I don't fit in anything else today, I want to fit in _____." If your answer was God, tell Him. He delights to have His children put Him first.

SPIRIT SONG

Knowing what's right usually isn't our problem. Doing it is. We know we should keep our mouth shut instead of demanding our rights or to give up control instead of retaliating, but that's more than we can muster on our own. Thankfully, Jesus wants to fill us with His life. As we lean on Him, the perfect Lamb of God, we become lamb-like as well.

Isaiah 53:7 says that Jesus "was oppressed and afflicted, yet he did not open his mouth; he was led like a lamb to the slaughter, and as a sheep before her shearers is silent, so he did not open his mouth." Jesus knew when defending Himself was not part of God's plan. Despite His pain, He resisted the temptation to make events go His way. He didn't run over people's right to choose, even when they chose to act like the devil himself. Nothing evil was able to change Him from being a forgiving, caring person.

He wants to fill us with these same lamb-like qualities. It doesn't mean that we should sit back and let whatever happens, happen. We're responsible to ask, seek, and knock. When God answers with His plan, we can trust that He will give us what we need to cooperate with it.

Sometimes God needs to defend us. At other times, we have to let others feel the consequences of their sin before they will realize the truth. And at times, God needs to judge and settle the score. It's more than we can do, but not too much for our lamb-like Savior who lives in us. As He fills us, He supplies all we need to be forgiving, caring people.

The next day John saw Jesus coming toward him and said, "Look, the Lamb of God, who takes away the sin of the world!"

—JOHN 1:29

Prayer

Give up your right to anything God doesn't want you to have or be. It will make room in your heart for more of Jesus.

I WANT TO BE WHERE YOU ARE

Some days don't you just hate for your quiet time to end? Wouldn't it be great if you could keep that heightened awareness of God's presence with you all day? Don't you wish you could hang on to the joy and peace it brings? When you feel like that, what you're really longing for is heaven.

We'll never be fully at peace until we're in our true home. Some days we long for it more than others. When we're weary from life's struggles, we want to go where God reigns supreme, where everyone and everything obeys His will perfectly, where we're known and loved completely, and we're so certain we belong that we could shout, "I was made for this!"

But the best thing about heaven will be our reunion with the One we love. God's glory in all its fullness will completely penetrate and transform us. He will satisfy every longing we ever had. We'll be with the Creator, Sustainer, and Source of all joy. It's so wonderful that the Scripture writer could only say: "No eye has seen, no ear has heard, and no mind has imagined what God has prepared for those who love him" (1 Corinthians 2:9 NLT).

One day we won't be asking God to do anything for us or give anything to us because we'll have it all. We'll have Him! Until then, we pray and sing, "I just want more of Your presence!"

One thing I ask of the Lord, this is what I seek: that I may dwell in the house of the Lord all the days of my life, to gaze upon the beauty of the Lord and to seek him in his temple.

—PSALM 27:4

Prayer

"I just want to be with You" may be the best words a parent can hear from his or her child. Imagine His delight as you tell him how you long to be with Him.

I OFFER MY LIFE

God never wastes our pain. It doesn't matter whether you brought it on yourself or it was inflicted on you. God doesn't compartmentalize your life into usable and unusable experiences. He will use it all for His glory if you'll let Him.

The events and actions that may have hurt you the most can speak the loudest to a hurting world. Lost people hunger for someone who understands their woundedness. They need to know those who wrestle with nagging questions and who don't get instant relief. Christians still fall down and get lost. Believers don't have it all together.

Christians who are transparent enough to admit they've been bumped and bruised by life will change the world. When we give up trying to impress people with our perfect image, God's grace shines through.

All that you are, all that you have, all your regrets, all your acclaim, all the joy and all the pain—lay these things before God to let Him use for His glory. What have you experienced that showed that God's grace was strong enough to sustain you, pursue you, and even use you? You may never understand why God allowed your pain, but you can be sure that as you tell the world of God's grace, He will get the glory.

Though I walk in the midst of trouble, you preserve my life; you stretch out your hand against the anger of my foes, with your right hand you save me.

—PSALM 138:7

Prayer

What difficulties are you facing today? God can take your hurts, disappointments, and imperfections and speak through them. Offer them to Him today.

LORD, BE GLORIFIED

How much do you want to see God glorified? If it's just a little, play it safe and only do those things you're sure you can in your own strength. But if you want to see God glorified a lot, then follow Him to places where you'll need Him to be your indispensable necessity.

God is always up to something new, and He invites you to join Him. Whether it's a new career, a new ministry, a new relationship, or a new act of obedience, He wants you to take risks outside your comfort zone. His ideas of what He can do in and through you are so much bigger than your own, you'll have to stretch to grasp them.

Each time you step out in faith you'll move closer to the next challenge, and the next, and the next until you live in a way that depends on God every moment. Such a life brings God much glory!

So, how much are you willing to need God? And how much do you believe He can do? He loves to use the simple things to confound the wise, the weak things to shame the strong, and the lowly things to overcome the great. Follow His call as you pray for Him to be glorified in your life today and every day.

And whatever you ask in My name, that I will do, that the Father may be glorified in the Son.

—JOHN 14:13 NKJV

Prayer

It's often difficult to tell whether the call we're hearing is from God or our own ego. Let the Holy Spirit examine your motivations to clarify whether you are hearing something that needs heeding or something that needs healing.

SANCTUARY

Have you ever looked so hard for God in your life that you forgot He was right there—inside you? Maybe you were so intent on finding His purpose or knowing His will that you missed the fact that all day He was giving you ideas, whispering that He loved you, and encouraging you to keep going.

You're not alone. Paul had to remind the church at Corinth that they were temples of the Holy Spirit if Christ had come to live in them (1 Corinthians 6:19). If he were writing today, Paul might call these believers "sanctuaries," just as this song expresses a strong desire to be a living sanctuary for the Lord.

As a sanctuary, God wants us to be a safe place for others to come in order to experience His love. He wants us to be a refuge for souls who are hurting and a strong arm for those who have been burdened. No, we don't have to work miracles; we just have to connect people with the miracle worker. As we relinquish our role to Him, our lives become a holy place for others.

The life of Jesus in you may be the only sanctuary some people ever enter. Believe in that life and nourish it through prayer and Scripture. Then the God who lives in you will welcome others to know Him, too.

Do you not know that your body is a temple of the Holy Spirit, who is in you, whom you have received from God? You are not your own; you were bought at a price. Therefore honor God with your body.

—1 CORINTHIANS 6:19-20

Prayer

How pure and holy is your sanctuary?
Ask God to clean out the things that distract you from Him.
Receive His grace so your life will be a safe place for others.

NO OTHER NAME

Do you believe that Jesus rules over the universe? Even more crucial, do you believe He rules over your life—your past, your present, and your future? Before your story ever began, He knew it beginning to end. He has only allowed in it the people He created. He has only let happen the events He already knew He would use for your good. Nothing in your life has taken the Lord by surprise.

In His supreme sovereignty, Jesus understands everything inside you. He knows all your motivations, feelings, thoughts, immaturities, hidden faults, and hindrances. You are no surprise to Him. He has never said, "If only I'd known better, I would have changed that." He's always known it all!

If you wrestle with what might have been, exalt Jesus to His proper place. The Creator and Ruler always knew what would be. Nothing has happened by accident. You're in this place and time by His design. He is there too, reigning supremely over it all.

But our High Priest offered himself to God as one sacrifice for sins, good for all time. Then he sat down at the place of highest honor at God's right hand.

—HEBREWS 10:12 NLT

Prayer

Ask God to help you let go of all that "should have been" and accept His exalted rule over your life.

MORE LOVE, MORE POWER

Close athletic contests are exciting for fans and players alike. Good athletes enjoy playing against someone who is an even match. Rivals challenge us to reach for every ounce of skill and power we possess. They push us to new levels in our game.

The same is true in our spiritual lives. Few of us would volunteer for a mission that required us to daily struggle for a higher level of love and power. But since our enemy is great, we're required to press for more. In fact, thanks in part to Satan's challenges, we can know great victory. What joy would there be in overcoming a weak enemy?

Relying on ourselves, we'd never overcome such a formidable foe. But as we let go of all that defeats us, we make more room for Christ to fill us. He replaces our unforgiveness, regrets, and doubts with His love, peace, and power as we worship Him. There's no limit to what we can receive because there's always more of Him to have.

In the end, it's really no contest because the One who lives in us is greater than the one who lives in the world. Ever since the cross, Satan has been doomed to defeat. His advances will only serve to bring us into new levels of God's love and power.

You, dear children, are from God and have overcome them, because the one who is in you is greater than the one who is in the world.

—1 JOHN 4:4

Prayer

If you really want victory in your life, you first have to join the winning side. Dedicate all your heart, mind, and strength to God's glory. Then let Him fill you with all you need to overcome your enemy.

I GIVE YOU MY HEART

How badly do you want to be free in Christ? It usually takes getting fed up with the world's empty promises, tired of Satan's traps, or sick of our own stupid impulses before we really want to be free. Until that point, we stay bound by our stray affections.

Satan deceives us into thinking that we should only give God part of our heart, as if that way we could get the best of both worlds: our own selfishness and God's goodness. The truth is that the very thing we refuse to surrender imprisons us. We never experience the freedom of walking with God and enjoying His presence until we let go.

If God is trying to wrestle you to the ground to give in, know that whatever you let go of is nothing compared to knowing Him. His love and peace are so much more real, more stable, and more lasting. You won't believe you didn't give in sooner.

God always finds more for us to surrender—hidden attachments and unhealthy desires. By giving them all to Him, they lose their power to control us. Little by little, He sets us free to love and worship Him. That's a freedom worth surrendering for.

Blessed are they who keep his statutes and seek him with all their heart.

—PSALM 119:2

Prayer

Ask God to show you what you may be hanging on to instead of Him. Then ask for the faith in His goodness, power, and love to be able to give it up and be set free.

MAKE ME A SERVANT

Throughout the Bible, we read of God choosing humble servants to convey His power.

Where would Naaman be without his wife's servant girl sending him to Elisha to be healed? Where would Jesus be without Mary accepting God's will as the handmaiden of the Lord? Where would the Christian church be without Paul and Timothy? Where would we be without Jesus, the One who came to serve and give His life as a ransom for many?

These servants, and countless others like them, humbled themselves in order to lift up others. Their lives didn't revolve around developing their spiritual gifts, finding something great to do for God, or even becoming the best they could be. Instead they asked: "Who can I help?" "What can I do to fit in with God's plan?" "What need is God calling me to meet?" "How can I obey?" As a result, they changed the world.

Your humble service can do the same. Trust that whatever God has put in you He can work powerfully through. Whatever your gift, use it to serve others. Then people will hear the powerful message of God's grace: They are worth being loved.

For even the Son of Man did not come to be served, but to serve, and to give his life as a ransom for many.

—MARK 10:45

Prayer

Ask God to examine what holds you back from serving others.

CREATE IN ME

How good is your vision? Your eyes may be twenty-twenty, but spiritually we see with our hearts. That's why Paul's prayer for the church at Ephesus was that "the eyes of your heart may be enlightened" (Ephesians 1:18). Are you seeing God as clearly as you'd like?

When our hearts are dirty, our vision is impaired. Like this songwriter, we need God to come and clean us.

Sometimes we aren't seeing God in our lives and we don't even know where we're "off." We just know something's not right. That's when it's helpful to pray some questions and ask the Holy Spirit to do some probing. "How have I been resisting what You've been trying to teach me?" "Is there something true about You, God, that I haven't been believing?" As we open the door, the Holy Spirit reveals our sin and is able to remove any detriments to our vision.

God is always at work (John 5:17). He wants you to know Him better and better. He longs for you to see how much He loves and cares for you. He wants what's best for you and is working to bring you into all of it. If you can't see that, it may be time to pray the words of the song and let God clean out your heart.

Create in me a clean heart, O God; and renew a right spirit within me.

—PSALM 51:10 KJV

Prayer

A clean heart can have a powerful effect on the world.
Don't try to rush God into using you before
He's done what He needs to in your heart.

REFINER'S FIRE

*I*t's humbling to read Luke's introduction to his story about the Pharisee and the tax collector who went to the temple to pray (Luke 18:9-14). Luke says that Jesus told the parable "to some who were confident of their own righteousness and looked down on everybody else." In other words, "Listen up, all of you who focus on doing all the right things but miss how off you really are."

That was the Pharisee's problem. He was so busy tithing and sacrificing that he was blind to the judgmental attitude of his heart. In his self-righteousness, he missed God's desire for him to receive mercy and then pass it on to others.

When we focus on our outward actions, especially how we compare to others who act worse, we too are in danger of missing the depth of sin in our own hearts. That's where God wants to do His major work. As we let Him examine our desires and attitudes, our righteousness is revealed for what it is—a flimsy substitute for confidence in God's mercy.

You can trust God's love and kindness toward you. He sits like a refiner of silver, closely watching over you as He purifies you. When the "dross" is burned away, what is left is a beautiful piece of silver in which the refiner can see His reflection. The process may be painful at times, but God is cleansing you so that He can see His reflection in you.

He will sit and judge like a refiner of silver, watching closely as the dross is burned away.

—MALACHI 3:3 NLT

Prayer

Unless God reveals the sins in our hearts, we'll probably never see them. Let Him examine your attitudes. Remember, the fire of His love is strong enough to purge any sin.

WE ARE AN OFFERING

Can God be trusted? Is He really as good as He says He is? Since the Garden of Eden, people have wrestled with these questions. We know we should surrender wholeheartedly to Him, but doubts tempt us to withdraw, trust ourselves, and take no risks.

We will never know anyone more deserving of our surrender.

God promises to give us all good things: "He who did not spare his own Son, but gave him up for us all—how will he not also, along with him, graciously give us all things?" (Romans 8:32).

God promises to be faithful, even when we're faithless: "If we are faithless, he will remain faithful, for he cannot disown himself" (2 Timothy 2:13).

God promises to never abandon us: "Never will I leave you; never will I forsake you" (Hebrews 13:5).

God promises to give us peace no one can take away: "I have told you these things, so that in me you may have peace..." (John 16:33).

God promises to take us home to be with Him: "I am going there to prepare a place for you...I will come back and take you to be with me that you also may be where I am" (John 14:2-3).

Give Him complete control. You'll find Him completely trustworthy.

Offer yourselves to God, as those who have been brought from death to life; and offer the parts of your body to him as instruments of righteousness.

—ROMANS 6:13

Prayer

Ask God to reveal the fears that hold you back from surrendering to Him. Examine them in light of His truth and walk in the confidence of His love for you.

ALL I ONCE HELD DEAR
(KNOWING YOU)

We spend so much time and effort trying to know what we cannot know—what trials lie ahead; how our children will turn out; what God might do through us. Thankfully, the secret of getting ahead in the spiritual life isn't what we know but whom we know.

When we let go of all we cannot figure out, we get to know God. That's not an accident. God planned life to work that way. Instead of pursuing Him, we can easily slip into pursuing answers or his plans. But when we do that, our intimacy with Him always suffers.

God reveals Himself to those who put Him first. He entrusts His plans to us (Psalm 25:14) and graciously imparts Himself to us when we want to know Him more than anything. His goal is to draw us into a relationship so strong that we'll trust Him even without the answers.

If you've been frustrated by God's silence, it could be that you're asking the wrong questions. As hard as it might be, let go of needing to know anything besides Him (even if that means knowing you're loved or knowing God's will). Make needing to know God your only pursuit. He will not keep you clueless as to the rest. It's just that He never wants you to forget that it's all about a relationship with Him.

Continue your love to those who know you, your righteousness to the upright in heart.

—PSALM 36:10

Prayer

The apostle Paul considered everything a loss compared to the surpassing greatness of knowing Christ Jesus (Philippians 3:8). Set aside your other pressing needs in prayer today and pursue knowing Him.

HE IS ABLE

We don't have all of the answers. But fortunately, we don't have to handle it all! We don't have to be consumed with our problems as if it's all depending on us. Knowing God can handle our concerns frees us to live balanced lives.

God wants us to experience rest and play as much as He wants us to work hard. Jesus came that we might have and enjoy our lives (John 10:10) and not be bound by anxiety or dread. As much as we'd like it, we don't have to know the answers to these questions: Where will God lead me? How will He resolve this? When will I get relief?

Relief comes when we're content to live the questions. When we embrace just the step in front of us, we can revel in the anticipation of what God will do with all the rest. Whatever lies ahead will be good, because God will be there and He is always good. He always gives us what we need.

God is preparing your circumstances so that everyone who sees you will acknowledge that you are a person whom the Lord has blessed (Isaiah 61:9). It's your inheritance as God's child. Jesus died to give it to you. Receive it. Live the questions and let God accomplish the rest.

Cast all your anxiety on him because he cares for you.

—1 PETER 5:7

Prayer

Sometimes we get so concerned with the future, we miss the step right in front of us God wants us to take. Tell God everything that concerns you, put it in His hands and then live as if you are in His will. Ask Him for the faith to believe He is guiding your steps even when you don't have all the answers that you would like.

HERE I AM, LORD

When God needed a faithful leader for Israel, He called Samuel. And He literally called. "The Lord came and stood there, calling as at the other times, 'Samuel! Samuel!' Then Samuel said, 'Speak, for your servant is listening'" (1 Samuel 3:10). When He needed a prophet for Israel, Isaiah answered the call: "Then I heard the voice of the Lord saying, 'Whom shall I send? And who will go for us?' And I said, 'Here am I. Send me!'" (Isaiah 6:8).

God may not call you to serve Him as clearly as He did Samuel or Isaiah. Instead, He may call in a quieter, but no less certain way. However it's packaged, God is calling you to love people the way He does. Where do we get the power to love people who may wound us, offend us, or not deserve it in our minds? Only by seeing them as broken, blind, and in need of a Savior—at exactly the same place we would be if Jesus hadn't rescued us. Jesus' love never forgets that this is what we are. He doesn't expect perfection. He isn't surprised when we fail. He knows we would be empty if He didn't fill us, broken if He didn't heal us, and alone if He didn't belong to us.

That's the message He asks us to share with others. He's calling you. How will you respond?

A new command I give you: Love one another. As I have loved you, so you must love one another.

—JOHN 13:34

Prayer

Is God's call clear in your life?
If not, ask Him to put his desires on your heart.
As you step out, you'll find out what He wants.

GIVE THANKS

Human-made religions center on what people can do for their god. But Christianity centers on what God has done for us. He gives us His Son as a continual source of comfort and freedom, even when we have nothing to offer in return. To receive Him, we only need to let go of trying to save ourselves and rely on Him alone to save us.

This requires admitting our weaknesses and allowing God to use them to show Himself strong. That's humbling! And oh how we fight it. We want to be loved for being so good, not for being so needy. Yet God knows this is exactly what we are. Instead of being put off by our inabilities, He encourages us to come to Him. He knows that only people who have come to the end of themselves rely on Him. God has a limitless supply of hope and strength for people who recognize their need. No matter how "poor" we may feel, we are the richest people in the world, all because of what the Lord has done for us. For this, we give thanks.

He gives strength to the weary and increases the power of the weak.

—ISAIAH 40:29

Prayer

Give thanks to God for all He has done for you.
Invite Him to show Himself strong in a difficult situation,
and thank Him for the opportunity to rely on Him.

GIVE THANKS

Give thanks—to whom? To the Holy One, God Himself. Why? Because He has given Jesus Christ His Son. Given Him for what? To die on a cross and save us from our sins. Give thanks—how? With a grateful heart.

If we really think about it, we are overwhelmed: God sent His one and only Son to die a cruel death on a cross. That's how much He loves us, rebellious, evil, contentious, sinful people. We don't deserve such love. We don't deserve to have someone die for us—and yet Someone did. God looked down upon His glorious creation, now stained by sin, and He knew He would act to bring us back to Himself. He could not simply overlook sin, change His mind, or decide that maybe sin isn't so bad after all. Sin had to be punished, but He took the punishment upon Himself through His Son. When Jesus shed His blood on the cross, He was paying the punishment for our sins. Now, when we accept His sacrifice, we are made right with God.

Give thanks, and do so with a grateful heart! We would have no hope for eternity if not for the Holy One who has given Jesus Christ, His Son, for us.

For God so loved the world that he gave his one and only Son, that whoever believes in him shall not perish but have eternal life.

—JOHN 3:16

Prayer

Thank the Lord for giving Jesus Christ, His Son, to take
the punishment your sins deserved. Thank Him
with a grateful heart for all He has done for you.

ALMIGHTY

A mother asked her preschool daughter, "What are you drawing a picture of?"

The little girl unabashedly replied, "I'm drawing God!"

"But, sweetheart, no one knows what God looks like."

Continuing to pull her pencil across her tablet the young artist sighed, "They will when I'm done!"

Try to explain God and you'll quickly discover that you're in over your head. Nobody can explain who God is, what He looks like, why He works as He does. Yet when Jesus draped Himself in human skin and entered our world, He gave us a glimpse of God. The apostle John put it this way: "The Word became flesh and made his dwelling among us" (John 1:14).

But that was two millennia ago. What about when the "Word" doesn't become flesh but simply remains a book on the table? Well, that's when we need to open that book and discover for ourselves more about God. We may not be able to see God, but when we look into His Word, we learn what He is like. We discover, among other things, that He is almighty, glorious, most holy, faithful. What adjectives can you add to the list?

> *Now to the King eternal, immortal, invisible, the only God, be honor and glory for ever and ever. Amen.*

> —1 TIMOTHY 1:17

Prayer

Spend some quiet moments in the Father's presence.
As you ponder his creation, consider how the Lord has
earned the titles "almighty," "holy," and "faithful."

VICTORY CHANT

Nothing is quite like a college football stadium when the home team comes from behind to win the game. The rhythm of pounding drums echoes through the stands. The foot stomps and cheers of approving fans are thunderously loud. An amazing victory demands an appropriate response.

Christians have even more reason to celebrate. What Jesus accomplished on the cross was far more important than any game. Although He was sidelined for three days, He returned from the grave to erase any doubt as to what He had done. Once and for all, Jesus won our eternal salvation and defeated death. But the King of kings not only conquered death, He invaded our self-centered hearts, freeing us from ourselves.

So we owe Him our praise. We hail Him—Lion of the tribe of Judah—who will one day open the scrolls and usher the end of history as we know it. And we will be with Him forever because of what He has done for us. It's our privilege to celebrate His victory with songs of praise, expressions of joy, and prayers of gratitude. His love truly does free us to sing. So how about it? Have you sung yet today?

Then one of the elders said to me, "Do not weep! See, the Lion of the tribe of Judah, the Root of David, has triumphed. He is able to open the scroll and its seven seals."

—REVELATION 5:5

Prayer

Repeat the first phrase of "Victory Chant" over and over aloud. Thank Him for freeing you to sing praises to Him.

JESUS IS ALIVE

People of all ages gathered in a small Baptist church in rural Bangladesh to view a screening of the "Jesus" film. The small building was so crowded that little children had to sit on the floor while rows of adults stood in the back. During the crucifixion scene, weeping and gasps of disbelief could be heard as the dark-skinned audience looked on in horror. As the Bengalis watched, they vicariously sensed the drama of the moment. It was as if they actually could feel the agony of Jesus' pain and the disappointment of the disciples. In that emotional moment, one young boy near the makeshift screen jumped to his feet and cried out, "Don't be afraid. He gets up again! I saw the movie before."

Whether we say, "He gets up again," "Christ is risen," or "He's alive!" the reality of the Resurrection should not be reserved for only one Sunday a year. The message of Easter is the foundation of our faith every single day of our lives. Because Jesus defeated death, He is not bound by space, time, or distance. He's alive! Jesus lives forever! Write in block letters across your calendar, "Every day is Easter!"

> *Because Jesus lives forever, he has a permanent priesthood. Therefore he is able to save completely those who come to God through him, because he always lives to intercede for them.*
>
> —HEBREWS 7:24-25

Prayer

Spend some quiet moments rehearsing the "crosses"
you are currently carrying in your life. Then thank
Jesus that because His cross did not defeat Him,
He is alive today to help you carry yours.

April 4

MOURNING INTO DANCING

Mourning. Unless you see it spelled, the mere mention of the word suggests the delight of a breathtaking sunrise or the fresh start each daybreak promises. In reality, however, "mourning" means just the opposite. Those who mourn are sorrowing. Their soul is lost in a long, seemingly endless night.

Mourning is part of life in an imperfect world. The Bible tells us that "the wages of sin is death" (Romans 6:23). When sin came into the world, death tagged along. When death takes loved ones, we mourn. That is a natural process—we should. In fact, it is healthy to grieve for a time. There is indeed "a time to weep and a time to laugh, a time to mourn and a time to dance" (Ecclesiastes 3:4).

Of course, we will miss the person and feel the sorrow; but in the midst of mourning, God promises daily mercy and grace. The time for laughter and dancing will return, for God will lift our sorrows. He approaches us and asks us to dance. Though circumstances may be difficult, He alone can waltz us away from the brink of despair and envelop us with His everlasting arms.

Then maidens will dance and be glad, young men and old as well. I will turn their mourning into gladness; I will give them comfort and joy instead of sorrow.

—JEREMIAH 31:13

Prayer

If you are in mourning because of some loss in your life,
pour out your heart to the Lord. Admit your
feelings candidly. Ask Him to sweep you off
your feet with a sense of His presence.

GREAT IS THE LORD

Remember playing with a magnifying glass when you were a child? Maybe you discovered its power when you used it to focus a ray of sunlight. (I wonder how many insects have been burned to a crisp on sidewalks and driveways.) Even if you weren't so mischievous, you soon realized how that small oval piece of glass could transform the words in a comic book. Simply holding the magnifying glass above the page made those little letters become huge.

The psalm writer says over and over again that the Lord is great. That is His way to describe the immeasurable qualities of the Lord of the universe. Obviously, one five-letter word is not nearly adequate to support the weight of God's glory. But it provides us with a magnifying glass of sorts with which to examine His goodness and enlarge His worth (at least in our eyes). When we see God's greatness, we realize that He alone is worthy of glory and praise. That's what happens when we take the time to focus on the Lord. He doesn't get any bigger than He already is. But from our perspective, He is greater still. Lift up your voice—great is your Lord!

> *Great is the Lord and most worthy of praise; his greatness no one can fathom. One generation will commend your works to another; they will tell of your mighty acts.*
>
> —PSALM 145:3-4

Prayer

Pray with your eyes wide open. In fact, hold a magnifying glass over Psalm 145 and pray the words of the psalmist aloud. Allow the larger-than-normal letters to boost your confidence in the Lord's worthiness.

WE GIVE THANKS

Within a couple months of the September 11 terrorist attacks on the World Trade Center and the Pentagon, United States troops defeated Taliban strongholds. For the first time in decades, Afghan women were allowed to appear in public without having their faces covered. The return of the government to the people of Afghanistan represented a milepost of victory. But, the war on terrorism would require additional offensive operations.

Similarly, followers of Christ live between the inauguration and the culmination of His rule. When Jesus came to earth, He staked the boundaries of the kingdom of God. But what He announced through His teaching and validated by His death and resurrection are not complete. The initial, and crucial, battle has been waged. The deceiver of our souls has been dealt a fatal blow and his doom is certain. But the kingdom has not been fully established. The Father, in His time and according to His purposes, will complete the victory. The Son will return to reign in power. Meanwhile, we have reason to give thanks. Lift your voice in a joyful song. After all, the battle is the Lord's. One day, all nations will bow to Him. Read the last chapter of His book. We win!

"I am the Alpha and the Omega," says the Lord God, "who is, and who was, and who is to come, the Almighty."

—REVELATION 1:8

Prayer

Pray for those who have been victimized by evil.
Ask the Lord to draw near to them with His mercy and
compassion. Thank Him that the justice consistent with
His holiness and love will eventually come to pass.

I WILL BLESS THE LORD

"Ah-choo!" When someone sneezes in your presence, what do you say? You either say "Guzundheit!" or "God bless you!" And for good reason. For a brief moment, a sneeze has interrupted a person's heartbeat. The mindless response that we automatically say is actually a prayer for God to care for the person.

The dictionary definition of "bless" is to consecrate, sanctify, or bestow divine favor upon something or someone. We ask God to bless our homes. We ask Him to bless our nation. We can also entreat the Father to bless our children.

Have you ever wondered why we say "Bless the Lord"? How are we capable of blessing the Lord? Now there's a conundrum. But wait! If the Lord blesses us (and He does), then when we are called to bless Him (which we are), it means that we are invited to return the compliment. With words, attitudes, behavior, and songs on our lips, we willingly reflect back His goodness as a way to honor His greatness. In other words, we are showering our Creator with adoration and gratitude. So go ahead, let everything you do and say bless His holy name.

Enter his gates with thanksgiving; go into his courts with praise. Give thanks to him and bless his name.

—PSALM 100:4 NLT

Prayer

Tell the Lord that you want to bless Him—that is, you desire
to reflect back to Him the blessings He has so generously
given you. Then ask Him to show you how to do it!

I WILL MAGNIFY

"No, I don't want to spend eternity in heaven!" The fourteen-year-old girl's emphatic words surprised her pastor-father. "Yes, I know Jesus will be there and I want to see Him, but I can't get all that excited about floating on a cloud plucking a harp!"

For a teenager on the verge of adulthood, spending forever singing the same songs over and over sounded boring. The problem for this young woman was her definition of heaven. Nowhere in Scripture is eternity painted with such mundane colors.

According to the book of Revelation (where we get our most descriptive, albeit symbolic, picture of heaven), a lot of activity goes on in the presence of the Lord. And what's more, we are told that the King of kings and Lord or lords will be reigning. Have you ever heard of a monarch reigning where the subjects are allowed to just sit around? Not on your life! And not in your after-life either! There will be so much wonder, beauty, and meaning to our existence that we will find ourselves exulting in our identity as the bride of Christ and willingly exalting Him in all that we will be doing.

I heard a loud shout from the throne, saying, "Look, the home of God is now among his people! He will live with them, and they will be his people. God himself will be with them."

—REVELATION 21:3 NLT

Prayer

Meditate on the concept of being with Jesus
eternally in heaven. Thank Him that although
you don't comprehend it all, you can be sure you
will be there, ready to do whatever the King desires!

I BELIEVE IN JESUS

An old spiritual asks, "Were you there when they crucified my Lord?" Obviously, we can't answer a literal yes. The Savior died two millennia ago. Those who were there at the foot of that blood-stained cross included disciples, soldiers, and passersby. They saw more than they could fully understand. The sinless Son of God was subjected to cruel punishment and a heinous execution. But the true injustice was the fact that Jesus took on Himself the shame and guilt of all sin of all time.

Before He died, those who stood around heard Him say, "It is finished" (John 19:30). Curiously, in the language Jesus spoke, what He actually said could be translated, "Paid in full!" In other words, Jesus allowed our moral debt of holiness to be paid in full by Him. By His sinless life and sacrificial death, Jesus was willing to foot the bill.

Then to prove He had the moral reserves to actually cover what He offered to pay for, He defeated death. Because of the Resurrection, Jesus is standing in our midst. Next time you reach for your credit card or checkbook, thank God that you are covered when it comes to financing your eternity.

God has purchased our freedom with his blood and has forgiven all our sins.

—COLOSSIANS 1:14 NLT

Prayer

Express your gratitude to the Lord for His unmerited
mercy in your life. Ask Him to soften your heart to
the gift of salvation that is so easily taken for granted.
Ask His help to forgive those who have offended
you in light of the debt He has paid in your life.

WE BRING THE SACRIFICE
OF PRAISE

"Did you get anything out of church today?" the critical husband asked his wife as they drove to their favorite diner for Sunday dinner. "I kept waiting to hear something I could take with me that would last me through the week," he continued.

Sadly, that comment is heard in many cars between the church and Sunday lunch. In many situations, the sermon or the service has not been planned so that worshippers have a sense of what they are to do in light of what they've sung, prayed, or heard.

But no matter how lacking a sermon or service might be, the pastor and worship leader are not entirely to blame. When we enter the sanctuary on Sunday morning, we cannot expect simply to take. By definition, those who come to worship have something to give. To worship means to "offer worth" to the object of their worship. We have the responsibility to offer the sacrifice of praise. We may not leave church having gotten much out of it, but the question we need to ask ourselves is this: In our singing, praying, listening and thinking, did we offer the Lord a gift? What did He get out of the service?

> *Through Jesus, therefore, let us continually offer to God a sacrifice of praise, the fruit of lips that confess his name. And do not forget to do good and to share with others, for with such sacrifices God is pleased.*
>
> —HEBREWS 13:15-16

Prayer

Before you ask God for anything in your prayer
time today, spend some extended time reminding Him
(and yourself) how faithful and good He has been to you.
Write down ten reasons that He is worthy of your praise.

SING HALLELUJAH TO THE LORD

Many songs include the word "hallelujah" in the lyrics. Centuries before the birth of Christ, songs were composed that incorporated that hauntingly beautiful Hebrew word that simply means "praise God." Before David ascended Israel's throne, he penned hymns of praise. Exiled Jews in Babylon sang "hallelujah" to the Lord as they called on Him for deliverance. They sang that familiar word when, at long last, they made their pilgrimage back to Jerusalem.

And then there were the disciples of Jesus who, upon realizing the One raised from the dead was indeed the promised Messiah, recast the ancient word to praise the Lamb of God. From the first century on, psalms, hymns, and spiritual songs are generously punctuated with "hallelujah." It was no accident that George Frederic Handel included the "Hallelujah Chorus" in his immortal oratorio *Messiah.* He had to. No retelling of the life of Jesus or the rehearsal of God's faithfulness in history to His people could avoid it. Through the years, it has become a universal word. The same in any language. And the language of worship is incomplete without it. No wonder it will be part of heaven's vocabulary. Allow "hallelujah" to fall from your lips multiple times today.

> *Then I heard what sounded like a great multitude, like the roar of rushing waters and like loud peals of thunder, shouting: "Hallelujah! For our Lord God Almighty reigns."*

> —REVELATION 19:6

Prayer

No need for many words today. As you go to prayer, slowly repeat "hallelujah" over and over again. Vary your volume. Speak this wonderful word with expression.

KING OF KINGS

On a hot summer day in the Middle East, a twelve-year-old boy climbs an olive tree in the courtyard near his home. In the distance, above the sound of bleating sheep, he hears a quiet cadence of drums. He climbs higher in the tree. Straining his eyes, he sees a parade of people on the horizon.

Leading the way is a solitary figure. He is naked except for a loincloth. And he is dancing. The people who follow on his heels are obviously happy. As the throng draws closer to town, the boy can hear the sounds of singing. And then he sees it: a golden box hoisted on parallel poles, carried by men in royal garb. Following in step, two men hold high a royal banner. The banner bears King David's insignia. The man at the front of the procession is the king, leading the Ark of the Covenant back to Jerusalem as a child dancing before the King of all kings.

If you had been that child, chances are your heart would have pounded with excitement as you listened to the tambourine chatter and the people sing. Fortunately, worship of the same King is still possible today.

David, wearing a linen ephod, danced before the Lord with all his might, while he and the entire house of Israel brought up the ark of the Lord with shouts and the sound of trumpets.

—2 SAMUEL 6:14-15

Prayer

The Lord is indeed King of all kings and Lord of lords.
Imagine what that means. As you approach Him in prayer,
remind yourself that He is able to doing anything.
All authority and dominion are His.

GLORY

For more than two hundred years Americans have referred to their flag as "Old Glory"—and for good reason. The red, white, and blue recalls the days of glory when courageous soldiers fought to save the footings of democracy that had only recently been poured. They were glorious days indeed. So when our flag flutters overhead, illuminated by the late afternoon sun, patriotic hearts mark double time.

But the glory we speak of when referring to the Most High God is of another kind. It is not stirring memories of yesteryear. It is hardly patriotism or pride. The glorious majesty that surrounds heaven's throne invites our wonder and awe. Like a magnet, it draws from the depths of our hearts exuberant adoration as well as hushed reverence. This glory is not a nation's flag. It is the banner of praise that flies from deep within hearts that are aware of the One who has washed them clean.

Thus, the glory of God is that which radiates from His invisible yet holy presence. But it is also what is due Him. To that end, give Him the glory He deserves by reminding yourself today that you are a citizen of the kingdom of heaven.

Praise be to the Lord God, the God of Israel, who alone does marvelous deeds. Praise be to his glorious name forever; may the whole earth be filled with his glory. Amen and Amen.

—PSALM 72:18-19

Prayer

As an offering of praise, think of the word "glory"
as an acronym. Come up with words that ascribe
worth to God that begin with each of those five letters
(for example: gracious, loving, ordering, righteous, yielding).

I WILL SING OF THE MERCIES OF THE LORD

When Gunder Birkeland whistled a tune, his wife and children knew he wasn't feeling well. That was his unique way of dealing with chronic pain. As a child, Gunder contracted polio and succumbed to the crippling powers of the disease that left his feet twisted, his back hunched, and his body wracked with pain. Although Gunder learned how to cope with constant discomfort, some days were just plain hard. On those days, he whistled.

As he grew up, Gunder discovered the unconditional acceptance of a loving God. He learned that a forgiven heart was far more important than an attractive physique or a pain-free life. Once he trusted Christ as his Savior, Gunder began to recognize the many blessings a day could bring. He credited the Lord with profitable business deals, wisdom to raise three kids, and the desire to reach out to those who struggled with health issues like he had. Mercies, Gunder called them. God's undeserved mercies.

Something else Gunder did signaled how grateful he was for God's many blessings. He sang—not very well, mind you. He couldn't carry a tune five feet. But that shriveled little body contained a huge heart that couldn't contain God's love without lifting his voice in praise.

As you know, we consider blessed those who have persevered. You have heard of Job's perseverance and have seen what the Lord finally brought about. The Lord is full of compassion and mercy.

—JAMES 5:11

Prayer

Thank the Lord for ways He has been merciful to you in the last twelve months. Be as specific as you can. Then sing of the mercies of the Lord with a song of praise—and it doesn't matter how well you can sing!

ANCIENT OF DAYS

Of all the names for God, Ancient of Days is probably the most obscure. It's a name that sounds as old as the hills or as ancient as ancient history. And that is exactly what this reference to the Lord is supposed to imply. It calls to mind the reality of the pre-existence of the Creator. Just try and fathom it. Before time began, God had been on the scene for millions of years. But no one was counting.

The six days of creation are difficult enough to grasp without attempting to step behind the curtain of time in hopes of finding the stage manager of the cosmos. No matter. We wouldn't be able to see Him anyway. The Ancient of Days cannot be seen with the human eye. Yet one day, all will see Him and bow down to worship Him.

Although God can't be understood, take comfort in knowing that beyond just willing your life into being, He wills to have a relationship with you. Now that's a truth you can take to the bank. It's a desire in the heart of God that predates Adam and Eve, but it's as current as this very day.

At the name of Jesus every knee should bow, in heaven and on earth and under the earth, and every tongue confess that Jesus Christ is Lord, to the glory of God the Father.

—PHILIPPIANS 2:10-11

Prayer

Confess your finite understanding to One who understands the end from the beginning. If you are struggling with an overwhelming issue that is beyond your control, candidly express your concerns to the Lord. Turn them over to Him.

OUR GOD IS LIFTED UP

From time immemorial, worship has been characterized by more than singing. In the days of the Old Testament, the people of God came before Him with chants and shouts. They paraded in the presence of the Most High with all kinds of instruments: flutes, lyres, harps, drums, trumpets, cymbals, tambourines. This included rhythmic movements—the lyrics of praise called for both verbal and body language. Championing the cause of God can't be accomplished by offering passive approval for what He has done.

If you've ever been to a championship college football game, you've felt the electricity of emotion. When the clock has elapsed and one team has won, the band lets loose with the school's fight song. The cheerleading squad bids all spectators become participants in the victory celebration. The players, having doused their coach with a ten-gallon container of icy water, proceed to lift him up on their shoulders and parade him onto the gridiron.

Although our worship celebrations are more controlled and sane than the frenzy of a football game, we have much to learn from those occasions. Lifting up the Lord requires more than lifting up a hymnbook. Let your singing be like joyful shouts to your Lord!

Praise him with the sounding of the trumpet, praise him with the harp and lyre, praise him with tambourine and dancing, praise him with the strings and flute, praise him with the clash of cymbals, praise him with resounding cymbals.

—PSALM 150:3-5

Prayer

Spend time imagining yourself in a setting where Psalm 150 was being acted out. Ask the Lord to help you sing with great joy, lifting up and glorifying Him.

LET THERE BE GLORY AND HONOR AND PRAISES

If you're old enough, you may remember that song The Byrds sang in the sixties: "For every thing, turn, turn, turn. There is a season, turn, turn, turn." Their lyrics came right out of Ecclesiastes, chapter 3. There is "a time to cry and a time to laugh. A time to grieve and a time to dance" (Ecclesiastes 3:4).

So what is the appropriate attitude for Sunday morning worship? Is there a time to laugh, as well as a time to cry? A time to grieve as well as a time to dance? Should we come into the presence of the Lord with thinking minds or throbbing hearts? Would you believe—both?

Jesus said we are to worship Him in spirit and truth (John 4:23). In other words, we don't have to arbitrarily choose. It's not an "either, or" but a "both, and." A sane, thoughtful, and prayerful encounter with the living God brings a smile to His face. But so does a passionate rehearsal of His faithfulness expressed with the emotional faculties He created in us.

Simply put, worship requires both honor and glory. The key is being alert to what seems appropriate and then responding accordingly.

Yet a time is coming and has now come when the true worshipers will worship the Father in spirit and truth, for they are the kind of worshipers the Father seeks.

—JOHN 4:23

Prayer

Pray for your pastor and worship leaders. Ask God to give them an ability to appropriately balance the necessary elements as they plan congregational worship.

WE WILL DANCE

What do you like most about going to a wedding? (I mean other than the frosting-laden cake and salted nuts at the reception.) Most likely it is the atmosphere of joy and beauty that defies description. Like they say, you've never seen an ugly bride. If the wedding is of someone you know well, your interest is elevated.

The occasion is far from ordinary. The music is carefully chosen and well rehearsed. Families, often separated by distance, are reunited. Vows of committed love are shared. God's counsel for marital success is offered by a robed cleric. Tokens of affection are exchanged. The congregation arrives appropriately attired and bearing costly gifts. And at many weddings the reception includes more than cake and nuts or coffee and mints. There might just be a sit-down dinner and—dancing!

No wonder the Bible pictures heaven as the union of Christ and His bride. It's a place of love, joy, music, laughter, reconciliation, long-overdue justice, and togetherness. Scripture calls attention to the marriage supper of the Lamb. The atmosphere will be thick with the presence of God Himself. No red carpet runner will do. Streets paved with pure gold, please! And would you believe even the "non-dancers" will dance?

Then the angel said to me, "Write: 'Blessed are those who are invited to the wedding supper of the Lamb!'" And he added, "These are the true words of God."

—REVELATION 19:9

Prayer

Get out your wedding album and review it in an attitude of prayer. Ask the Lord to intervene in areas of your marriage where you are currently struggling. But don't stop there. Ask the Lord to fill your heart with an increasing homesickness for heaven.

WORTHY, YOU ARE WORTHY

Jesus is worthy of our praise. The sooner we learn that, the sooner we will stop our busyness to sit in His presence, as Mary of Bethany did so long ago.

The story recorded in Luke 10 describes Jesus paying Mary and Martha a visit. Martha was stressed out about getting a meal on the table. Her sister Mary, however, was sitting at the Savior's feet, feasting on His every word. Martha asked Jesus to insist that Mary give her some help. But Jesus did not comply with her request, and the reason was clear. He wanted to teach Martha a lesson. He wanted the older sister to learn that there is more to life than the art of entertaining or a fixation with food. What Jesus saw in Mary was a portrait He wanted to hold up as an example of how to set proper priorities.

Mary had recognized that her friend from Nazareth was more than a carpenter. He was more than a rabbi. He was the long-awaited Messiah. He was worthy of her worship. He is worthy of our attention. He is worthy of letting all else wait. Don't neglect time in His presence today.

I call to the Lord, who is worthy of praise.

—2 SAMUEL 22:4

Prayer

Confess to the Lord your tendency to obsess over insignificant details that derail your devotion to Him. Spend quiet time in His presence.

A SHIELD ABOUT ME

Johnny hadn't meant to hurt anyone, least of all the family dog, Bruno. When the ten-year-old had unwrapped his last birthday present, he was so excited he just had to try it out. He had asked for a BB gun for his Christmas and his birthday for the last three years. But up till now, his parents thought him too young. Johnny raced into the wheat fields in back of the farmhouse and began shooting his new toy. He hadn't realized Bruno had run after him and ran right in line of the metal pellets. The dog had been badly hurt.

Johnny moped around the house unable to look anyone in the eye. But after several hours, his wise father sat beside his son and lifted his chin with his hand. "I know you are sorry for what happened," he said gently. "We all have forgiven you. It's time you forgave yourself."

Like Johnny, we know what it's like to be sorry for our sins. But too often we live with unnecessary regret and guilt. The Father desires to lift our heads and remind us we are fully forgiven. Why don't you let Him today?

But thou, O Lord, art a shield for me; my glory, and the lifter up of mine head.

—PSALM 3:3 KJV

Prayer

Picture yourself kneeling before the King of kings who is seated on His holy throne. Visualize the Lord reaching down and lifting up your bowed head. Hear Him say to you, "My child, because I love you, forgive yourself."

FIND US FAITHFUL

Alfred Nobel, after whom the Nobel Peace Prize is named, was originally known for his invention of a substance that nations would utilize in war. Nobel, a Swedish-born scientist, invented dynamite. How he decided to channel his energies in a more positive direction is a curious story.

It seems Nobel was sipping his morning coffee while reading the newspaper. As he turned to the obituaries to read what was said about his recently-deceased brother, he was shocked to see his name. The newspaper had inadvertently published Alfred's name instead of his brother's. What was a further shock to the great scientist was seeing that if he had in fact died, all the world would remember him for was "the invention of a deadly explosive." At that point, Nobel decided he would use his fortune to reward those who would dedicate their lives to the furtherance of peace. As a result of that decision, Alfred Nobel revised his own legacy.

How do you want to be remembered? As a success in your vocational field? As one who achieved great wealth? Or as one who successfully passed the baton of faith to those whom you had the opportunity to influence?

I have been reminded of your sincere faith, which first lived in your grandmother Lois and in your mother Eunice and, I am persuaded, now lives in you also.

—2 TIMOTHY 1:5

Prayer

Think about those who left a faithful witness in the world and passed the baton of faith to you. Thank the Lord for their influence in your life. Ask the Lord to use you in the same way in the lives of those who come behind you.

HOW BEAUTIFUL

Shirley's hands weren't pretty at all. They were calloused and wrinkled. She had worked hard for most of her sixty years. Raising three energetic children had taken its toll, as had her hands-on responsibility in the family trucking business. But Shirley's hands were not too weary to serve the Lord. Her hands gladly went to work for the body of Christ.

When Shirley was asked one Friday to bake bread for Sunday's celebration of the Lord's Supper, those same hands went to work willingly. The next month when the pastor asked if she would prepare the elements for communion, she excitedly agreed. With joy she poured grape juice and broke her homemade loaf into bite-size morsels. In fact, Shirley asked if she could serve the Lord in that special way each month. For years thereafter Shirley's "beautiful" hands set the table for God's people. It was obvious she had firmly grasped what Jesus had modeled—humbly laying down her life by giving what she had to offer for the sake of the Christ's church. What is it that the Lord would like your hands to do for the body of Christ? Your hands don't need to be "beautiful," they just need to be available.

And since I, the Lord and Teacher, have washed your feet, you ought to wash each other's feet. I have given you an example to follow. Do as I have done to you.

—JOHN 13:14-15 NLT

Prayer

Today as you go to prayer, don't fold your hands. Open them
as a gesture of availability. Confess to the Lord ways
you've held back serving His church. Determine to
use the gifts God has given you in ministry to others.

THIS IS THE DAY

As Olga Birkeland grew older, the arteries in her brain became restricted. Blood flow was limited, and her capacity of mental recall was impacted. Her family grieved the gradual loss of the mother and grandmother who had been the life of the party. Against the dark backdrop of the dreaded disease that stole Olga's memory, however, there shone a bright spot.

No matter what day of the week it was, this sweet Christian woman insisted that it was Sunday. "Today is Sunday and that means we're going to church!" she would say. "Aren't you going to get dressed? We don't want to be late." The profound experiences in worship that Olga had known earlier in her life had engraved themselves on the tissues of her brain. Somewhere deep in her failing mind, she wanted it to always be Sunday.

In a way, Olga Birkeland was right. For the Christian, everyday is the Lord's Day. Each morning announces His promise of His presence complete with grace and mercy. Since each day is one that the Lord has made, we have every reason to anticipate something wonderful.

Rejoice in this day that God has made and has given to you!

This is the day the Lord has made; we will rejoice and be glad in it.

—PSALM 118:24 NKJV

Prayer

Instead of praying your typical prayer, make a to-do list for what you need to accomplish today. As you write down each item, commit it to the Lord and ask His help.

NEW EVERY MORNING

Go ahead. Picture yourself in South Texas at a Christian dude ranch. Needing a change of pace, you've come to the right place. The work you'll be doing all day is backbreaking and draining. But as you work alongside real-life cowhands, you find yourself grateful for a body that functions as God created it. This work is so different than what you're accustomed to, it almost seems like recreation.

Later, with other campers, you join the staff around a blazing campfire. The crackling logs explode, shooting sparks skyward. As you look overhead, you see what appear to be millions of crushed diamonds against black velvet. Someone strums a guitar; another picks up a harmonica. Before long, an unrobed choir of untrained voices breaks forth in praise to God for another day of grace. You sing along with all your heart because you are mindful of daily mercies like never before. It's a little piece of heaven on earth.

Now, take that same attitude toward life and God's gracious provision and live it today, in your home, neighborhood, and work. Indeed, this is the day that the Lord has made—so rejoice and be glad!

Because of the Lord's great love we are not consumed, for his compassions never fail. They are new every morning; great is your faithfulness.

—LAMENTATIONS 3:22-23

Prayer

As you find your favorite chair to spend some
time in prayer, take along a blank sheet of paper.
Contemplate the gift of an unblemished new day
that promises new evidence of the Lord's mercies.

HOLY LOVE

The Oregon Coast is a thing of beauty. The craggy rocks that define the shoreline are quite a contrast from the smooth sandy beaches of California. But the long, rugged shoreline of the Northwest boasts romance and personality. The blue waters of the Pacific drench mile after mile of tidewaters in which grow tall evergreen trees. The approaching waves fall like the pages of a book blown by an unexpected breeze.

Anyone who has spent time beachcombing along Reedsport, Florence, or Lincoln City knows that what is lovely and beautiful to look at is at the same time a power to be reckoned with. Lives are lost each year off the Oregon Coast by those who failed to respect the mysterious force that churns beneath the tranquil, glass-like sea.

The Lord is at once loving and holy. He is not to be taken lightly or dismissed as sentimental. That His love is beautiful to behold (not to mention life-changing when embraced) cannot be disputed. But His is a holy love that demands reverence and awe. When we come to Him aware of who He is, we can drink in the unequalled splendor of the Almighty God who has demonstrated His never-ending love that is deeper than the deepest sea.

The mighty oceans have roared, O Lord. The mighty oceans roar like thunder; the mighty oceans roar as they pound the shore. But mightier than the violent raging of the seas, mightier than the breakers on the shore—the Lord above is mightier than these!

—PSALM 93:3-4 NLT

Prayer

No words need be spoken in the Lord's presence today.
Simply linger in reverent silence aware of
the ocean-like power of His holy love.

COME AND FILL ME UP

"You may not feel thirsty, but you need to be drinking all the time." The tour guide smiled as he gave his warning. But it was obvious to the group of tourists in Israel that he was serious. Because they had never toured the Middle East before, they listened carefully.

The guide continued, "Because of the intense summer sun, your body loses more fluid than you realize through perspiration. Don't just drink when you are thirsty. Keep sipping throughout the day. If you don't, you'll begin to dehydrate."

At times, we open the Bible desiring to drink in the Lord's presence. During those moments, the Lord seems close, and we can't ignore our thirst for more of Him. On other occasions, however, the thought of spending time with the Father seems like an obligation or an interruption in our routine. We don't feel thirsty for the Living Water. Any seasoned traveler on the path of faith would warn us that we need to "drink" all the time—whether we feel thirsty or not. Life saps us of what we can only find in the Lord's presence.

Make sure that you take time to irrigate your soul today.

O God, you are my God, earnestly I seek you; my soul thirsts for you, my body longs for you, in a dry and weary land where there is no water.

—PSALM 63:1

Prayer

In addition to your regular time of personal worship,
stop and pray each time you take a coffee break today.
As you take a sip, allow the Lord to swallow up
the little worries that have plagued your mind.

THE POWER OF YOUR LOVE

Nome, Alaska, came to prominence during the days of the Yukon Gold Rush. Today it is primarily known as the terminus of the Iditarod sled dog race. This little town of three thousand people is situated on the Bering Sea and perched on the permafrost that the Native Americans of the north call "tundra."

If you've been in Nome in both the summer and the winter, you might think you are in two different towns. During the summer, the muddy dirt roads in front of wood frame houses are littered with abandoned cars, rusted-out washing machines, and broken furniture. Once the snows come, the garbage-strewn town is a virtual fairyland. A blanket of white covers all the unsightly litter. But, as you might expect, when the spring thaw comes, reality returns.

Except for the power of God's redeeming love, our lives would be much like Nome. From time to time, we could successfully cover the ugliness of our guilt and shame, but not for long. What is buried eventually is exposed. What we could not bring about on our own, however, God has done by His amazing grace. He has replaced our garbage with His goodness.

The power of God's love has made you clean—completely clean.

"Come now, let us argue this out," says the Lord. "No matter how deep the stain of your sins, I can remove it. I can make you as clean as freshly fallen snow. Even if you are stained as red as crimson, I can make you as white as wool."

—ISAIAH 1:18 NLT

Prayer

Ask the Lord to change, renew, your heart. Ask Him to strip away your weaknesses and deal with your sin by the power of His great love.

AMAZING LOVE

Maybe you have seen that stunning painting that depicts Christ's amazing love. A person stands behind a dark-haired man who is no longer strong enough to stand on his own. But it's not just anybody who is bearing him up with strong, embracing arms. It's Jesus!

Upon closer examination, you see the details in this portrait of love. The man being held by the Lord is stained with blood. In his limp hand, he still grasps a hammer. From the context of the scene, we are left with the unmistakable impression that Jesus is holding the person responsible for His crucifixion.

But that man with the hammer is more than just the man in the painting. He represents each of us. Although the Roman soldiers were the ones who drove spikes into Jesus' wrists, they acted on our behalf. Our sin caused Jesus to be tortured and to die. Indirectly, we nailed Him to the cross. Yet, guilty as we are, Jesus comes behind us and holds up. Talk about amazing love. That's exactly what it is.

When confronted by the reality of God's amazing love for you, how do you feel? How can you respond?

This is real love. It is not that we loved God, but that he loved us and sent his Son as a sacrifice to take away our sins.

—1 JOHN 4:10 NLT

Prayer

Picture yourself in that famous painting. Feel the arms
of Jesus holding you up. Release your sense of guilt in
shame and allow them to fall at your feet—and His.

DRAW ME CLOSE

*T*he Bible has many stories about blind people being healed by
Jesus. Perhaps the most dramatic, however, is that of Bartimaeus.
As this blind beggar sits by the side of the road, his hope is nearly
gone. Jericho's famed groves of trees provide shade for the sight-
less man, but nothing can shield him from the sense of worthless-
ness and shame.

One day as the townsfolk chatter amid their typical routines,
Bartimaeus overhears talk that arrests his attention. The miracle-
working rabbi from Galilee is approaching the village. He has
heard of the amazing feats this carpenter-turned-teacher has
performed. In his lonely heart he dares to wonder if Jesus might
have the power to heal him.

No doubt you know the rest of the story. As Jesus draws close,
Bartimaeus cries out, "Jesus, Son of David, have mercy on me!"
(Mark 10:47). Even though the crowd tries to silence the beggar,
he cries out all the more. Blind Bartimaeus was so needy, he had
nothing to lose. He longed to be drawn close to the Lord with the
cords of love. And Jesus did not disappoint him.

Whatever disables your faith today, call out to this same Jesus
and let Him draw you to Himself.

*Then I pray to you, O Lord. I say, "You are my place of refuge. You are
all I really want in life."*

—PSALM 142:5 NLT

Prayer

Take your cue from Bartimaeus. Sit cross-legged on the
floor and close your eyes. Admit your need to the Lord
and reach out your arms. Call out to Him by name.

JESUS, WHAT A WONDER YOU ARE

Early one Sunday, Pastor Troy left for church with his young family. As he carried his little daughter Lesley to the car, she spotted a bright star. Pointing with her stubby finger, she shrieked.

"That's a morning star, sweetie," her daddy explained. He then began to sing, "Twinkle, twinkle little star, how I wonder what you are. Up above the world so high, like a diamond in the sky. Twinkle, twinkle little star, how I wonder what you are." Little Lesley slipped her thumb in her mouth and laid her head on her daddy's shoulder. A child's wonder had been acknowledged.

Our first introduction to the subject of stars is not all that scientific. Long before we came to understand their chemical consistency or distance from earth, our parents serenaded us about their wonder. There was no need to fully explain their origins or function in order to appreciate their majesty.

Similarly, we don't need a seminary education to understand the wonder of the one the biblical writers call "the Morning Star." His gentleness, purity, and kindness shine down through history and from the pages of God's Word. Even a child can sense His splendor. But it takes a lifetime (and then some) to wonder about all that He is.

Show the wonder of your great love, you who save by your right hand those who take refuge in you from their foes.

—PSALM 17:7

Prayer

Step outside late at night or early in the morning and look to the twinkling stars overhead. Allow that silent chorus of praise to stimulate your delight in your Creator's power.

JOY OF MY DESIRE

Kathy looked ten years older than the date her birth certificate boasted. Not bad for a forty-year-old woman who had already lived two lifetimes. Starved for love as a kid, she rebelled as a teenager and sought the physical affection of any man whose attention she could attract. She had a baby out of wedlock, and then another. In addition to the disgrace of her family, the pressures of raising children on her own took their toll. Kathy turned to alcohol and then drugs. But the buzz and the high never filled her emptiness. She baked pies as a way of supporting herself and her two kids.

One Sunday, on a lark, Kathy decided to attend a little country church half a mile down the road. One of her best customers attended there. What this modern-day Samaritan woman found in that place was a whole lot more than she bargained for. She met Jesus. In His embrace of grace, her definition of love was rewritten. She had found what she had been looking for.

All around us are women and men at some well, trying to quench a thirst that can only be satisfied in the unconditional love of the Lord. Be on the lookout for them today. Point them to the One who can satisfy their desire and give them joy.

But the water I give them takes away thirst altogether. It becomes a perpetual spring within them, giving them eternal life.

—JOHN 4:14 NLT

Prayer

Ask God to open your eyes (and your heart) to someone who is longing to know the love only He can supply.

IN THE LORD ALONE

Swiss Army knives are great tools. In one little device, you have a virtual tool kit in your pocket. In addition to an all-purpose knife, you have a screwdriver, a bottle opener, a pair of miniature scissors, a corkscrew, and a nail file. With your Swiss Army knife at hand, you'll be in a position to whittle your way through all kinds of knotty challenges. You will even be a hero to someone whose eyeglass screw has just come loose.

In a much larger scale, that's what the living Lord desires to be to those who worship Him. In Him we have more than a Creator. We have a Savior, a Healer, a Guide, a Defender, a Father, and a Friend. In Him we have the solution to our frailty and sinfulness. In Him we have a supreme Judge and Servant Leader. In Him alone we have all we would ever need.

No wonder when Jesus commissioned His followers to go into every corner of the world on His behalf, He only equipped them with the promise that He would be with them.

Wherever you go and whatever you face, Jesus is with you—and He's all you need.

Neither height nor depth, nor anything else in all creation, will be able to separate us from the love of God that is in Christ Jesus our Lord.

—ROMANS 8:39

Prayer

On a slip of paper list the various roles the Lord has played in your life since you surrendered to His rule.

YOU ARE MY GOD

In Psalm 22, we are privy to King David's deeply intimate thoughts. Reading those haunting verses is like looking over his shoulder while he makes an entry in his personal journal. It's obvious that David is in much distress. As far as he is concerned, God is on vacation. "My God, my God, why have you forsaken me?" he cries.

But look again. Even though David feels forsaken by God, he expresses his doubt in prayer. Does that surprise you? This psalm is a prayer to God. Wouldn't you think that if David really felt God was nowhere to be found, he wouldn't waste his breath complaining? Not so. There is something in David that causes him to believe that God is still within earshot, even if it seems as though He's gone for good.

After all, David knows this God very well. He's been in a tight spot a time or two before, and the Lord has always come through. David's words betray his underlying belief that the Lord is his God. For David, this relationship is the fruit of a number of years of walking together.

The Lord is your God as well. And as such, He can handle your honest doubts and fears. Don't fear to express to Him your thoughts and feelings.

For he has not despised or disdained the suffering of the afflicted one; he has not hidden his face from him but has listened to his cry for help.

—PSALM 22:24

Prayer

Write a letter to God. Use friendship language.
Share your fears and hopes. Go ahead and use stationery.
Fold it in an envelope and tuck it in your Bible.

YOU HAVE BEEN GOOD

Here's a song worth playing over and over again. The more you listen to it, the more you want to sing along. This waltz-like melody invites our hearts to dance. Even without lyrics, this tune in three-quarter time can lift the most downcast spirit. It pulls the drapes away from the window of our hearts and lets the sunlight of God's love shine in.

But the song's poignant words join hands with the memorable melody and together they circle around our worshiping hearts. The lyrics point out that God's faithfulness and goodness from which we have benefited have touched the lives of countless generations before us. They paint a series of word pictures that remind us on the cloudiest of days that ours is a God who cannot withhold His penetrating presence from us.

Martha Stewart, the consummate entertainer and homemaker, is known for her signature expression, "It's a good thing." Well, thanks to Twila Paris, we can claim a signature expression by which we greet the Lord each day: "You have been good, Lord."

You are forgiving and good, O Lord, abounding in love to all who call to you. Hear my prayer, O Lord; listen to my cry for mercy.

—PSALM 86:5-6

Prayer

Today as you pray, simply say, "Lord, it's a good
thing that..." and then finish the statement
with something good that the Lord has done.

THY LOVING KINDNESS

U"Up, Daddy, up!" Kristin reached her arms up in the air. "Hold me, Daddy!" Even without words, the two-year-old's desire could have been discerned. But added together, the plea was unmistakable. As far as little Kristin was concerned, being in her father's arms was better than life itself. Loving her dad the way she did, she wanted to nuzzle his neck and kiss his face. He had earned her love because he had earned her trust.

When we chronicle the many ways that God has intervened on our behalf, we have every reason to trust him as a reliable loving Father. He has proven Himself over and over again. Sometimes we, like tantrum-prone toddlers, are strong-willed enough to deny His goodness. But, when we come to our senses and are willing to be honest, we are forced to admit that His loving kindness is, in fact, better than life.

Next time you are in a praise gathering and those around you extend their arms to heaven in adoration, picture yourself as a young child desiring to be held by your Father. Lift your hands unto Him. "Hold me, Daddy. Hold me!"

Because your love is better than life, my lips will glorify you. I will praise you as long as I live and in your name I will lift up my hands.

—PSALM 63:3-4

Prayer

Before coming before the Lord with your
laundry list of personal requests, spend several
minutes glorifying Him with your lips.

WE HAVE COME INTO THIS HOUSE

There is a legend about a Greek immigrant who walked from Lewiston, Idaho, all the way to Washington, D.C., during World War II. This man dearly loved his adopted country. He was too old to fight, but he wanted to find a way to help pay for freedom. Gus determined he would use his feet and his willpower to raise money for the war effort. He would ask his family and friends to give a penny to the war effort for every mile he walked.

Although the trip took Gus several months, by the time he approached the nation's capital, news of the Greek American had reached the president. He and the first lady sent word to the weary walker that they would like to have dinner with him in the White House. You can imagine the pride that pounded in Gus's heart as he entered the mansion at 1600 Pennsylvania Avenue. With reverence and joy, he respectfully deflected every question the president asked him. He simply wanted to enjoy the ambiance and pay his respects to the leader of the free world.

When we enter the Lord's house, we are to do so with a sense of celebration and respect. Worship is all about God. Our concerns and preference are to take a back pew. Worship is an invitation to forget about ourselves and magnify the Lord.

Speak to one another with psalms, hymns and spiritual songs. Sing and make music in your heart to the Lord, always giving thanks to God the Father for everything, in the name of our Lord Jesus Christ.

—EPHESIANS 5:19-20

Prayer

When you enter the Lord's house this coming Sunday,
focus on forgetting about yourself, magnifying
the Lord, and worshiping wholeheartedly.

WHATEVER IS TRUE

The image is disturbing. A frying pan sits atop a kitchen stove. The announcer's voice says, "This is your brain." Then we see someone crack an egg and empty its contents into the sizzling skillet. Once again the announcer speaks. "This is your brain on drugs."

Sadly, countless teenagers with incredible potential have scrambled their brains by indulging in mind-altering drugs. But there is no turning back. Once the damage is done, the results are irreversible.

A mind is a terrible thing to waste. But that not only is true with regard to drug abuse; it also has to do with the content we upload into the precious organ God gave to each of us. It is true (sometimes alarmingly so!) that we become what we think about. No wonder the apostle Paul was so insistent that the Christians in Philippi guard their minds by filtering their thoughts. If he were around today, he would challenge us with the same words.

With what do you fill your mind? Make sure it is true, noble, right, pure, lovely, admirable, excellent, and praiseworthy.

Finally, brothers, whatever is true, whatever is noble, whatever is right, whatever is pure, whatever is lovely, whatever is admirable—if anything is excellent or praiseworthy—think about such things.

—PHILIPPIANS 4:8

Prayer

Be aware of your thoughts today. Consider if they
are pure, right, noble, and true—or if you would
need less lovely adjectives to describe them!
Ask the Lord to help you think purely.

YOU ARE THE MIGHTY KING

Peter had his share of embarrassing moments. His tongue boasted footprints from the sandals that fit his feet. But one time Peter resisted the temptation to put his foot in his mouth.

Jesus asked the disciples what kind of press He was getting in the marketplace. "Who do people say the Son of Man is?" (Matthew 16:13). And His friends shared what they had heard as they had traveled around Israel. But then Jesus posed a follow-up question: "Who do you say I am?" And with enviable confidence Peter responded, "You are the Christ, the Son of the living God" (Matthew 16:15, 16).

If Jesus were to ask you the same set of questions, you probably could answer quite easily who people in your circle of influence think He is: either the Son of God or a respected religious prophet or teacher. Not much has changed in two thousand years. But how would you answer the second question? The temptation is to answer it the way Christians whom we admire would answer it. But Jesus would not be content with the stock answer. He wants to know who you say He is. If He isn't yet the Mighty King in your life, you can do something about that.

For to us a child is born, to us a son is given, and the government will be on his shoulders. And he will be called Wonderful Counselor, Mighty God, Everlasting Father, Prince of Peace.

—ISAIAH 9:6

Prayer

In the quiet of a reflective moment, listen for Jesus to ask you who He is in your life. Be honest. Then ask Him to become even more influential in your life.

JESUS, WHAT A BEAUTIFUL NAME

An angel caught a young teenage girl by surprise. The surprise element only grew when the angel proceeded to tell Mary what God had in mind. Before leaving her, the angel implied that a book of baby's names would not be a necessary purchase. She was to call her baby "Jesus." But had Mary been told at that moment how the world would eventually be touched by the name of her Son, she would have been astounded.

In Mary's day, "Jesus" was a fairly common name. It was the Aramaic equivalent of "Joshua." What was uncommon were the circumstances surrounding this particular Jesus' birth, His life and ministry, as well as His death and resurrection.

Today, baby boys are still named Jesus, especially in Latin American countries. But whenever you hear the name of Jesus without reference to a last name, there is no doubt about who is being talked about. It is the beautiful Savior with the beautiful name whose grace transforms the pain and sorrow of an ugly world and makes it a beautiful place to live.

"Jesus"—speak and sing that name with joy!

And his name will be the hope of all the world.

—MATTHEW 12:21

Prayer

Make the name of Jesus a work of art. Regardless of your
artistic abilities, take your kid's crayons or markers
and print "Jesus" in the middle of a blank sheet.
Thank Him for the hope His name brings.

AS WE GATHER / THE STEADFAST LOVE OF THE LORD

In the early 1970s something remarkable was happening in Costa Mesa, California. A pastor by the name of Chuck Smith walked the beaches of Orange County, sharing his faith in Jesus with long-haired hippies. As many gave their hearts to the Lord, Pastor Chuck suggested they gather for Bible study. Handfuls of converts became hundreds. Calvary Chapel became known as the church by the beach where lives were being changed nightly.

Pastor Chuck welcomed the new musical influences the converted hippies brought with them to Bible study and worship. He celebrated their gifts and invited them to write songs of praise to the Lord. The result was a movement in religious music that continues to this day.

The two songs that comprise this medley were part of the first wave of what we now refer to as praise and worship music. The evidence of changed lives, worship gatherings that were truly celebrations, and Spirit-inspired songs that reflected contemporary culture all bore witness to the steadfast love of the Lord that is continually new.

Regardless of your age, experience, or knowledge, you can sing your new song to the Lord.

It is of the Lord's mercies that we are not consumed, because his compassions fail not. They are new every morning: great is thy faithfulness.

—LAMENTATIONS 3:22-23 KJV

Prayer

Thank God for the way praise music has touched
your life and that of your family. Sing one of your
favorite songs to the Lord—just you and Him.

THE GREATEST THING

Wheaton College has had its share of notable graduates—including evangelist Billy Graham and martyred missionary Jim Elliott. These men left Wheaton with the school motto engraved on their hearts: "For Christ and His Kingdom."

In the days that followed September 11, 2001, the world was introduced to yet another graduate of Wheaton College. Todd Beamer, a 1991 graduate, was one of those on the United Airlines plane that crashed in rural Pennsylvania, a plane that was likely headed toward another target in Washington D.C. Todd and others on the plane with him are credited with leading an attack against the terrorists who had killed the pilot and commandeered the cockpit. Realizing he was about to die, Todd used the on-flight phone to call home. Unable to reach his wife, he prayed the Lord's Prayer with the Air Fone operator as a testimony to his faith. Then he said good-bye and turned and uttered the phrase that has now been heard all over the world: "Let's roll!"

Knowing Christ and living for Him and His kingdom was Todd's highest priority. As a result, knowing that death was coming was not the end of the world. It didn't deter him from one final act of courageous Christian service. Living for Christ and His kingdom can motivate you to greatness too. Let's roll!

I want to know Christ and the power of his resurrection and the fellowship of sharing in his sufferings, becoming like him in his death.

—PHILIPPIANS 3:10

Prayer

Claim Wheaton College's motto as your prayer for today.
Listen in your heart for ways the Lord will make aspects
of that motto possible as you go about your tasks.

HIDE ME IN YOUR HOLINESS

Do you recall the lullaby your mom used to sing to you as she rocked you to sleep? Probably not. And if your kids are pretty well grown, you might not even remember the lullabies you sang to them when they were babies. There are many from which to choose, but all nighty-night melodies have the same purpose: to provide an atmosphere of peace in which a little one can fall asleep.

When you think about it, all lullabies are designed to calm the spirit and comfort the soul. Even the lyrics are the kind of thoughts you'd want to fill your mind with at the end of the day.

After a grueling day of stressful decisions, anxious commutes, difficult encounters, and people issues, you want to relax in the presence of God. You want to confess your shortcomings and express your longings. As if with a blanket of protection, you desire for the Lord to hide you in His holy presence. Now there's a formula for a good night's sleep.

You are my hiding place; you will protect me from trouble and surround me with songs of deliverance.

—PSALM 32:7

Prayer

Tonight, surround yourself with a lullaby from God by reading your favorite psalm. As you prepare to fall asleep, make the words of His song a comforting chorus of your prayer.

THE SWEETEST NAME OF ALL

When he was born, his mama named him Walter. But when Walter Payton grew up and started playing for the Chicago Bears, his fans called him "Sweetness." This Chicago legend had the heart of a fierce competitor as well as the gentle heart of a compassionate person. On a team of tough football players, many of whom lacked some of the relational skills or social graces of other professions, Sweetness was a refreshing balance. When he died a few years ago in his early forties, Walter Payton had left the world a sweeter place.

No one in the Bible ever referred to Jesus as "Sweetness." Somehow that would have minimized the reverence of which He was worthy as the Messiah. But in a bitter world, where hate mocks love and justice is often pinned to the mat by power, Jesus came as the sweet foretaste of a glorious new world. Jesus was the sweet fragrance of life in a decaying world where death has taken a premature bow. His words of life were like honey.

No, Jesus was never called Sweetness, but His gentle, compassionate manner with children and society's outcasts was definitely more like sugar than vinegar. He desires to be the sweetener in your life as well. And He will be if you simply spend time in His presence each day.

How sweet are your words to my taste, sweeter than honey to my mouth.

—PSALM 119:103

Prayer

Ask God to help you evaluate attitudes or patterns in
your life that leave a sour taste in people's mouths.
Seek His help to do just the opposite.

PEOPLE NEED THE LORD

Next time you are at the mall, conduct your own people survey. You'll need a clipboard, a sheet of paper, and a pencil. But don't worry. You won't need to ask questions. Just position yourself on a bench near to where shoppers walk as they trek from store to store. As people pass by, look in their faces. Write down descriptive words that describe what their faces convey. Do they look happy? Tired? Sorrowful? Pained? Bored? Energized? Depressed?

If they pass close enough to you, look into their eyes. What do you see? Light? Emptiness? Life? Passion? What about the body language you witness in the posture of individuals? Are they in love with life? Are they in a hurry? It's amazing what you can infer about people's level of contentment with life just by observing their countenance and actions.

If you could only peek into the souls of the people passing you, your heart would break. Yes, people need the Lord. You can see it in their eyes and on their faces. And because they need the Lord, they also need you to tell them about Him.

Who can you tell about the Savior today?

When he saw the crowds, he had compassion on them, because they were harassed and helpless, like sheep without a shepherd.

—MATTHEW 9:36

Prayer

Ask the Lord to give you eyes to see people in your
world the way He does. Ask Him to break your
heart with the things that break His heart.

LIFT HIM UP

*I*f you have ever watched a weightlifting competition on television, you can describe the scene. A muscle-bound contestant resembling Hercules strides onto the stage wearing a body suit. As he prepares to reach down for the massive weights, his face takes on a certain aura. The lifter's eyes are closed. It's as if he is praying. Actually, he is lost in deep concentration. As he collects his thoughts, he is marshaling his strength for what is about to take place. And then after several moments of personal preparation, the athlete quickly jerks the bar up and pushes it over his head.

What a great parallel for the person who prepares to worship the Lord. In order to lift up the name of Jesus, we must thoughtfully prepare for what we are about to do. We need to focus our thoughts on the One we desire to worship. Closing our eyes to better concentrate, we may feel the need to confess wrong attitudes or sinful behavior. We no doubt will want to rehearse in our heads how the Lord has demonstrated His strength in the midst of our weakness. Much like the weightlifter who must mentally prepare himself for that which tests his limits, the awesome task of lifting the name of Jesus higher and higher requires us to go through a series of warm-up exercises.

I will praise you as long as I live, and in your name I will lift up my hands.

—PSALM 63:4

Prayer

Prepare to enter the Lord's holy presence by asking
Him to reveal unconfessed sin in your life.
Once He has, claim His offered forgiveness.
Then spend some moments reflecting on His faithfulness.

HOSANNA

Kids love parades. Something about a festive procession fuels their innate enthusiasm. The floats are beautiful. The bands are loud. The clowns are engaging. Have you ever seen an unhappy child while a parade passes by? Come to think of it, at parades adults most resemble their happy-go-lucky children. Smiles abound. Cares are absent.

Jerusalem's children lined the dusty road as a parade passed by one Sunday long ago. No clowns or bands. No flower-covered floats. No drill teams in this parade. But a dignitary was there. I guess you could say He was the Grand Marshal. The children cheered, but they were not alone. Their parents applauded and sang as the solitary figure riding a donkey came into view. "Hosanna! Hosanna in the highest!" they sang. They waved branches from palm trees. They carpeted the cobblestones with their capes and cloaks. The one on the donkey ironically was the King of the cosmos. It must have been quite a scene.

It's a scene that we are able to recreate every time we come as children into the Lord's presence. With joy and confidence we recognize there is no need to worry, for He is Lord of all.

The crowds that went ahead of him and those that followed shouted, "Hosanna to the Son of David! Blessed is he who comes in the name of the Lord! Hosanna in the highest!"

—MATTHEW 21:9

Prayer

Close your eyes and picture yourself at that
Palm Sunday parade. Feel the enthusiastic joy.
Think of words that you might have called out as
you saw Jesus' smiling eyes looking in your direction.

THE RIVER IS HERE

*I*f you have ever had the privilege of traveling in Israel, you have probably visited Jerusalem, Bethlehem, and Nazareth. If you were fortunate, your tour also included the Jordan River, which connects the Sea of Galilee and the Dead Sea. Consider yourself truly blessed if your itinerary encompassed Banias.

Banias (or ancient Dan) is the small territory to the north of Israel where the snow melt of Mount Hermon cascades into flowing streams of fresh water before emptying into the Sea of Galilee. This lush green region feels like the Garden of Eden must have been. Unspoiled and fresh. Colorful and beautiful. As you walk the dirt paths at the base of the waterfalls, the churning sounds of the turbulent streams sound like a rhythmic melody.

What begins way up on the mountain as melting snow is in actuality the genesis of the Jordan River. What a great metaphor for the way the presence of a holy God flows into our lives. With small trickles of His grace and rivulets of His mercy, the river of God becomes a current that carries us with power each day of our lives. But we have a choice. We can dam the flow or let the Lord have His way. What will you choose today?

> *They are like trees planted along the riverbank, bearing fruit each season without fail. Their leaves never wither, and in all they do, they prosper.*
>
> —PSALM 1:3 NLT

Prayer

Thank God for the river of His love that flows
continuously from His heart. Thank Him
that it represents cleansing and healing.

SHOUT TO THE NORTH

Jesus never claimed to be one of many ways to God. With an exclusive confidence that angers the contemporary critic of Christianity, Jesus announced that He is "the way, the truth, and the life." Furthermore, without even pausing to take a breath, the Savior said, "No one can come to the Father except through me" (John 14:6 NLT).

Someone has joked that to say that "all religions lead to God" is like saying that to call home all you need to do is simply dial any seven digits you choose. All calls end up at the same place. Only a fool would try that approach. Obviously, every set of numbers but one would be wrong.

The truth is that Jesus is the Savior for all. He did not die for only a certain type of person. He died for the world He created. He seeks a relationship with people of every color, every language group, and every culture in every country of the world. What might initially sound exclusive or narrow is, in fact, grounded in glorious inclusiveness. We are invited to call out to the ends of the earth that God so loved the world that He gave His only Son that whoever believes in Him will not perish but have everlasting life.

Messenger of good news, shout to Zion from the mountaintops! Shout louder to Jerusalem—do not be afraid. Tell the towns of Judah, "Your God is coming!"

—ISAIAH 40:9 NLT

Prayer

The "shout" is a biblical form of praise. Why not try it?
In your prayer closet, the basement, or alone in
the woods, go ahead and cheer the Lord with
a "hallelujah" or an "I praise You, Jesus!"

YOU ARE GOD

We are imperfect people who have a tendency to be capricious, moody, and unreliable. We say one thing and do another. We make promises only to let those easily spoken words fall from our lips and break in a million pieces on the ground. We were created in God's image, but we are damaged goods. Sometimes we resemble our Creator; sometimes we fail the likeness test miserably.

In contrast to our unpredictability, God is constant, true, and faithful. He can only be consistent with Himself. The Scripture tell us that He is incapable of change. What He promises, He does. What He prizes, He continues to treasure. What He demands, He continues to expect. Although some would argue to the contrary, His Ten Commandments have not become ten suggestions. His fallen world is still a world for which He continues to accept responsibility and is one over which He maintains complete control.

Simply said, our changing views about God don't alter God. Our inability to accept His truth does not invalidate its accuracy. God is God and will always be. This is a terribly frightening and yet a very comforting reality. It is a reality that invites our praise.

Every good and perfect gift is from above, coming down from the Father of the heavenly lights, who does not change like shifting shadows.

—JAMES 1:17

Prayer

Admit to God your tendency to be hot or cold (even lukewarm) toward Him. Ask Him to increase your faithfulness. Celebrate the fact that He cannot change.

YOU ARE MY KING

"There's no such thing as a free lunch," they say. That old axiom means that there has to be somebody footing the bill somewhere. Those who make their way to a soup kitchen or a rescue mission don't have to pay at the door. They are welcome. But someone has contributed to this agency so it could provide for others.

The same could be said for heaven's handout. Looking down on His fallen creation, God saw us in our need. We could not repair the rift that separated us from our Creator. Heaven was designed to be our ultimate home, but without some kind of intervention we would be forever homeless. A holy God who is wholly compassionate designed a rescue mission that would bridge the breach. He would offer us complete forgiveness, residency in heaven, and full inheritance as sons and daughters. But the only way He could accomplish this was to punish His perfect Son by placing on Him all our guilt, shame, and selfish ambition. Grace would be free, but it would come with an unbelievably costly price tag.

No wonder we call it "amazing" grace. In light of all Jesus did to purchase our salvation, no wonder we claim Him as the King of our lives.

For you know the grace of our Lord Jesus Christ, that though he was rich, yet for your sakes he became poor, so that you through his poverty might become rich.

—2 CORINTHIANS 8:9

Prayer

Consider the contrasts that distinguish us from our great God. Think about what the Father paid that we might freely claim His love.

ONCE AGAIN

The kitchen table represents the heart of a family unit. Around it, a memorized grace is offered, meals are shared, and memories are made. Parents rebuke, siblings tease, heartaches are confessed, and jokes are tried on for size. To this same table, grown children who had married and scattered return, time and time again to see the folks and recall the good old days. When a family member dies, the kitchen table serves as a magnet drawing the mourning to assigned places.

In much the same way, the communion table at church serves as the family gathering place. As we gather around this family table, memories are recalled that point to the death of our elder Brother who willed that we would forever gather in His name. Like the one in the home in which we grew up, this is also a table where we can expect the Father's discipline, assurance of His forgiveness, and the opportunity to celebrate the privilege of being a family.

Whenever you have an occasion to enjoy the Lord's Supper, once again you are given an opportunity to think about Jesus' sacrifice and embrace the inheritance of His grace. Thank Him for the cross, for by it you have been saved.

He canceled the record that contained the charges against us. He took it and destroyed it by nailing it to Christ's cross.

—COLOSSIANS 2:14 NLT

Prayer

Use a cross pendant or a cross on the wall as a visual aid. Think about the cross on which the Savior paid for your salvation. Ponder His suffering. Meditate on His love.

POUR OUT MY HEART

*I*f you knew for a fact that God heard you every time you prayed, you'd be inclined to keep praying, right? If you were convinced that God caringly bent His ear in your direction whenever you approached Him with something that was on your heart, you'd be more apt to come clean with Him. So why do we typically struggle to maintain a regular prayer time?

Maybe it's related to questions we have about how prayer works. If God is really interested in what we have to say and if He actually listens to the cry of our heart, does He actually answer the prayers we offer up?

Scripture is definitive about this. It assures us that God answers every prayer we pray—every single one. His answers aren't always the ones we're expecting or hoping for. But He always responds. As someone has wisely observed, "Sometimes God replies with yes, sometimes with no, sometimes with wait."

So don't look at prayer as an obligation that you need to do to please God. Accept it as a wonderful privilege to pour out your heart to Someone who cares for you more deeply than anyone else in the world.

> *Trust in him at all times, O people; pour out your hearts to him, for God is our refuge.*
>
> —PSALM 62:8

Prayer

It's called "emptying prayer." Take out a blank sheet
of paper and write as fast as you can all the "stuff"
in your heart about which you are concerned.
Transfer the title of these worries to the Lord.

BLESS HIS HOLY NAME

*I*t's the funniest thing. You are stopped at a red light when you look over to your right, and there in the car next to you is a nattily dressed businessman engaged in an animated conversation—with himself. A classic case of insanity. The driver smiles, punctuating his thoughts with hand gestures. One moment he is losing it with laughter. And then before the light has changed to green, he is chewing himself out royally. Oh, now you see it. He isn't talking to himself after all. His car is equipped with a wireless phone attached to the sun visor.

Quite possibly, those who observed King David on his throne thought he was off his rocker. He did not have a miniature cell phone clipped to his royal robes, yet he was talking to himself. The Scriptures bear witness to that. And based on what the Word of God indicates, nothing about David's practice betrayed mental illness. He spoke to his soul.

Come to think of it, following David's practice might very well prevent mental illness or emotional captivity. When we command our inner beings to rejoice in the Lord, we place ourselves in position to do more than just respond to negative feelings or unexpected circumstances. By talking to ourselves, we discover the benefits of being proactive.

Bless the Lord, O my soul; and all that is within me, bless His holy name!

—PSALM 103:1 NKJV

Prayer

Instead of reeling off requests of what you want God to do for you, picture yourself in the presence of the Lord, all the while speaking aloud to your soul. Remind yourself how wonderful He is.

I SING PRAISES

Robert Schmidgall was the beloved pastor of the 4,000-member Calvary Church in Naperville, Illinois. He and his wife, Karen, had planted the church in their living room thirty years earlier. Through their influence, hundreds of people had put their trust in Christ and discovered the indescribable joy of worshiping Him. Bob Schmidgall loved to sing praises, and he continued to lead the congregation in singing praise.

On January 3, 1998, two days after he had celebrated his fifty-fifth birthday, Pastor Bob collapsed while having breakfast with a friend in a local restaurant. He was dead by the time he hit the floor.

On the day of his funeral, the sanctuary of Calvary Church was packed to capacity. Seated among members of the congregation were the mayor, city council members, and ministerial colleagues. It should have surprised no one that, as Pastor Bob's casket was rolled up the center aisle and positioned near the communion table at the front of the church, the congregation was led in singing this song, "I Sing Praises." Because that was this pastor's stated goal in life, it was only appropriate that these lyrics would mark his death.

What song would epitomize your life and Christian commitment?

Praise the Lord. Sing to the Lord a new song, his praise in the assembly of the saints.

—PSALM 149:1

Prayer

Thank the Lord for those pastors, Sunday school teachers, and church leaders whom He has used in your life to sow and nurture faith. Ask the Lord to use you in the lives of others.

THE POTTER'S HAND

*T*he story is told of a master pottery maker in Peru. Having heard of the distinct quality of his work, people from all over the world traveled to the outskirts of Lima in search of his unpretentious shop. It was an uncovered cluttered workspace exposed to the intense rays of the South American sun. As a result of forty years of continuous labor, the potter's sun-baked skin resembled the dark reddish-brown clay he shaped into beautiful pots and bowls.

What distinguished this artisan's pottery was a small indentation that every piece boasted. The notch-like feature at first glance might be considered a flaw. But it was not. It was the result of a claw-like digit on the potter's right hand. He was born with it instead of a thumb. The shriveled stub and its permanent sharp fingernail imprinted the clay as it was fashioned in its final form. What had been a source of endless humiliation as a child had become the signature of success.

Although our Creator's fashioning hands are not deformed, as He shapes us into His image, the evidence of His fingerprints in our lives render us valuable and priceless in His eyes. Celebrate the worth He sees as He looks at you today.

Yet, O Lord, you are our Father. We are the clay, you are the potter; we are all the work of your hand.

—ISAIAH 64:8

Prayer

Hold out your hands in front you. Observe the tiny
blotches, the wrinkles, the unique markings of your palm.
Allow the mystery of your hands to remind you of the
loving purpose with which the Potter shaped your life.

LIFT HIGH THE LORD
OUR BANNER

Ever since September 11, there has been a renewed interest in flying Old Glory. Miniature flags flutter from antennas as cars fly down the freeway. Giant flags hang majestic and motionless in food courts of shopping malls. Residential neighborhoods are punctuated by the prominence of stars and stripes positioned on front porches.

When our freedoms are threatened, our fearful hearts beat as one. We are willing to proudly gather under the banner of our country without concern of being criticized. When war looms, there is no room for cynics.

Obviously, "Old Glory" has its place. But we who are citizens of another kingdom know that the Lord is our glory. He is our banner. He is the emblem of our salvation. He is our standard of righteousness. Because the cross has staked His claim in the soil of our souls, it is only right that we pledge to Him our allegiance.

Songs that remind us that we are subjects of the King do not undermine the love of our country. They provide us with a necessary reality check that when all is said and done, our kingdom has yet to fully come.

But we are citizens of heaven, where the Lord Jesus Christ lives. And we are eagerly waiting for him to return as our Savior.

—PHILIPPIANS 3:20 NLT

Prayer

Thank God for the blessings and privilege of living in a
country that allows you the freedom of worship, and ask
Him to remind you of the goodness of your heavenly home.

MIGHTY WARRIOR

When you think of commanders-in-chief, who comes to mind? Ulysses S. Grant? Robert E. Lee? George Patton? Dwight D. Eisenhower? In the United States, the term refers to the President. He is the head of all those in the armed services. He is the apex of the military chain of command. No wonder a trumpet fanfare hails his entrance whenever he enters a room. He is vested with total authority and willingly bears the responsibility for the nation's defense.

Referring to Jesus as the Commander-in-Chief of the cosmic battle of the ages is appropriate. It's a great word picture. Christ went head to head against the guerilla-like strategies of Satan and won. Thinking of Him as the mighty warrior who stands with us as we face our daily spiritual skirmishes encourages us. Although we may feel as though we are all alone on the front lines, nothing could be further from the truth. Our warrior is with us, leading us through the trenches and providing us with a barrack of protection. Going before us, His shadow falls upon us and envelops us with safety.

Then Jesus came to them and said, "All authority in heaven and on earth has been given to me."

—MATTHEW 28:18

Prayer

Admit your feelings of weakness and vulnerability to Jesus.
Confess your need of His protection and strength.
Picture Him helping you put on your spiritual armor.

HOW GREAT IS YOUR LOVE

"How deep is your love?" Long before the Bee Gees posed that question as a way of measuring romantic affection, the apostle Paul considered it in terms of God's love. Digging to the point of bedrock, Paul strained with everything he had to try and picture for us the dimensions of our spiritual security. The pile of words that resulted from his dredging expedition fills the eighth chapter of Romans.

Suffice it to say, there is no way that we can comprehend the greatness of God's love. It goes beyond our ability to understand or communicate (let alone measure). To say it is higher than a mountain and wider than the heavens is only the beginning. The love of God is the source of our faith, the destination of our hope, and the means by which we can love Him in return. Far more than some adolescent definition of infatuation, God's love is the unfathomable, indescribable atmosphere that allows us to breathe spiritually. In His unconditional love, acceptance, and forgiveness is the oxygen of life. Consciously breathe in His love as you go about your day.

For I am convinced that neither death nor life, neither angels nor demons, neither the present nor the future, nor any powers, neither height nor depth, nor anything else in all creation, will be able to separate us from the love of God that is in Christ Jesus our Lord.

—ROMANS 8:38-39

Prayer

Thank the Lord for His love that is so high, wide, deep, and long that it always surrounds you.

I LIFT MY EYES UP (PSALM 121)

The ancient city of Jerusalem was not all that big. "The Ophel," as the city of David was called, was about a mile long and a half-mile wide. This rectangular-shaped strip of land gently sloped north across the Kidron Valley from the Mount of Olives. In this same section of land Solomon would later build the temple of the Lord.

Because of the topography of the area, the location of Israel's capital city was always a concern. It was precariously perched among the Judean hills. Because taller hills encircled the city, Jerusalem was vulnerable to sneak attacks by her enemies.

The King James Version of Psalm 121 is beautiful poetry, but it offers a misleading translation. "I will lift up my eyes to the hills from whence cometh my help" gives the impression that the hills were a symbolic source of strength. They were not at all. They were a source of fear. Fortunately, newer translations remedy the situation. Because the king lifts his eyes up to the mountains, naturally he wonders where his help will come from. And gratefully he can answer for us based on his past experiences. His help will come from the Lord who made heaven and earth. When you need help, you need only to lift your eyes to heaven. From there, your help will come.

I lift up my eyes to the hills—where does my help come from? My help comes from the Lord, the Maker of heaven and earth.

—PSALM 121:1-2

Prayer

What mountains are making you feel dwarfed today? What issues leave you feeling intimidated or afraid? Lay them before the Lord and express gratitude that God promises His help.

EXALT THE LORD

Have you ever been caught in an unexpected rain shower on a warm spring day? Because the weather forecaster didn't anticipate this sudden change in barometric pressure, he or she failed to advise you of the need for an umbrella. As a result, you got absolutely drenched. But you didn't mind all that much. It was a warm rain, and heaven's "tears of joy" actually felt kind of nice.

It's a bit odd. Being caught unawares and getting soaked do not exactly define an ideal situation. But if the above scenario has ever been your plight, you know how delightful it is. You wouldn't want it any other way.

Something just as unexpected and wonderful is the refreshing presence of the unseen Lord. You can't see Him, but you feel Him near. This beautiful praise song is a mellow reminder of how perfect our lives can seem even when they are lived against the backdrop of big disappointments. We exalt Him when we relax in the knowledge of His sovereignty.

I will cause my people and their homes around my holy hill to be a blessing. And I will send showers, showers of blessings, which will come just when they are needed.

—Ezekiel 34:26 NLT

Prayer

Stop right now. Don't go any further. Your plans
for the day will wait. Spend the next five minutes
realigning your perspective. Claim the promise
that the Lord is with you in all that you do.

GREAT ARE YOU LORD / GREAT IS THY NAME

Back in the sixties, Tony the Tiger loved to growl out his reaction to his special cereal: "They're gr-r-r-eat!" he'd say. It was an advertiser's clever attempt to get us kids to bug our parents to buy that cereal. Well, even though it's probably been quite a while since you last had a bowl for breakfast, you have to admit they were good. Maybe even very good. But great?

Life is filled with all kinds of special things—favorite foods, heartrending music, breathtaking beauty, poignant moments with family, career milestones, birth, maturity, reconciliation, and so much more. As incredibly moving as these experiences are, however, we do ourselves a disservice if we are quick to claim that they are great. Only God is great. Only He is deserving of such a five-star rating. Only He is perfect. Consider this acronym: "God Rules Everything Always Terrifically." Now that's gr-r-r-eat!

As with the word "love," when we overuse a word that is to be used sparingly, it loses its punch. Next time you catch yourself saying something is really "great," rewind the tape and replace the adjective. Meanwhile, take time today to be conscious of all that is great about our great God.

Great is the Lord and most worthy of praise; his greatness no one can fathom.

—PSALM 145:3

Prayer

Come up with your own acronym for God's greatness
using the five letters of the word "g-r-e-a-t."
Meditate prayerfully on your great God.

I WILL SERVE THEE

*I*n the film version of *Annie*, that little red-haired orphan girl is chauffeured to Daddy Warbucks' mansion. Mr. Warbucks' assistant describes to Annie all the wonderful opportunities that await her. She will be able to have tennis lessons, go swimming, shop for new clothes, and choose what she would like for dinner. The list goes on and on.

Because Annie is accustomed to earning her keep at the orphanage, when she is asked what she would like to do first, the little orphan girl stops to think, then says, "I think I'll do the windows first and then the floors so in case I spill water on the floor I can mop it up while scrubbing." When told she doesn't have to do any chores in her new home, Annie can't believe it. It sounds too good to be true.

Being adopted into the family of God is a lot like Annie's experience. Becoming heirs of God is nothing we can earn. It's a free gift. Salvation and eternal life are bequeathed to us. All the same, recognizing what has been given to us (and can't be taken away), we are overwhelmed with love and want to serve the Lord as a way of saying thanks. What we do is a way of expressing our love.

But be sure to fear the Lord and serve him faithfully with all your heart; consider what great things he has done for you.

—1 SAMUEL 12:24

Prayer

Before you ask God to do something for you today,
make yourself available to Him and listen for
ways that He might want you to serve Him.

UNTO THE KING

Legend records that when she was a little girl, Queen Elizabeth got separated from her parents while on a hike in a forest. Afraid and alone, the young princess followed a path until she came to a cottage. An elderly woman welcomed the child into her home and proceeded to brew a pot of tea. Elizabeth explained her plight and asked for help. The woman, in whose home the princess sought refuge, was most impressed with Elizabeth's etiquette and grace. Eventually she asked the child, "Are you someone special?" to which Elizabeth answered, "Oh no, mum. I'm no one particularly special. But my father is the king!"

What a wonderful picture of who we are and what we are called to be. In the grand scheme of things, we aren't all that insignificant. We are easily lost in the jungle of life. We are in need of others to help us find direction. But our Father is the King of the universe. He has everything under control and is not overcome by the challenges that steal our peace. As we focus our eyes on Him instead of the obstacles around us, not only will we discover an ability to cope, we will reflect His grace and beauty. As we look to Him today, those around us will see in us a family resemblance.

Now unto the King eternal, immortal, invisible, the only wise God, be honour and glory for ever and ever. Amen.

—1 TIMOTHY 1:17 NKJV

Prayer

Celebrate the freedom you have being a creature and not the Creator. Thank God that you are not responsible for holding the world together. Express gratitude that He is.

THE LORD IS HOLY

A preschool boy rushed into the kitchen while his mother was preparing dinner. Having played outside in a vacant lot since lunch, the little guy was covered with dirt, grass stains, and thistles. A forest of muddy footprints followed behind him as he hurried into the house. Before his mom could utter a word, Josh held up both arms and said, "I need a bath, Mommy. I'm a filthy dirty mess. Can you help me get clean?"

The consequence of living in a fallen world includes falling down and getting smudged with the filth that surrounds us. We are stained by the ugly talk we hear at work. The atmosphere of gossip, off-colored stories, and profanity rubs off on us. We get tripped up by jealousy, envy, and a desire to please other people. We get snagged by temptations that arouse our lower nature. Yes, we know what it feels like to need a bath. We are anything but holy.

Gratefully, the God we worship is holy and pure. He longs to cleanse us from the evidence of sin in our lives and in our world. Memories of that warm soapy washcloth with which our moms used to bathe us whet our desire to be clean before the Lord.

Cleanse me with hyssop, and I will be clean; wash me, and I will be whiter than snow.

—PSALM 51:7

Prayer

On a sheet of paper, jot down thoughts or actions that marked your life in a negative way today. Admit your weakness and wrongdoing to the Lord. Accept His cleansing.

HIS NAME IS JESUS

Christians have been singing songs of praise since the first century. One of the very first songs they sang is actually recorded in correspondence Paul wrote to the church in Philippi. In the second chapter of Philippians, he incorporates lyrics into his letter about the incarnation of God's Son. Those ancient words underscore the uniqueness of Jesus. They celebrate the fact that His name is above every other name.

The life and ministry of Jesus bore witness to the truth that nothing could derail the locomotive power of His love. The lame walked, the blind saw, the dead were raised to life. When Jesus encountered need, He sowed seeds of hope. And the reason was clear: He had the upper hand.

Throughout history, those who claim the name of Jesus watch walls of resistance fall. The name of Jesus continues to take precedence over every other name that defines humanity today: sinner, blindness, prisoner, and orphan. It is a name that is elevated above death, demon possession, drug addiction, or divorce. It is a name that we are given permission to speak when confronted with the giants that dwarf us each day. All we need to do is speak it boldly and watch the Lord intervene on our behalf.

Therefore God exalted him to the highest place and gave him the name that is above every name, that at the name of Jesus every knee should bow.

—PHILIPPIANS 2:9-10

Prayer

Softly say the name of Jesus over and over again.
Each time you say it, picture it rising to the top
of the pyramid of pain and problems in your life.
Thank Him that He is king of your mountain.

ALL CONSUMING FIRE

Following the collapse of the two towers of the World Trade Center, the smoldering rubble burned for months. As bodies were retrieved and debris carried away, smoke continued to curl toward the sky, reminding us of a tragedy we'd rather forget. Gratefully, the burning eventually ceased as peace returned to our hearts.

Scripture tells us that our God is an all-consuming fire. Unlike the hell on earth that follows the invasion of an enemy, His is not a fire that blazes without purpose. His eternal flame is a purifying fire. It is fueled by His holiness. It is spread by His desire that we be holy too. His smokeless flame aims to burn away our impure motives and consume our wayward thoughts. With the heat of a refiner's furnace, the Lord desires to rid us of anything that would stand between Him and us.

Although the ravaging smoke of September 11 speaks of the sin in our world that God wills to quench, the blazing fire of an Olympic torch or the flickering flame of a dinner-table candle can be a helpful reminder of the presence of a holy God. He is the God of every nation and a God who focuses His cleansing love in our direction.

Therefore, since we are receiving a kingdom that cannot be shaken, let us be thankful, and so worship God acceptably with reverence and awe, for our "God is a consuming fire."

—HEBREWS 12:28-29

Prayer

Light a candle and ponder the dancing flame.
Read the verse from Hebrews and ask the Lord what
impurity in your life He desires to burn away today.

ALL THINGS ARE POSSIBLE

Linda Gregoriev thought her life was over. Her husband, Steve, had just died, leaving her with five adopted children under the age of twelve. This forty-something schoolteacher doubted she would ever marry again. "Who would want a widow with five kids?" she wondered. As far as she was concerned, it would more likely that she be kidnapped by a Middle Eastern sheik than find a husband.

But Linda had not given her Savior the credit He deserved. As a committed Christian, she knew that Jesus delights in drilling doors through steel curtains. But a lack of faith prevented her from believing the Lord for such a miracle in her situation. Nonetheless, the Lord was determined to surprise Linda with proof that He is the God of the impossible.

Enter a recently converted recovering alcoholic by the name of Larry. Making himself available to do "fix-up" projects around Linda's home, Larry found himself falling in love. The widow's contagious smile and compassionate heart won his. Not only were the two married, within two years they were accepted by Wycliffe Bible Translators as field staff in South America. All things possible? You'd better believe it.

Jesus looked at them and said, "With man this is impossible, but with God all things are possible."

—MATTHEW 19:26

Prayer

Think about some situation in your life or that of an acquaintance where the Lord lived up to His reputation as the God of the impossible. Then praise Him!

BLESSED BE THE LORD

Early in the sixteenth century, only those schooled in Latin could read the Scriptures. That basically meant the leaders of the Catholic Church. Martin Luther thought something should be done about that. It seemed discriminatory. But because of his determination to change the situation, he found himself imprisoned in a German castle. His heinous crime? Translating the Bible into the language of his countrymen. As he contemplated his fate, he was able to contrast his impenetrable confines to the fortress-like protection that God offers to every Christian.

Luther picked up his quill and, dipping it in a bottle of blank ink, scrawled lyrics about the security of the believer that could be sung to a popular drinking tune. Yes, nearly five hundred years later Christians are still singing, "A Mighty Fortress is Our God."

Martin Luther was right. We are secure in the protection of a loving God. Even when we are misunderstood or falsely accused, we are not defenseless. We may feel vulnerable to attack or weak as can be, but God is an ever-present help in time of need.

God is our refuge and strength, an ever-present help in trouble. Therefore we will not fear, though the earth give way and the mountains fall into the heart of the sea.

—PSALM 46:1-2

Prayer

What has you locked in a prison tower? Some unsubstantiated fear? Let the Lord remind you that He is your tower of strength. Ask Him for the faith to trust Him.

WE BELIEVE

What do we believe? This song, taken from the ancient Apostles' Creed, condenses the Christian faith into a few lines that describe what believers across the world believe. While we may have different opinions about many things, we are in complete agreement about these: We believe in God the Father, the Creator, and in Christ, His Son, who was born of a virgin, suffered to save us, and then rose again. We look forward to life everlasting.

The God to whom we cling by faith is the One who made all there is. And though He calls each star by name, He also calls us His own children. In His eternal heart of love, He conceived of a way to embrace a sinful world. We believe this Way to be the Truth and the Life.

We believe He's the Savior of all. Jesus became the innocent victim of suffering as He died for us. But He pried Himself free from death's icy fingers, and flew to the realm of heaven beyond to a seat of high honor reserved only for Him since before even time began.

Our beliefs aren't owned only by us. We share them with millions who commune with us from Christ's cup, all the while looking up with grateful hearts, thankful for our forgiveness and for the life yet to come.

We believe that Jesus died and rose again and so we believe that God will bring with Jesus those who have fallen asleep in him.

—1 THESSALONIANS 4:14

Prayer

Contemplate Jesus Christ, the risen and glorified Lord, seated on His throne. Come boldly into His presence, convinced that He died to make your relationship with Him possible.

BEHOLD WHAT MANNER OF LOVE

Hugh Everett struggled with self-esteem, and for good reason. Six months after he was born, his unwed mother determined she could not raise him. He was deposited at an orphanage. For the next two years, little Hugh was farmed out to foster home after foster home. Each time, he was returned and branded un-adoptable. At last, a couple unable to conceive took Hugh home. Curiously, shortly thereafter the couple succeeded in having a child of their own. Favoring their natural-born son, the couple often ignored Hugh. He grew up aching to know the love of birth parents he would never meet.

Although the family in which he was raised was not religious, one of the requirements of his adoption was that he be provided religious instruction. As a result, each week the couple would drop Hugh off at Ruth Morton Baptist Church down the street from their home. At this small church, young Hugh Everett heard about a Heavenly Father with whom a relationship of love is possible. Hugh responded with eagerness and the ache in his heart desiring to belong was at long last filled.

Today Hugh Everett is an esteemed author of some thirty biographies. In each book he celebrates more than the story of God's faithfulness in the life of his subject. He also celebrates his own sense of identity.

Celebrate the love you have received from God, parents, spouse, children, and friends.

Behold, what manner of love the Father hath bestowed upon us, that we should be called the sons of God: therefore the world knoweth us not, because it knew him not.

—1 JOHN 3:1 KJV

Prayer

Thank God for the parents He gave you (even if they were less than ideal). Now, contemplate the perfection of parental love that your Heavenly Father channels in your direction.

STAND IN THE CONGREGATION

Back in the 1960s, the Mexico branch of Wycliffe Bible Translators was housed in Mexico City in an old hotel called "the Kettle." Wycliffe's founder William Cameron Townsend would often lead Sunday night gatherings. There was enthusiastic singing with those in attendance requesting songs that affirmed the life-changing power of the gospel. Among those would be any number of translators who had come into the city to get supplies before returning to their assigned location in remote tribal villages.

"Uncle Cam" would call on these missionaries to stand and give a report on their work. With joyful expressions and testimony of the tangible evidence of the Spirit's work, these translators would give praise to God and encouragement to the support personnel. Something is refreshingly authentic about eyewitness accounts of God at work.

What was true in a missionary setting half a century ago is no less true today. When we allow for God's people to stand up in the midst of the congregation and tell what they have seen and heard, the church is strengthened and faith grows. Next time you are given an opportunity to bear witness to God's faithfulness in your life, stand and deliver.

I will give thee thanks in the great congregation: I will praise thee among much people.

—PSALM 35:18 KJV

Prayer

Think back to times when you heard the "saints" in your home church extol the goodness of the Lord. Allow those memories to grease the skids of your faith as you approach your Father in prayer.

I WILL BLESS THEE, O LORD

Many reasons could be given for why we raise our hands when we praise the Lord. For one thing, it's biblical. The psalm writer invited God's people to lift holy hands in the sanctuary. It's also a physical demonstration of need. We are calling on the Lord and requesting His attention. Besides that, it's a symbol of humility. If, when our hands our extended, our palms are open and facing up, we approach the Lord expressing our emptiness. We are, in a manner of speaking, acknowledging our dependency on Him.

Maybe it helps to think of it like this: When we were in school, the teacher would often ask those who knew the answer to raise their hands. Well, how about it? We who follow Jesus claim that He is the answer to our alienation with God and each other. If we have accepted Jesus' free gift of salvation, we not only know the answer, we have the answer. It makes sense then, in the context of worship, that we raise our hands high to remind ourselves that we know that the One we worship is the answer to every need we bring with us to church.

If you have been reluctant to raise your hands, why not let yourself go? Be bold. If you know the answer, don't be shy.

Thus will I bless thee while I live: I will lift up my hands in thy name.

—PSALM 63:4 KJV

Prayer

Let body language join with the words of your mouth in prayer today. Kneel in the Lord's presence as an indicator of reverence. Lift your hands as a symbol of praise.

ROCK OF MY SALVATION

Rocks are solid, sure, unmovable. Whether they are part of a strong formation like the Rockies, the awesome depth of the Grand Canyon, or the rugged beauty of the Badlands, we somehow know that they are here to stay. David celebrated that reality by picturing his God as a Rock—offering a certain salvation, strength, hope, and yes, even inspiration. David spent many years running from a wicked king and hiding in the rock formations of Israel that provided fortress-like protection. Those rocks would prove to be his salvation. For those who feared wild beasts or beast-like robbers, a well-placed chunk of limestone could be a lifesaver.

As we face life's difficult circumstances, God is our Rock. In Him we hide. We trust in Him, knowing that He is immovable, unshakable, standing forever. As the mountains provided safety for David, so God helps us in our time of need, providing a safe place. Nothing can hurt us when we are standing on our Rock of sure salvation.

The Lord lives! Blessed be my Rock! Let God be exalted, the Rock of my salvation!

—2 SAMUEL 22:47 NKJV

Prayer

Since God promises to be our Rock and give us a wall of protection, read a favorite promise you've underlined in your Bible before pouring out your heart to the Lord.

ALL WE LIKE SHEEP

Myopia. Even though it sounds like utopia, it's a not even close. Myopia is the ultimate condition of nearsightedness. It's a case of looking out for ourselves. And based on what we read in the Bible, it's congenital.

We are all born with this "I" disorder. From the very beginning, we seek our own way, see what we want to see, and close our eyes to others. In all reality, at the center of sin is a preoccupation with "me." That's why sin is sometimes written this way: s-I-n.

But God's vision for our lives is not restricted by our blindness. When we admit our selfish orientation and seek healing, God focuses His grace in our direction with laser-like precision and deals with the "I" of s-I-n. And the beauty of God's remedy is this: It does more than heal our individual situation; it has national implications. When we come before Him as a nation and admit our myopia, He restores our ability to look to Him as the moral compass of our country.

This melodic song draws us into an attitude of contrition and confession. Allow it to move you to identify an "I" infection that may be preventing you from seeing God in all His fullness.

All we like sheep have gone astray; we have turned every one to his own way; and the Lord hath laid on him the iniquity of us all.

—ISAIAH 53:6 KJV

Prayer

Pray for your nation. Ask God to show His mercy
in grace, not only in your life, but in your land.

MEEKNESS AND MAJESTY
(THIS IS YOUR GOD)

Oxymorons are word couplets that negate one another. They are paired opposites like "jumbo shrimp," "now then," "genuine copy," and "recorded live." Some of them can be humorous, such as "Microsoft Works," "military intelligence," or "airplane food."

When it comes to describing Jesus, oxymorons are neither funny nor ordinary. We can't seem to come to terms with His identity without allowing for descriptions that defy normal categories. He is the God-man, the Morning Star, the Suffering Messiah, and the Servant King.

In this wonderful hymn by Graham Kendrick about the Incarnation, we are posed with another oxymoron: meekness and majesty. In fact, the lyrics of this song are filled with contrasts. And when you stop and think about it, ours is an oxymoronic faith. The "simple mystery" of salvation is a portrait of opposites. We die in order to live. We give in order to receive. The first shall be last. In poverty we become rich.

Before doing anything else today, why not watch and pray?

For even the Son of Man did not come to be served, but to serve, and to give his life as a ransom for many.

—MARK 10:45

Prayer

Celebrate the mystery of your faith. As difficult as it might be for you, talk to the Lord without needing to understand how prayer works or why He allows what He does.

TO HIM WHO SITS
ON THE THRONE

It was her dad's fiftieth birthday party. Even though she wanted to stay up, Lauren's mom insisted she go to bed before the company arrived. With the doorbell and all the voices, laughter, and music, the four-year-old could not fall asleep. So when her curiosity could stand it no longer, Lauren slipped out of bed and quietly descended the staircase. To her disappointment, the French doors leading into the living room were closed. Lauren was wise enough to know that it would not be smart to open the doors and walk in. So, stepping up on her tiptoes, the curious child peeked through the keyhole near the door latch. What she saw was unlike any birthday party she'd been to. It was magical!

When it comes to heaven, the writers of the New Testament don't go into specific detail, but they do provide us a keyhole through which we can peek. Far more wonderful than the most elaborate birthday party, heaven promises to be a worship festival that defies words. The music will be breathtaking. The beauty will be thrilling. The glory of God's presence will leave us straining for words. As the old gospel hymn puts it, "What a day of rejoicing that will be!"

In a loud voice they sang: "Worthy is the Lamb, who was slain, to receive power and wealth and wisdom and strength and honor and glory and praise!"

—REVELATION 5:12

Prayer

Think about heaven. Ask God to fill your heart
with a desire to go there. Who waits for you there?
Thank the Lord for their influence in your life.

HONOR AND GLORY

Some years ago, a magazine published an issue with breath-taking pictures that were processed in 3-D format. Each copy of that particular issue included a disposable pair of glasses that enabled the viewer to see what was not clear to the naked eye. Those who wore the special lenses were treated to the scenery in impressive detail.

In personal worship, we are privileged to draw near to the unseen Christ. When filtered through glorious music and devotional insights, the eyes of faith are able to lock in on evidences of the Lord that might otherwise be missed. Songs like "Honor and Glory" remind us that the God we worship and adore is beyond our ability to see. Nonetheless, He is not beyond experiencing.

The lyrics of songs sometimes repeat over and over again. It's not because the writer ran out of words. Rather, it is because repetition helps us focus on the beauty of the Lord's presence in our lives. Repetition helps us meditate and in meditation, our vantage point is improved.

Adore your wonderful Lord, again and again!

Now to the King eternal, immortal, invisible, the only God, be honor and glory for ever and ever. Amen.

—1 TIMOTHY 1:17

Prayer

Take a phrase from your favorite praise song and repeat it over and over again in your head. Allow the truth of those few words to usher you into the presence of invisible God who desires to reveal Himself to you.

I'VE FOUND JESUS

During the Jesus People movement of the seventies, churches of every imaginable denomination joined together in a unified effort to evangelize our country. In a campaign sponsored by Campus Crusade for Christ, believers all over the nation placed bumper stickers on their cars which read, "I Found It!" When curious commuters saw the slogan, it was hoped that they would ask the driver, "What did you find?"

As is often the case, well-intentioned ideas breed cynical or antagonistic responses. Before long, some cars bore bumper stickers that read, "I Never Lost It!" Sadly, those who mocked the joy of finding life's ultimate destination continued down a one-way street in the wrong direction.

After several months, the "I Found It!" campaign had run its course, but not before the population of Christ's Kingdom had increased by several thousands. But all these many years later, Jesus continues to be found by those willing to admit that they have a need of Him.

You will seek me and find me when you seek me with all your heart.

—JEREMIAH 29:13

Prayer

Think about the day you met Jesus. Remember how you felt?
Thank Him for all He has done for you.
Pray for family and friends who still need to meet Him.

TRADING MY SORROWS
(YES, LORD)

The residents of Naperville, Illinois, continue to talk about it. On July 16, 1996 the summer skies opened and refused to close until seventeen inches of rain had fallen. It was a record amount of rainfall. Sump pumps were unable to keep up with the accumulating water in basements. Hundreds of thousands of dollars of furniture and clothing was destroyed. Inflatable rafts allowed neighbors to navigate streets that were too deep with water for cars to drive through.

As is often the case, after the torrential rain, lightning, and thunder had done their damage, the storm moved to the east. The memorable night of unimaginable destruction gave way to a morning of brilliant sunshine and clear blue skies.

According to the psalmist, life is filled with other kinds of storms. The floodgates of pain, sorrow, and fear let loose and drench us with despair. But he quickly adds that the rising of the sun will bring a change in the forecast. Sorrow may last for the night, but joy returns in the morning. If you are in the midst of the flood, grab hold of God and hang on. The end is in sight. Joy will come.

Weeping may endure for a night, but joy comes in the morning.

—PSALM 30:5 NKJV

Prayer

Go ahead and admit your pain and fear to the Father.
He desires to carry you through the storm you're facing.
Trust Him that the weather will soon be changing.

WHY SO DOWNCAST

Chelsea Thomas was born with Moebius syndrome. No matter how much she wanted to smile, for the first seven years of her life, she couldn't. It was physiologically impossible. Little Chelsea was born without a key nerve that transmits the "smile signal" from her brain to her face. As a result, even when she was happy, her face was sad.

Fortunately for Chelsea, a team of doctors in California operated on the seven-year-old in 1995. They removed a muscle and a nerve from her leg and transplanted them beneath the surface of her face. And as you might imagine, Chelsea Thomas has something to smile about.

Whereas Moebius syndrome is a very rare condition, unhappy Christians are only too common. We are easily swayed by the circumstances that come our way or our emotional response to those circumstances. The lilting melody and simple lyrics of this song drive home a simple truth: Those who belong to the Lord have no cause to be downcast. Because the Lord has taken responsibility for our lives and our future, we have reason to lift our heads up and be grateful.

Why are you downcast, O my soul? Why so disturbed within me? Put your hope in God, for I will yet praise him, my Savior and my God.

—PSALM 42:5-6

Prayer

Don't focus on what you need; give praise to the Lord for all He has given you already. Celebrate His faithfulness. And as you pray today, smile.

ONLY YOU

A few hundred years after Jesus personally taught His disciples about the innate hunger of the human heart for the Father, Augustine personally attested to the same. He wrote, "Thou hast made us for thyself O God, and our hearts are restless until they rest in thee." Many centuries later Blaise Pascal sang his own version of the same song. According to this brilliant philosopher, every person is born with a God-shaped vacuum that He alone can fill.

Everyone who has ever lived has attempted to prove that he or she is the exception to the rule. We seek to fill the hole in our soul with pleasure and power and entertainment and friendship and status and wealth. But in our attempt to be in a league of our own, we find that we have struck out.

Only God can satisfy the longings of our hearts. That's the way He made us. And the reason He did is so that He can have the exclusive joy in making us complete. What's incredibly wonderful is the joy that is ours when we simply quit trying to find our joy outside of Him.

Even strong young lions sometimes go hungry, but those who trust in the Lord will never lack any good thing.

—PSALM 34:10 NLT

Prayer

Sit back. Put your feet up. Take deep breaths. Take a
few moments to accept the fact that you have just cause to
rest in the Lord. He is the destination of your life's search.

THE HEART OF WORSHIP (1)

Scotty couldn't believe it. His birthday party was a total failure. He had invited about a dozen boys in his kindergarten class. On Scotty's birthday, each boy came dressed up in his Sunday best bearing a brightly-wrapped present. But upon coming through the front door, the invited guests gathered the birthday boy and sang "Happy Birthday" while holding on to their gifts. When the song was over, as quickly as they had come, the boys were gone. And they didn't even leave the presents.

As unthinkable as that scenario is, sometimes that's how we approach the Lord's Day. We show up at His house looking a little nicer than we ordinarily do. We come prepared to give Him our hearts. At first everything seems to be on track. We follow the lead of the praise team and sing a medley of worship choruses with feeling and expression. But when the singing stops, it's as if we've disconnected.

It's good to remind ourselves that even though we sometimes refer to "praise singing" as worship, what we do the entire time we are at church is worship. The essence of worship is relating to the One whose day it is. It's all about Him, not just the songs.

Worship the Lord with gladness; come before him with joyful songs.

—PSALM 100:2

Prayer

Ask God to give you a desire to enter into the whole of the worship service this coming Lord's Day. Express your willingness to worship Him in truth as well as in spirited singing.

THE HEART OF WORSHIP (2)

*I*t's all about Jesus. We would do well to make this song our refrain—not just on Sunday morning during worship, but every day. In essence, for the believer, every day should be "worship-full," for every moment is given to us by God's grace. And if every moment is considered as an opportunity to worship God, then every moment is all about Him.

What an effect it would have on our lives if we stopped and realized, "It's not about me." What peace we will gain when we understand that whatever happens in our lives is because "It's not about me; it's about Him." When things don't go the way we want, we understand that it's not about us, it's about God's bigger picture, God's glory. When we face suffering and difficulty, we understand that it's not about us, it's about Him. Whatever fills our days, whatever God calls us to do in any moment, we can remember that if we do that job, we are doing it for Him because it's all about Him. That infuses whatever we do—even the mundane and ordinary—with eternal significance.

It's not about us; it's about Him.

So whether you eat or drink or whatever you do, do it all for the glory of God.

—1 CORINTHIANS 10:31

Prayer

As you go through your day, consciously remind yourself that your life is not all about you. Instead, it's all about God—serving Him, glorifying Him, sharing Him with your world.

TAKE MY LIFE

It's the kind of unrehearsed comment you'd expect to hear on Bill Cosby's "Kids Say the Darnedest Things." The interviewer was asking children about their career aspirations. When a certain little girl was asked what she wanted to do when she "got big" like her mommy, she replied, "Go on a diet!"

Sometimes the thoughts we have about our future goals are different than what God has in mind. He isn't all that concerned about our career or geographic plans or our retirement dreams. His desires for our tomorrows have more to do with the kind of people we are becoming inside. The color of the collar we wear to work isn't nearly as important to Him as our character.

As we stand with our backs to His spiritual growth chart, He measures the degree to which our hearts need to be formed, our minds need to be transformed, and our wills need to be conformed. It's a measuring process that occurs every day for the rest of our lives.

The key, of course, is to let God do His work, to say to Him daily, "Take my life—all of it!"

Do not conform any longer to the pattern of this world, but be transformed by the renewing of your mind.

—ROMANS 12:2

Prayer

Review the qualities of the fruit of the Spirit (Galatians 5:22-23). Ask God to evaluate each quality while you quietly listen in His presence for His response.

ARMS OF LOVE

We love the way the sweet lyrics of this song sound—we love envisioning ourselves in our Father's arms of love. But the truth is, there are times when we aren't aware that that's exactly where we are.

You most likely have read a poem called "Footprints in the Sand." That inspirational poem was written by Margaret Powers. In it, she describes the plight of a person who felt abandoned by God in his or her darkest hour only to discover that he or she wasn't abandoned at all. The single set of footprints didn't belong to the person in pain walking the beach alone. They were the Lord's. The reason there was only one set was because the person in crisis was being carried.

Margaret Powers has lived the truth of her verse. Shortly after writing "Footprints," her poem was stolen and distributed throughout the world. For over two decades, the poet received neither recognition nor royalties. At long last, her ownership of the poem was proven. Looking back on this grave injustice, Margaret attests to the "arms of love" that held her. Although some days she didn't feel the Lord close, He never let her down. Perhaps you can relate.

Even to your old age and gray hairs I am he, I am he who will sustain you. I have made you and I will carry you; I will sustain you and I will rescue you.

—ISAIAH 46:4

Prayer

Rest in the arms of the Lord. Thank Him for those
everlasting arms that never tire or lose their strength.

BREATHE

The air is charged with emotion. Bystanders feel the negative energy. Desperate young parents are frantically searching a large downtown department store for their two-year-old child. Somehow, somewhere, their baby wandered off when they were looking at new furniture. Store security is collecting information from the panicked parents, all the while attempting to calm them. Strangers join the search efforts.

Without warning, a grandmotherly woman walks into view with the child in her arms. The sudden heroine has saved the day. But even as the little boy's eyes meet his mother's, he continues to sob uncontrollably. The fear he has felt thinking that he has lost his mommy and daddy is all consuming. Between heaves and sobs, he literally struggles to take in a breath.

No doubt you've seen a similar scene. Your heart goes out to both the child and the parents. But have you ever pictured yourself as a lost child desperately fighting to breathe, all the while longing for the arms of your Heavenly Father? That is a poignant portrait of our dependence on God that we never outgrow.

Run to His arms, and take a breath!

As the deer pants for streams of water, so my soul pants for you, O God. My soul thirsts for God, for the living God. When can I go and meet with God?

—PSALM 42:1-2

Prayer

Draw near to the Lord as to a parent. Cast yourself on Him as one who cares for you and longs to hold you. Share with Him your deepest need.

ETERNITY

The story is told about a man and his teenage son who lived in a little village in Spain. One night the man and the teenager had a disagreement that left them both feeling betrayed. The next morning, when the father went to Paco's room to awaken him, he noticed that the boy's bed had not been slept in. The boy had run away.

A lump rose to the father's throat and refused to be swallowed. His son meant more to him than anything. The thought of being separated from his boy was too much for the man. Wanting to make amends and begin again, the father went to the post office in town and tacked up a large sign that read, "Paco, all is forgiven. I love you. Meet me here tomorrow. Papa."

The next day the father went to the post office hoping to be reunited with his son. To his amazement, in addition to his Paco, six other teenage boys by the same name stood there, each answering a call for love, each hoping it was his dad inviting him home.

Jesus' story of the prodigal son is more than just a parable. It is a story lived out in every generation in every culture. In fact, it is every person's story. It is an amazing story of a God who waits for our return to His open arms.

If you ever leave "home," remember your loving Father who waits and longs for your return.

"Let's have a feast and celebrate. For this son of mine was dead and is alive again; he was lost and is found." So they began to celebrate.

—LUKE 15:23-24

Prayer

Rewind your memory tape to your own rebellion from the Father and then replay the scene of falling into His arms. Thank God for His grace, mercy, and the promise of eternity with Him.

WE REMEMBER YOU

A memory-challenged fifty-year-old once wrote in his journal: "I've reached the age where once again I play at hide-and-seek. My playmates aren't the kids next door but facts I try to speak. It irks me so to know I know a certain name or face, but when I think I'm getting warm they're gone without a trace. So much of what I once recalled gets stuck inside my mind. Like popcorn hulls between my teeth, some thoughts get caught, I find. But gratefully, it's just a game. It's not a total loss. I'd do just fine if I could find a string of mental floss."

Forgetfulness doesn't just come with age. It's a consequence of living in a fallen world. We are born with a tendency to forget what God has done for us. That's why He made sure His people had visual aids and tangible memory joggers in both the Old and New Testaments. The ultimate symbolic memory aid is Communion, the Lord's Supper. It calls to mind the priceless investment God made to provide us the free gift of eternal salvation.

As you come to the table, remember what your Father did in sending Jesus and remember what Jesus did on the Cross.

And when he had given thanks, he broke it and said, "This is my body, which is for you; do this in remembrance of me."

—1 CORINTHIANS 11:24

Prayer

As you pray, look around the room at objects and
mementoes that call to mind God's blessings in your life.
Take several moments to remember His goodness.

LAMB OF GOD

*I*n technologically-savvy America, the landscape of most people's lives is not dotted with wooly sheep and bleating lambs. The pastoral scenes that once defined us are hung in galleries of history. About the only reference to sheep that remains a part of our vocabulary is that of "counting" them when we can't fall asleep.

Picturing Jesus as the Lamb of God is a bit of a shock to sophisticated minds. Yet it is this out-of-the-ordinary image that jars us from a culture of comfort and convenience and forces us to return to the world of the Bible.

Only as we enter into the mindset of the ancient Hebrews can we fully understand how Jesus is the Lamb of God. The smell of wet wool and dried blood was part of their life. The unmistakable aroma of roasted lamb and burnt flesh was essential to their faith. Innocent and helpless lambs were butchered as part of God's remedy for sin—until, that is, He offered His Son as the once-and-for-all sacrifice. Because of Him, the most innocent of all who have ever lived, children's pets could now be spared. But far more importantly, God's children could now live forever.

Jesus, the Lamb of God, your Lamb, died so that you could live.

The next day John saw Jesus coming toward him and said, "Look, the Lamb of God, who takes away the sin of the world!"

—JOHN 1:29

Prayer

Thank Jesus, the precious Lamb of God who took away the world's sin. Thank Him for letting you, a little sheep, join His flock and be led by Him.

DRAW ME CLOSE

Long ago and far away, when the story of our salvation was still being written, a teenage boy tended his father's sheep. His name was David and his passion was praise. As he reclined by the campfire keeping watch over the sleeping flock, he sang poetry he had composed to the Lord.

Perhaps, as he drew a lamb onto his lap, he thought of how he desired that God would draw him close and never let him go. Perhaps laying back and looking up at the moonless sky dotted with countless stars, David thought of God, desiring closeness, friendship, a warm embrace. "Draw me close to You, never let me go. You're all I want."

Then maybe, as a restless sheep awakened from its sleep and voiced discontent, the young shepherd ceased his lofty thoughts and attended to the needs of the flock. And maybe then a quiet voice within David spoke to him. "I know you and love you. Your praises fill My heart with delight. I am just as concerned for you as you are for your sheep. David, I am your shepherd. When you are with Me, you will never want for anything."

We don't exactly know what prompted David to pen Psalm 23. But it isn't beyond reason to think it was such a scenario. What we do know, however, is that as long as the Lord was his shepherd, David was not in want.

The LORD is my shepherd, I shall not be in want.

—PSALM 23:1

Prayer

Picture yourself a lamb cradled in your Shepherd's arms. Tell the Lord He's all you want and need. Then ask Him for the faith and ability to believe that with Him, you "shall not be in want."

SING OUT

The years had taken their toll. His body bore the evidence of numerous beatings and shipwrecks. His shoulders were stooped, his back bowed. His aging eyes strained to see the words on the parchment as he held his quill in his trembling hands. The apostle Paul was decades removed from the haughty young rabbi who had ridden toward Damascus on horseback. But the passion of that bounty hunter in pursuit of Christians was just as strong as he wrote a letter of encouragement to the believers in Colosse. He called this congregation to embrace the presence of the Lord by meditating on His Word, cultivating grateful hearts, and singing out with worshipful songs. We have no idea if this articulate spokesman for the gospel could carry a tune, but we do know that he knew the power of letting loose in praise to God. Paul prompted the Colossians to build a temple of tunes worthy of His glory. He knew that "the Lord inhabits the song of His saints and lives in their praises." So sing! Come to worship! Rejoice in all that the Father has done!

Let the word of Christ dwell in you richly as you teach and admonish one another with all wisdom, and as you sing psalms, hymns and spiritual songs with gratitude in your hearts to God.

—COLOSSIANS 3:16

Prayer

Thank the Lord for the way music brings you into
His presence. Sing out in a verse of a favorite
praise chorus as a way to expressing your love to Him.

I LOVE TO BE IN YOUR PRESENCE

*I*t was called Stand in the Gap. On October 4, 1997 more than one million men gathered on the mall in Washington, D.C., for a day of worship, prayer, and biblical instruction. It was an event sponsored by Promise Keepers, and those million men stood together to rejoice in what God had done and would continue to do in their lives. Chris Romig from Melbourne, Florida, was there. "Being in the midst of a multitude of men who are lost in wonder, love, and praise gave me a hint of what heaven will be like," he recalls. "I just wanted it to go on forever. It was a day I will never forget." For Chris Romig, being in the presence of the Lord (and a million other men) has impacted the way he approaches the Lord in personal worship every day.

Fortunately, the indescribable joy of worship isn't limited to joining with a million others. Worship is a gift the Holy Spirit makes possible every day of our lives. What a wonder to stand and rejoice in God's presence! What a privilege to lift our hands and raise our voices in praise to our awesome God! Maybe you stand alone in the quiet of your room. Maybe you stand in a tiny congregation. Wherever you stand, rejoice that you have the awesome privilege to stand in His presence and sing His praises.

> *How can I repay the LORD for all his goodness to me? I will lift up the cup of salvation and call on the name of the LORD. I will fulfill my vows to the LORD in the presence of all his people.*
>
> —PSALM 116:12-14

Prayer

Tell the Lord how you love to be in His presence.
Tell Him why you rejoice in Him. Then just sit
(or stand) quietly in His presence.

LIGHT THE FIRE AGAIN

Sometimes the fire in our hearts seems to die down to nothing more than glowing embers. Sin has done its work, guilt has doused the flame, fear has driven us away, love has grown cold. We want to light the fire again, but we are guilt-ridden and afraid.

It happened to King David. He had sinned with Bathsheba. He tried to cover it up, justify it, forget about it. But finally he found himself cornered by unconfessed sin. A kind of claustrophobia made peace of mind impossible. The inner fire of spiritual passion no longer burned. Lacking the fresh wind of God's breath, the fire in his heart was no more than a glowing coal. Only when confronted by Nathan the prophet did David come to terms with his sin. The king confessed his sin and pled with the Lord to rekindle his heart. The Lord heard him and lit his fire again. And the dying embers that had been doused by sin were re-ignited.

Are you wretched, poor, and naked? Has sin doused the flame of God's love in your heart? Do as King David did, for the remedy is the same. Confess your sin to God and ask Him to breathe new passion for Him into your heart. Ask Him to light the fire again.

Create in me a pure heart, O God, and renew a steadfast spirit within me. Do not cast me from your presence or take your Holy Spirit from me. Restore to me the joy of your salvation and grant me a willing spirit, to sustain me.

—PSALM 51:10-12

Prayer

As you look at the burning logs in your fireplace or light candles on the dining room table, praise God for His ability to fan your dying embers of faith into flame. If appropriate, confess your sin and accept His immediate forgiveness.

BETTER IS ONE DAY

"How lovely is your dwelling place," David wrote (Psalm 84:1). How lovely to Israel's king was the place of God's presence among His people—the tabernacle, the sacred tent where God's presence dwelt in the sacred Ark of the Covenant. Surely every time David approached the canvas walls of the tabernacle, his heart beat faster. It was a place of sacred symbolism. It was a place of mystery. It was God's house. There he felt protected and covered by the shadow of God's invisible wings. It was truly a sanctuary. A refuge. It was a foretaste of heaven, where David could prostrate himself before God, drink in His beauty, and experience the only thing in life that could truly satisfy. For him, one day there was better than a thousand elsewhere.

The Lord desires that we experience the same. Does your soul long, even faint, for God's presence? Do you seek to see Him, to find Him when you worship? Do you long to draw near to Him? Then, like David, simply come into His presence. Seek Him every day in the quietness of your prayer time; seek Him every week in the sanctuary where you worship. You will find more satisfaction in His presence than you could ever find anywhere else.

Better is one day in your courts than a thousand elsewhere; I would rather be a doorkeeper in the house of my God than dwell in the tents of the wicked.

—PSALM 84:10

Prayer

Thank the Lord for your church, your place of worship
where you can meet Him. Ask Him to give your
heart satisfaction in His presence. Ask Him to
refresh your spirit as you worship Him this week.

HIS BANNER OVER ME

While doves coo and sparrows fly overhead, the royal musicians play within the great hall. A long table piled high with fruits, cheeses, and smoked meats groans under the weight of such a spread. Can't you picture it? But as appetizing and impressive as the banquet fare obviously is, what impresses you isn't just this meal fit for a king. You are amazed that you've been invited to the palace. The gilded walls reflect the glory of the king's power and sovereignty. His highness has chosen you to share his feast. The engraved invitation boasting the monarch's seal is in your trembling hand. "I humbly request your presence at a banquet given in your honor."

"In my honor?" you wonder. "What have I done to deserve any honor?" As your eyes drink in the intoxicating beauty around you, you see it—there it is at the apex of the vaulted ceiling. It's a tapestry of thick, rich fabric woven with threads of gold. The scripted words announce with silent dignity and sincere affection, "I love you. You are mine!"

Jesus, the King, says to you today, "Come to My banqueting table. I love you. Join Me in celebration. What have you done to deserve honor? Nothing. You are here simply because I desire for you to be here. You see, I am yours and you are Mine. My banner over you is love."

He has brought me to his banquet hall, and his banner over me is love...I am my beloved's and my beloved is mine.

—SONG OF SONGS 2:4; 6:3 NASB

Prayer

Jesus sent you an invitation to His banquet. Have you responded? He loves you. Enter into the place of honor beside Him. Thank Him today for loving you and for inviting you into His presence.

THE BATTLE BELONGS TO THE LORD

Some days we feel like we're on a battlefield. Whether it is in our homes, on our jobs, in our churches, or at our schools, we wonder how we will face what has become, for all intents and purposes, a battle against an enemy. We wonder if we have the courage to fight.

Young David found the courage. While his brothers scoffed at his naiveté and the waiting giant sneered at his defenseless vulnerability, David refused to be intimated. His knees may have been knocking, but his heart was pounding with confidence that God would defend His honor. After all, David said, "the battle belongs to the Lord." Standing up to Goliath wasn't David's battle; it was God's. David was simply willing to be the means by which God would glorify Himself. And by the time the sling had shot its single stone, God had done just that. The giant was brought to his knees, mortally wounded. Through His willing servant, God had fought—and won—the battle.

What battle do you face today? This song encourages you not to stress out contemplating and strategizing ways to survive seemingly impossible skirmishes. God still delights in defending Himself when His honor is at stake or His children are at risk. Chances are, the battle you are facing today isn't really yours at all. Take courage, and let the Lord glorify Himself through you.

Everyone gathered here will know the LORD does not need swords or spears to save people. The battle belongs to him, and he will hand you over to us.

—1 SAMUEL 17:47 NCV

Prayer

What battle are you entangled in right now? Confess your fears and your wounds to the Commander in Chief. Use this time of prayer to remind yourself that the Lord has offered to fight your battles for you. Ask Him to glorify Himself through you.

BOW DOWN

Isaiah bowed down. He couldn't help himself. In the year that Israel's beloved King Uzziah died, the soon-to-be prophet had a vision of the Lord. There in the temple, in the shadow of the Almighty's throne, the great I Am revealed Himself. It was unmistakable. As the words of the song suggest, His awesome presence filled the room and Isaiah worshiped like he had never worshiped before. There was a consuming fire to be sure, and the temple filled with smoke. The angels sang of God's glory. A seraph brought a live coal from the altar and, with its touch, purified Isaiah's mouth and cleansed his sinful heart.

In the midst of the vision, a voice was heard. "Whom shall I send? And who will go for us?" (Isaiah 6:8). It was the Lord speaking. It was a worship encounter Isaiah would never forget. And Isaiah answered God's call.

Gratefully, life-changing worship encounters are not limited to Old Testament prophets. The Lord's awesome presence fills the room whenever your heart bows humbly before Him. And when you sense His presence, don't be afraid to enter in. You have been invited to join saints and angels in the chorus of praise to Him—now and forevermore.

In the year that King Uzziah died, I saw the Lord seated on a throne, high and exalted, and the train of his robe filled the temple.

—ISAIAH 6:1

Prayer

Ask God to make known His presence to you as you worship Him. Come before Him with the confidence of knowing you are His child, yet with the humility of knowing that you are there by His grace alone.

AWESOME IN THIS PLACE

One day we will enter God's presence, going past the gates of praise until we are standing face to face with our Savior. What a joyous moment it will be when we look upon His countenance and see the fullness of His grace! Our response? To bow down and say, "You are awesome in this place!"

On September 19, 1997, contemporary Christian musician Rich Mullins left this world and entered God's presence. The song that is most associated with Rich Mullins is "Our God is an Awesome God." With those memorable lyrics, he used a word that captured the essence of God's unapproachable glory. The word "awesome" conveys the indescribable quality of our unequalled King.

When David Billington sat down to write a song of praise, he used the word "awesome" to describe his personal pilgrimage past the gates of praise into the presence of the living Lord—not in death, of course, but in life and in worship. Death will one day bring us face to face with Jesus, but in this life we can experience the awesome nature of God whenever we come into His presence with worship, praise, and thanksgiving. He is indeed an awesome God—beyond comprehension, worthy of all praise, worthy of our lives.

He was afraid and said, "How awesome is this place! This is none other than the house of God; this is the gate of heaven."

—GENESIS 28:17

Prayer

As the lyrics of this song suggest, "raise" your life to the Lord. You can accomplish that by offering God your hopes, dreams, heartaches, and regrets.

LET YOUR GLORY FALL

*I*t may have been the same upper room where Jesus and His disciples had shared one last supper. Twelve had fit a whole lot more comfortably than one hundred and twenty, but no complaining could be heard. Instead, the gathered believers were engaged in passionate prayer.

What were they praying? The Bible does not tell us, but we have a clue in Jesus' words to His followers, "Wait for the gift my Father promised" (Acts 1:4). They were waiting, and surely praying that whatever the gift was, they would use it well.

And then it came. The mysterious sound of a gale force wind. The flames, "tongues of fire," spontaneously igniting on their heads. Then the Spirit's presence manifested in foreign languages "declaring the wonders of God" (Acts 2:11). Those who stood on the streets below, who had journeyed to Jerusalem for the Feast of Pentecost, had come from a variety of nations. The words they heard were in their own languages. As the Holy Spirit descended on the disciples, the glory of God fell. That day the Church was born!

God is still in the business of working miracles and growing His Church. Like these early believers, pray that God's glory would fall, making His people strong in His might. Pray that He would make you ready to make a difference in your world for Him!

Suddenly a sound like the blowing of a violent wind came from heaven and filled the whole house where they were sitting. They saw what seemed to be tongues of fire that separated and came to rest on each of them.

—ACTS 2:2-3

Prayer

Don't wait for the sound of a windstorm or tongues of fire.
The Spirit came into your life the moment you believed. Now
ask the Lord to so fill you with His glory that your world will
see and know that you have been with Jesus.

THINK ABOUT HIS LOVE

Noted songwriter Walt Harrah grew up in Wenatchee, Washington, where his dad was pastor of Calvary Bible Church. From most any place in the small town on the Columbia River, Walt could look up at the jagged mountains that ringed this valley of fruit trees. The entire scene spoke of the majesty of the Creator. From the pink blossoms of the apple orchards to the forest-green fir trees that outlined the foothills of the Cascades, the glory of God's power was obvious. In the worship chorus that Walt penned, "Think about His Love," he invites you to wrap your mind around the indescribable reality that you are loved by the Creator of the cosmos. You are more than forgiven; you are more than acceptable; you are, in fact, the very object of His affection. Think about His love, His goodness, and His grace. Understand that there is nothing you can do that would cause the Father to love you more than He already does. Conversely, there is nothing you could ever do that would cause Him to love you any less. Even if you stray away, His love will find you.

Just imagine such love. It is as high as the heavens; it is without measure; it is completely satisfying.

My mouth will tell of your righteousness, of your salvation all day long, though I know not its measure.

—PSALM 71:15

Prayer

Don't feel the need to speak a prayer today. Just think about the Father's love. Ponder ways He has lavished His grace upon you in spite of the fact you didn't deserve it.

LOVE YOU SO MUCH

"How much do you love your daddy?" a playful mom asks her highchair-bound baby. The child doesn't know that her father has just come home from work and is standing directly behind the highchair. Spreading her thumb and index fingers an inch apart, the mother continues, "Do you love him this much?" The toddler, obviously tickled, giggles. The inquisitive mother holds her hands a foot apart and repeats the question. "Do you love your daddy this much?" The child begins to shake her head back and forth while smiling from ear to ear. "Well, how much do you love your daddy?" With an unmistakable twinkle in her eyes, the child sits as high as she can in her chair and stretches her little arms open as wide as they will go. And Daddy's heart melts with joy.

There is nothing quite so precious as a little child's sincere expression of love for a parent she adores. Our Father in heaven is moved by our demonstrations of affection. He loves to see hands raised, heads bowed, and knees bent. He loves it when we say, "I love You so much, Jesus." And when we recall what happened at Calvary, we can't help but respond that way. After all, Jesus reached out His arms on a cross and said, "I love you this much!"

"Lord," Peter replied, "you know I love you."

—JOHN 21:15

Prayer

Jesus encouraged us to become like children in the Father's presence. Go ahead and lift your arms to the Lord in prayer as an expression of your need. Tell Him, "I love You so much."

REJOICE

It was an amazing parade. In fact, it had only one person in it! A beloved teacher on a burro. As the palm trees swayed in the warm wind, a crowd of people lined the cobbled road that led from the village of Bethany to Israel's capital city. Word had spread throughout Jerusalem that the miracle worker from Nazareth was winding His way down the Mount of Olives through the Eastern Gate to the city. People whose lives had been touched by this unorthodox rabbi gathered. Waving branches from the nearby trees, children and their parents called out their praise. "Hosanna! Blessed is He who comes in the name of the Lord." They removed their outer garments and used them to carpet the road as their King approached. They rejoiced as the grand marshal of that first Palm Sunday parade drew near. And why wouldn't they? He was their only hope for peace, justice, and freedom.

He is our only hope as well. Do you desire peace in your soul, in your world? Do you long for freedom—from fear, from addiction, from pain? Do you seek justice where there is none? Then wait for the Messiah to come. The peace, freedom, and justice you seek may be given in a portion today; but one day they will be yours forever. Rejoice in the Lord! Rejoice!

They took palm branches and went out to meet him, shouting, "Hosanna! Blessed is he who comes in the name of the Lord! Blessed is the King of Israel!"

—JOHN 12:13

Prayer

With the "palms" of your hands, express your love of Christ. Open them and hold them up, asking the Lord to fill your hands with His peace, His freedom, and His justice.

SING TO THE LORD

Do you think the Lord gets tired of hearing us sing the same old hymns and praise songs? Perhaps. After all, He's the One who inspired the psalmist to write, "Sing to the Lord a new song." But then again, maybe He calls us to sing new songs for our own benefit. When we simply voice the same words over and over again, their freshness fades. The truth of the text remains unshakable, but when our familiarity with a song allows us to sing its words without thinking about what we are singing, that particular song has ceased to serve us well. It's when those oldies but goodies have worn thin, when we are merely mouthing words, that the Lord knows we need to sing to Him a new song. He wants our worship to be real, not rote. When we willingly and consciously express our love to the Lord, He delights in what He hears. He knows we mean what we say. We are also more apt to worship with delight when our minds are engaged in what our mouths are singing.

So sing to the Lord a new song or an old song—but sing it with passion, sing it with all your heart, glorifying the King of kings!

Oh, sing to the LORD a new song! For He has done marvelous things;
His right hand and His holy arm have gained Him the victory.

—PSALM 98:1 NKJV

Prayer

Thank the Lord for the gift of new things that keeps your walk of faith an adventure. Thank Him for the gift of a new day and all that it promises. Sing a song of praise to Him.

BECAUSE WE BELIEVE

What do you believe? I mean, in a nutshell, what would you say are the foundational beliefs of Christianity?

The question is important. Look around and you'll see all kinds of fellow Christians with a huge variety of opinions on so many different matters—what music to use in worship, how to dress, what degree of involvement with the world is acceptable, how to spend their money. While Christians can agree to disagree about all kinds of matters, there are some bedrock issues on which we all must agree in order to call ourselves Christians.

We believe in the Trinity—the Father, the Son, and the Holy Spirit. We believe in our unity as Christians. We believe in the Bible, God's Word, as utterly infallible. We believe that Jesus was born of a virgin and therefore fully God and fully man. We believe that He was resurrected and that He will one day return.

These are the foundational truths of the faith. While Christians can hold a variety of opinions about many different matters—and while we may have to learn to agree to disagree in many cases—we all agree on these. That's what makes us family. That's what gives us unity with believers in the next block and on the other side of the world.

And now you also have heard the truth, the Good News that God saves you. And when you believed in Christ, he identified you as his own by giving you the Holy Spirit, whom he promised long ago.

—EPHESIANS 1:13 NLT

Prayer

Thanking God for each of the foundational truths
of our faith. Thank Him for fellow believers all
over the world who have been saved by God's grace.

WHO CAN SATISFY MY SOUL LIKE YOU?

Is there ever a time when you feel truly satisfied? A great meal can leave you satisfied—for a time. But soon you'll be hungry again. A great vacation can leave you tan and rested—for a time. But soon you'll feel tired and stressed once more.

The rock band The Rolling Stones had a hit back in the sixties called, "I Can't Get No Satisfaction." Judging from the looks of Mick Jagger and his and aging band members, the cost of their continued search for something that would satisfy has been considerable. That classic hit remains in their repertoire. When you stop and think about it, isn't it sad to be known by a song that reveals that all the money, women, and fame you've enjoyed have brought no satisfaction?

But that's a reality for all of us. There is no satisfaction, for no one can satisfy our yearning souls other than the One who created our souls and their yearnings in the first place. Learning to trust in the Lord and rely on Him to provide what we need is the key to finding satisfaction. No wonder Dennis Jernigan asks us in this penetrating song, "Who could ever be more faithful and true?" It's the same reason John Piper has gone on record to say, "God is most glorified when we are most satisfied in Him."

And my God will meet all your needs according to his glorious riches in Christ Jesus.

—PHILIPPIANS 4:19

Prayer

No one can satisfy you, comfort you, or love you
more than God. Are you looking for something today?
Ask Him to send His living, refreshing rain into your life.

HOLY, HOLY, HOLY (HOSANNA)

On a sea of glass as clear as crystal you take your place among the twenty-four elders and the four living creatures surrounding the throne. The angelic choirs are in full voice. Their trumpets blare, their cymbals crash, their harps fill the room with indescribable music. But that's not all that fills the room. The glory of the Creator God hangs heavy in the air. As you draw your breath, you can't help but sense the weight of the atmosphere. It is unlike anything you ever experienced on earth. But your breathing isn't labored; you can breathe just fine.

There is something you can't do very easily, however. It's difficult to stand up. Falling on your face in gratitude and in expression of your love is the only posture appropriate when in the presence of the Holy One.

> *Then I looked and heard the voice of many angels, numbering thousands upon thousands, and ten thousand times ten thousand. They encircled the throne and the living creatures and the elders.*
>
> —REVELATION 5:11

Prayer

Get down on your knees (if possible put your face
to the ground) and linger for several moments in
silence before the Lord. Forget about yourself
and humble yourself before the King of kings.

OUR GOD REIGNS

"How lovely on the mountains are the feet of him who brings good news," states Isaiah 52:7. Lovely feet? Yes, though looks can be deceiving. Some feet are callused and bruised, but they refuse to rest. They keep climbing, stumbling forward, bleeding at times, finding a way when the path up the mountain is not discernible. They are feet on a mission, providing mobility for those with a message to convey—but it is no ordinary message. Whether in a scrolled parchment or leather-bound book, the message is indeed Good News: God has not forgotten us. He is not far away. Though it appears at times as though He has been dethroned, He has not. Our God reigns!

Because God reigns, those who carry that message have lovely feet indeed. Old Testament prophets like Jeremiah and Joel, first-century martyrs like Stephen and Peter, these were people on a mission: The news must be delivered; the message can't be delayed. It is no small wonder, then, that lovely feet continue to bring the Good News. Such feet are found on persecuted pastors in Romania, in the straw sandals of missionaries serving in Africa, in the sheepskin boots of servants in the Ukraine, and even in Florsheim shoes in suburban America.

Are your feet beautiful? Yes indeed, for wherever they take you, the rest of you goes—bearing the Good News that our God reigns!

How lovely on the mountains are the feet of him who brings good news, who announces peace and brings good news of happiness, who announces salvation, and says to Zion, "Your God reigns!"

—ISAIAH 52:7 NASB

Prayer

Pray for the pastors at your church. Ask God to encourage their hearts and to give them endurance for the path their ministry requires that they walk. Ask God to give you "lovely feet" so that everywhere your feet go, you are bearing the Good News.

FAITHFUL ONE

*I*f you've visited Yellowstone National Park, you've likely taken the time to see Old Faithful. Just a few hundred yards far from that historic old lodge is that legendary geyser, the most photographed geyser in the world. With predictable regularity, that underground cauldron spews a vertical column of hot spring water anywhere from 90 to 180 feet into the air. Contrary to popular opinion, Old Faithful does not show off once an hour. The old gal lets off steam on average every seventy-five minutes. Sometimes there are fifty-five minutes between performances and other times more than twice that long. You can't set your watch according to Yellowstone's natural wonder. Her faithfulness is a bit fickle.

Quite different, however, is the faithfulness of the One who created Old Faithful. The Lord is the Faithful One, so unchanging. We can depend on Him. He is never late. Although we do not always understand His priorities, He is always punctual. In His time, He always comes through. His faithfulness overarches our entire lives. In fact, the psalmist says His faithfulness reaches to the skies. Now there's an image that challenges Old Faithful!

For great is your love, reaching to the heavens; your faithfulness reaches to the skies.

—PSALM 57:10

Prayer

On a sheet of paper write, "God has shown His faithfulness to me by..." Make a list of obvious times the Lord has come through for you when you wondered what you would do.

WHAT A FRIEND I'VE FOUND

*I*f anybody needed a friend, she did. No one paid her the time of day. Her life was punctuated with loneliness. For twelve years she'd been housebound. A dreaded disease dogged her steps. Doctors could offer no hope for healing her humiliating feminine disorder that left her slowly bleeding continuously. As far as she was concerned, it was a slow death. It left her "unclean"—no friends, no corporate worship, no hope.

But then she found a friend. His name was Jesus. Yes, you know the story. It's found in Luke, chapter 8. Hoping for a miracle and longing for companionship, the unnamed woman refused to lose all hope. She persisted in her plan to at least touch the robe of the rabbi. The disciples thought Jesus was overreacting when He said someone had "touched" Him. They were, after all, in a crowded street. But Jesus knew what had happened. The faith of a determined (and very sick) woman had been rewarded. The smile that crept across Jesus' face reassured the woman that faith like that would get her a long way. In fact, it still does. When we refuse to accept our plight apart from the Lord and move in His direction, we are rewarded with His friendship—now and eternally. Praise God!

"Daughter," he said to her, "your faith has made you well. Go in peace."

—LUKE 8:48 NLT

Prayer

Make a personal inventory of how the Lord exhibits
qualities of friendship in your life. Voice those qualities
in prayer. Ask Him for His help as you seek to be that
kind of a friend to those in your sphere of influence.

CREATE IN ME A CLEAN HEART

Isn't it amazing? The one credited as being a man after God's own heart was hardly squeaky-clean. David had a heart that was polluted by lust and deceit. In fact, many scholars think that when David penned the words of this song (read Psalm 51:10), he was dealing with the sin of adultery.

But before we get too judgmental, let's take a trip to the bathroom mirror. Like David, we are in need of more than freshening up. Our hair may be combed, but our heart is dirtied by sin. As we stand in front of our reflection, we stand in need of forgiveness. We need clean hearts. When David recognized his sin, he pled with God not to cast him from His presence or to remove His Spirit, but to instead give him a clean heart and restore the joy of his salvation.

Fortunately, God has anticipated our need and stands ready to remove the grime of guilt. In fact, when we became His children (through His grace and our faith), He removed our stone-cold hearts that were stained and unwashable and replaced them with pliable hearts that can be cleansed. That's what accounts for the fact that a sin-prone king could still be called a man after God's heart. David found he couldn't live with unconfessed sin in his life and experience spiritual joy. Neither can we.

I will sprinkle clean water on you, and you will be clean; I will cleanse you from all your impurities and from all your idols. I will give you a new heart and put a new spirit in you.

—EZEKIEL 36:25-26A

Prayer

As you stand before the bathroom mirror, take a good long look at the person looking back at you. Ask the Lord to bring to mind transgressions that need confession. Ask Him to cleanse your heart.

THERE'S SOMETHING
ABOUT THAT NAME

When the mighty angel entered that humble home in Nazareth unannounced and called Mary by name, the teenage girl must have looked like she'd seen a ghost. Gabriel recognized Mary's fear and told her not to be afraid. Then he told her something that would have seemingly frightened her more. Even though she wasn't married and was still sexually innocent, she was about to have a baby. Not just any baby, however. This child "will be great and will be called the Son of the Most High" (Luke 1:32). This child would be the promised Messiah. The angel instructed Mary to give her child an Aramaic name: Jesus. Like the Hebrew equivalent, Joshua, the name means "the Lord saves."

Curiously, it's a pretty common name. Millions of Jewish boys have been named Joshua. The same with countless Hispanic mothers who have named their sons Jesús. But only the sinless Son of Mary has ever offered living—and dying—proof that the Lord has saved us from our sins. He did it on the cross. The reason there is something about the name Jesus is because there is something unique about the One who was given that name. He is Master, Savior, and eternal King. He is Jesus, who saves us from our sins.

You will be with child and give birth to a son, and you are to give him the
name Jesus.

—LUKE 1:31

---•---

Prayer

Use the name of Jesus as a meditation focus. Say it over and
over again audibly. As you speak His name, allow the Holy
Spirit to bring to mind aspects of His character and salvation
that you need to hold on to at this time in your life.

---•---

BLESS HIS HOLY NAME

*I*f you know where to go, you can still find a soul-stirring worship service in a seventeenth-century gothic church in Europe. But that isn't the norm. Most limestone cathedrals are more apt to be museums or art galleries than gathering places of growing Christians. Gratefully, stained-glass windows or flying stone buttresses aren't prerequisites for praise. As far as God is concerned, your heart can be a cathedral.

Worship is, by definition, a response. We see the great things the Lord has done and we must respond. We can't help ourselves. We want to express our wonder and gratitude. We want to bless the One who blesses us by parading our praise in His presence. Worship acknowledges the worth of God demonstrated in the work He does.

Every day, every moment, can be filled with worship. Bless the Lord with all that is within you. Recognize that He has done great things. Thank Him for His countless blessings in your life. Bless His holy name.

Bless the LORD, O my soul: and all that is within me, bless his holy name. Bless the LORD, O my soul, and forget not all his benefits: Who forgiveth all thine iniquities; who healeth all thy diseases; Who redeemeth thy life from destruction; who crowneth thee with lovingkindness and tender mercies; Who satisfieth thy mouth with good things; so that thy youth is renewed like the eagle's.

—PSALM 103:1-5 KJV

Prayer

Prayers don't have to be spoken. They can be written. Go ahead and "pray with a pencil." Find a sheet of paper and list the "great things" the Lord has done in your life this past calendar year. As you jot each item down, express gratitude in your heart.

July 22

COME AND WORSHIP

Worship has so many aspects. We come before God. We bow before His throne. We arise and lift our voices in order to make His glory known. We offer thanksgiving. We praise.

Who worships? The royal priesthood, the holy nation—believers who have been called from every tribe and nation to show forth His praise and show forth His power. There's a call to one and all. And what a high and holy calling it is!

Sometimes we feel that our spiritual life is separate from our "regular" life. We forget that we have been called to worship. We know that pastors have a holy calling and they devote their lives to various aspects of worship. But our pastors aren't the only ones who have a holy calling from God. All believers from every tribe and nation have been called to "arise and worship."

Have you heard the call? Today is the day; now is the hour. Believers have entered God's kingdom and become His priests—able to step into His presence. So enter His courts. Listen for His voice. Whether you bow, arise, sing, give thanks, or glorify—let all that you do worship the Lord!

No longer will anything be cursed. For the throne of God and of the Lamb will be there, and his servants will worship him. And they will see his face, and his name will be written on their foreheads.

—REVELATION 22:3-4 NLT

Prayer

Worship is a unique privilege of those made in
the image of God. Thank Him for this opportunity.
Ask Him what He thinks about the way you worship.

JESUS, MIGHTY GOD

Although there is no record of what Jesus looked like, a painting by a Chicago artist in the 1940s has influenced many people's opinion. Warner Sallman's "Head of Christ" is the most recognized likeness in the Christian world. But that brown-toned image with the shoulder-length hair and gentle eyes is only one man's guess. If it were up to you, how would you depict Him?

Judging from the way many people talk about Jesus, they'd draw a rather weak-looking character afraid of His own shadow. A full reading of the New Testament (and especially the Book of Revelation) would call such an image shortsighted. The Jesus of the Bible is kind and approachable, but He's also bold, challenging, and shrewd. He overturns tables in the temple and puts overly pious religionists in their place. He is Mighty God. He is the Rock, fortress, and defense. His conquering arm is always victorious. He causes His foes to tremble.

When you think of Jesus, remember His compassion and kindness. Thank Him for His great love for you. Then remember His awesome power and strength that bought your salvation and now guides and protects you. Thank Him for being your Rock, your fortress, and your defense.

His head and hair were white like wool, as white as snow, and his eyes were like blazing fire.

—REVELATION 1:14

Prayer

As you come into the Lord's presence, open the eyes of your heart to see a picture of your Savior—meek and mild, yet all-powerful and awesome. Thank Him for all He is to you.

O MAGNIFY THE LORD

Haystack Rock on the Oregon Coast is one of the most photographed rock formations in the world. Its recognizable shape accounts for its peculiar name. Silhouetted against fiery sunsets, Haystack Rock shows up in coffee table books and on posters and postcards. Every evening, professional and amateur photographers aim their cameras in her direction. The pictures can be breathtaking.

Curiously, Haystack Rock is virtually useless apart from its aesthetic appeal. Except for seagulls and seals taking refuge on its slippery slopes, it serves no practical purpose. It is too small for human habitation and too dangerous for climbing or diving. Obviously, the psalmist who compared the Lord to a mighty rock was not thinking of the scenic vista near Cannon Beach, Oregon. The Rock he had in mind was a towering monolith that would serve as a safe barricade from advancing enemies, the Rock that would be his salvation. No doubt what he pictured were the jagged rocks of the Middle East complete with limestone caves where those who were running for their lives could hide. Our Rock is more than just a photo prop, more than just a nice poetic picture. He is the Rock of our salvation. Blessed be that Rock!

> *The LORD is my rock, my fortress, and my savior; my God is my rock,*
> *in whom I find protection. He is my shield, the strength of my salvation,*
> *and my stronghold.*
>
> —PSALM 18:2 NLT

Prayer

Visualize a large boulder or rock formation. As you enter into the Lord's presence, allow yourself to feel safe in Him.

CELEBRATE THE LORD OF LOVE / GOD IS GOOD ALL THE TIME

A son and his father. Two men with heavy hearts. One left home to sow wild oats and quickly experienced the harvest of his folly. The other stayed at home longing for a boy he loved more than life itself. Although for different reasons, hearts once free were now imprisoned.

Years went by. As the son turned his back on a field of dreams (that had become a nightmare), he tried to imagine his father's reaction to his irresponsibility. A metronome of guilt slowly beat in his chest. As the father waited by the window each day, he sadly searched the horizon for evidence that his son was still alive. But each day that dawned with hope dissolved into despair. And then one day...

Yes, you know the story. Jesus told it. He described how the prodigal son did make it home only to find his father's response totally the opposite of what he'd expected. He also described the father's race to meet his son. Hearts once heavy had been traded in for hearts of joy.

Thanks to God's grace, that kind of swap still takes place. And when it does, this worship song says it all. So celebrate!

But we had to celebrate and be glad, because this brother of yours was dead and is alive again; he was lost and is found.

—LUKE 15:32

Prayer

If it's been awhile since you came clean with the Father, allow Him to wipe the slate. Confess and accept His forgiveness. Then celebrate!

ARISE AND SING

God had promised His people they would be uprooted for their blatant disobedience unless they repented, but they had blindly disregarded His warnings. Finally, God kept His promise and sent His beloved people into captivity in Babylon. This was no occasion for singing. They were being punished for their disobedience.

That generation died in captivity. So did the next. After seventy long years, God kept another promise—to return His people to their land. And so the Jews began returning from the sun-baked deserts of Babylon. God had delivered them from their captors. Children born in a pagan land were now grandparents on their way to see their "home" for the first time. With purposed steps, they progressed as fast as they could. As they looked over the shoulders, they smiled at one another. They didn't fear the possibility of enemy armies sneaking up behind them. Neither were they concerned about wild beasts. As Scripture records, there were a couple of unexpected travelers that overtook them—their names were "gladness and joy." As they contemplated God's goodness they retrieved their harps and started to sing.

When it seems you've lost a reason to sing, take your cue from the returning Jews. Recall the ways the Lord has delivered you. Then open your heart and rejoice!

They will enter Zion with singing; everlasting joy will crown their heads.
Gladness and joy will overtake them, and sorrow and sighing will flee away.

—ISAIAH 35:10

Prayer

Sometimes posture promotes praise. Stand up and
raise your arms to the sky. Sing the lyrics of
a favorite worship song to an audience of One.

HOW AWESOME IS YOUR NAME / WE LIFT YOU HIGH

Some words have the ability to scare us. They are singular words that pack a powerful punch. Words like "cancer," "Parkinson's," "Alzheimer's," "divorce." These words can take our breath away. They can make us give up all hope. They are fearful words, sad words, painful words that, when uttered, cause all of life to come crashing in around us.

The Bible reminds us, however, that there is a word that is more powerful still. That word is the Name that is above every name. That Name has power over drug addiction, alcoholism, and depression. It's a Name that can stare down unemployment, bankruptcy, and injustice. It's a Name that makes grief, loneliness, and fear pack their bags and flee.

One day Peter and John came across a lame beggar near the temple in Jerusalem. The man, deprived of his mobility, was hopeful for a couple of coins. But what he got was far beyond what he could have ever imagined. The two disciples confessed that they didn't have any money to give him, but expressed their desire to give him what they had. Reaching down they pulled the man up "in the name of Jesus Christ." Instantaneously, the man was healed.

How awesome is His name.

But Peter said, "I don't have any money for you. But I'll give you what I have. In the name of Jesus Christ of Nazareth, get up and walk!"

—ACTS 3:6 NLT

Prayer

There's a time for standing in the Lord's presence. There's also a time for kneeling. As you go to prayer, say the name of Jesus reverently, for it is the Name that is above all names.

REVIVAL FIRE FALL

Have you ever felt like your ability to trust God has taken a vacation without your knowledge (or permission)? Facing the pressures that park on our front porch every morning can rob us of whatever spiritual reserves we thought we had. We feel drained, perplexed, afraid, tired, overwhelmed. Perhaps you can relate to a spiritually weary Christian who confessed in her journal:

> *There's a power outage inside me. I've blown at least one fuse (if not more). There's no heat. No light. I wish I could say there's a battery backup, but there's not. All I have is a candle. Just one unlit wick and a book of matches. But at least my wick is dry, Lord, and therein is my hope. I'm counting on Your Holy Spirit to fall afresh (like it did at Pentecost long ago) and with purging flame to energize my empty life with holy joy, burning desire, and the warmth of Your passionate presence.*

You see, even when the power has gone out and you are left in the dark of doubt and discouragement, all you need is a flicker of faith and a sincere desire that the fire fall.

> *We also pray that you will be strengthened with his glorious power so that you will have all the patience and endurance you need. May you be filled with joy.*

—COLOSSIANS 1:11 NLT

Prayer

In what areas of your life are you feeling powerless?
Name those in prayer. Confess your need to God.
Ask Him to restore the power.

YOU ARE MY GOD

Someone once observed that it is possible to miss heaven by a mere eighteen inches. What he meant is this: You can believe in your head that a Supreme Being created the world and continues to be all-powerful, but unless that belief in your head makes its way to your heart, you are not a true believer. The difference is between acknowledging the existence of the Almighty and entering into a personal relationship with that God by surrendering your will and emotions to Him. God ceases to be a distant deity or a theological abstract. He is, instead, "my God." He is a personal point of reference. As such, He is approachable, accessible, and an indispensable part of our lives. No wonder while David was dodging those who were out to kill him in the desert, he cried out to the Lord. He knew that God was more than just God. The Lord was his God. And because the personal investment was a two-way reality, David knew that God would come through. When we reach the place where we have embraced the object of our religious thoughts with the arms of our heart, we have crossed the bridge from belief to faith.

O God, you are my God, earnestly I seek you; my soul thirsts for you, my body longs for you, in a dry and weary land where there is no water.

—PSALM 63:1

Prayer

The God to whom you pray is not a distant deity.
He is the One who created you and desires a
relationship with you. Thank the Lord that He
knows your name and hears you when you pray.

ABOVE ALL

The impact Jesus has had (and continues to have) on our world exceeds our ability to fully comprehend. When we think we have done our best to pile His influence into a mountain of meaning, we are humbled to discover He is above that. The truth is, He is far above all such attempts. No one can measure the magnitude of His significance. Jesus is above all nature and all creation. He is above all wisdom and anything people try to accomplish. He's above all kingdoms, wonders, and wealth.

That's also what Dr. James Allen Francis was going for in a sermon he preached on July 11, 1926 to the National Baptist Young Peoples' Union at First Baptist Church of Los Angeles. His challenging message was titled, "Arise, Sir Knight." Attempting to portray the unsurpassable greatness of Jesus Christ, he said, "When we try to sum up His influence, all the armies that ever marched, all the parliaments that ever sat, all the kings that ever reigned are absolutely picayune in their influence on mankind compared with that of this one solitary life."

And that one solitary life had influence on you because of His willingness to die, rejected and alone. For your sins He died. He took the fall and thought of you—above all.

Christ is the visible image of the invisible God. He existed before God made anything at all and is supreme over all creation.

—COLOSSIANS 1:15 NLT

Prayer

Because Jesus is truly "above all" there is nothing too difficult for Him to handle. Bring your concerns and cares to Him today. Thank Him for all He did for you, dying in your place.

LET THE PEACE OF GOD REIGN

Ask any passerby on the street, "If you could have one wish, what would you wish for?" More often than not, you'll hear the words, "I'd wish for world peace."

We hear the words and smile. A noble wish, for sure, but seemingly impossible. World peace? Not with terrorists and dictators. World peace? Not while human nature desires power and greed encompasses reason. World peace? An illusive dream, right?

Well, not so fast.

The Bible promises world peace when Jesus comes to reign. It's not an illusive dream—it's a reality. And believers, whether alive at His return or already in heaven, will get to enjoy that peace for all eternity.

But what about now? Is there any haven of peace in this crazy world? As we await God's reign on earth, we can experience His reign in our hearts. When we set our hearts on Him, running the race of time with Him by our side, we can let His peace reign. When we trust in the Holy Spirit to strengthen us, we can let His peace reign. When we let His healing power breathe life into us and make us whole, we can let His peace reign.

Open your heart to hunger for more of God. Let the Spirit saturate your soul. Let the peace of God reign.

And the peace of God, which transcends all understanding, will guard your hearts and your minds in Christ Jesus.

—PHILIPPIANS 4:7

Prayer

Ask the Lord to bring you His peace, no matter how "unpeaceful" your life may be right now. Allow the peace of God to fill your heart, strengthen you, and saturate your soul.

SONG FOR THE NATIONS

In the very beginning, long before time, a song was born. Over the silent chaos of the uncreated world, God hummed a tune. It was a song of life. Because it was a melody He couldn't keep to Himself, He spoke the worlds into existence and called for living beings. With lips of love He kissed those He created in His image, and with those same lips He whistled His timeless tune deep within their souls. But there the song remained locked. For centuries men and women mumbled on in a monotone life. Out of sync with the melody God desired for them, His people attempted to experience intimacy, meaning, and pleasure unaware of the lyrics of love in their hearts. God's song remained unsung.

But not forever. On a silent night in the little town of Bethlehem, God clothed Himself in the fabric of flesh away in a manger. And while some heard a baby's hungry cry, others heard the song of a God hungering for relationship with people. The baby grew and His voice grew strong. While some heard a rabbi teaching, others heard a virtuoso voicing the melody of grace. Singing of God's love in comforting tones, the Singer calmed the anxious. Whistling ever so gently as He'd heard His Father do in the beginning of time, He unlocked the song in women and men that they (and we) might sing it for the world.

I will sing of the mercies of the LORD for ever: with my mouth will I make known thy faithfulness to all generations.

—PSALM 89:1 KJV

Prayer

Prayers can be written as well as spoken. They also
can be sung. Using one of your favorite praise songs
(or even the Lord's Prayer), sing your praise to the Lord.

RISE UP AND PRAISE HIM

Have you ever noticed the rhythms of life that comprise our daily routines? From the metronome-like swipe of windshield wipers to the syncopated motion of a washing machine, from the graceful sweeping motion of willow tree branches bowing in the wind to the steady fall of raindrops, the world is replete with rhythmic activity. When is the last time you laid on your back and gazed at clouds bumping against one another as they crossed an afternoon summer sky? Do recall being stopped at an intersection by a flock of geese waddling across the road? What about that time you marveled at how your children spontaneously danced when joyful music filled the room?

When you stop and think about it, the world that the Lord created is a tapestry of motion. The earth spins on its axis. The moon orbits around us. The tides rise and fall. If you are willing, you can take your cues for worship from the world around you. Although there is a time and place for silence and quiet reflection, there is also a time to let yourself go and let your feet move in a joyful dance before the Lord. So rise up and praise Him—with all your heart, with all your soul, with all your might.

A time to weep, and a time to laugh; a time to mourn, and a time to dance.

—ECCLESIASTES 3:4 NASB

Prayer

Prayer can be spoken, sung, or acted out. There's a time
for each. As you play your favorite upbeat worship CD,
enjoy singing—yes, even dancing—before the Lord.

I GIVE THANKS

Saved sinners. That's us. We are oxymorons—a pair of words that don't belong together and actually seem to negate each other, like "found missing." We are sinners, deserving nothing more than death. But we are saved.

Saved sinners because we have been shown favor unending. Saved sinners because Jesus gave His life for us. Saved sinners because Jesus' blood has covered us and He has shown mercy to us.

Saved, but still sinners. Saved, but constantly facing our sinful nature that seeks to rear its ugly head without a moment's notice. A temptation flits across the screen of our minds, an evil thought or desire, a nasty word, a hurtful deed. Saved, but sinners. Jesus has saved us and continues to work in our lives to restore us again and again. Through this process of becoming more like Him, we slip and fall. We ask for restoration. And He always restores. Why? Because He is our gracious Redeemer. We belong to Him.

For by grace you have been saved through faith, and that not of yourselves; it is the gift of God.

—EPHESIANS 2:8 NKJV

Prayer

Are you facing struggles and temptations today?
Do you wonder how you, a sinner, can possibly truly be saved?
Talk to God. Repent and ask Him to restore you again.

NO GREATER LOVE

Picture a fire on a beach. An early morning breeze has energized the dying embers. Bread is warming. Fish is cooking. Jesus, no longer an inmate on death row, has risen from the grave. He is fixing His friends breakfast on the seashore. Can you smell it? After a night of trolling for trout, they are hungry. As they gather around their master chef, He kicks it up a notch and expresses His joy in their presence. It's a feast of friendship. But Jesus has more in mind than just waiting on their physical needs. He has spiritual needs in mind as well.

Approaching Peter, Jesus sees into the master fisherman's guilty heart. Having betrayed Jesus three times, Peter is filled with regrets that the resurrection has not fully negated. The Savior knows this and for that reason gives him the privilege of affirming his love just as many times.

"Simon son of John, do you love me?" Jesus asks three times.

And three times Peter responds, "You know I love You."

No matter how far your sins have taken you, come back to Jesus and tell Him you love Him. His love is so great that it can cover all sin and shame. There is no greater love than Jesus.

Greater love has no one than this, that he lay down his life for his friends.

—JOHN 15:13

Prayer

Stand at the toaster and smell the warm bread toasting.
As you smell this inviting aroma, picture the Lord
fixing you breakfast. Thank Him for the
practical ways He nourishes your life.

SHOW YOUR POWER

Perhaps He was meek, but Jesus was far from mild. He wasn't opposed to overturning tables in a temple when a show of strength was called for. Jesus could flex His righteous muscles when needed. He called the religious hypocrites a brood of snakes. He strongly reprimanded one of His disciples and said he was acting like an emissary of Satan. And why not? Jesus is God Himself, who had spoken into the darkness and created light.

But He also showed His power in less dramatic ways. Like the way He bucked the culture's way of minimizing women and children. Like the way He moved outside the margins of respectable society to touch lepers, lunch with tax collectors, and validate the poor. But perhaps the greatest power that Jesus displayed was the way He resisted the temptation to fight back. When falsely accused, He quietly listened. When physically attacked, He turned the other cheek. When given the chance to mount an army and prove His Messiah-ship with force, He opted to set aside His power and be overpowered and nailed to a cross.

And by doing that, He saved us. Now we can call upon His power every moment of every day. Need help? Ask the God of the universe, the God of your salvation, to show His power—to you!

When they hurled their insults at him, he did not retaliate; when he suffered, he made no threats. Instead, he entrusted himself to him who judges justly.

—1 PETER 2:23

Prayer

Ask the Lord to infuse you with His power when
you feel like striking back at those who offend you.
Ask Him for the power to show self-control.

DID YOU FEEL THE
MOUNTAINS TREMBLE?

If you've ever lived through an earthquake, you know all about trembling mountains. If you haven't, go ahead and ask someone who experienced the earthquake that struck the San Francisco Bay area several years ago. The date was October 17, 1989. While the brown hills surrounding the city shook, people of all ages cowered and ran for cover. The 7.1 quake collapsed a section of the Bay Bridge. The quake killed 62, injured 3,757 and left more than 12,000 homeless.

In an odd juxtaposition, game three of the 1989 World Series featured the San Francisco Giants and the Oakland Athletics. Ballgames and death struggles; shouts of joy from the stands and tears of grief from the homefront. The mountains had trembled, but life had gone on.

A day is coming when the risen Christ will reappear and the world as we know it will end. The mountains will tremble, the marketplace trading will cease, and justice will be weighed in the balances once and for all. Yes, the Bible does speak of earthquakes and end times. For those who have rounded the bases of faith and know they are headed for home, it will be the hope for which they have longed. For those still warming the bench in the dugout of doubt and skepticism, it will be one frightful double-header. A returning King and a cataclysmic Armageddon. The heavenly gates will fling wide to prepare the way of the risen Lord.

Nation will rise against nation, and kingdom against kingdom. There will be famines and earthquakes in various places.

—MATTHEW 24:7

Prayer

Spend a few moments in quiet contemplation.
Picture the world as it is now (war-torn, diseased,
sinful, etc.) and how it will be when Christ returns.

WE WANT TO SEE JESUS LIFTED HIGH

Jeers. Cheers. A cacophony of confusion. Emotions high. Unprecedented commotion. The crowd is gathered as if for a freak show. It's a Roman execution, and there in plain view just outside the gates of Jerusalem, three crosses lie on the ground. Three men are forced on their backs on the rough-hewn timbers. With mallets and spikes, Caesar's soldiers nail the condemned to the waiting wood. "We want to see Jesus lifted high!" The bloodthirsty cry from the rabbi's critics reverberates against the surrounding hills. And that day the misguided masses get what they call for. A thief, a murderer, and a rabbi are lifted up from the ground and hung out to die.

Now contrast that with those who claim a personal relationship with the once-slain Savior. Because of His undeserved death, they know life. Because He was lifted up, they will live forever. And when Jesus returns to earth as the righteous, victorious Lord, the grateful forgiven crowd will call out the same words that the bloodthirsty cried, but with a far different meaning. "We want to see Jesus lifted high!" And like those who had their wish granted that day 2,000 years ago, so will these. He will be high and lifted up on His glorious throne from which He will reign forever and ever.

Therefore God exalted him to the highest place and gave him the name that is above every name.

—PHILIPPIANS 2:9

Prayer

In your mind's eye, see Jesus lifted high on the cross.
Express your gratitude for His sacrifice. Thank Him
that He will soon return as the exalted King of all kings.

LET IT RAIN

As Courtney looked out the window at where the San Gabriel Mountains were supposed to be, all she saw was a thick brownish-gray curtain of sky. Amazed at atmospheric inversion that had trapped a dense layer of smog over the Los Angeles basin and rendered the craggy hills invisible, this visiting Canadian expressed amazement and dismay.

"All we really need is an old-fashioned gully washer!" her friend and California native Sarah said, agreeing with her houseguest's observations. "It's really ugly isn't it? But you know, nothing takes care of something as bad as this as a good rainstorm. As hard as it may seem to believe today, Los Angeles is still as beautiful as it was when its founders dubbed it the City of Angels."

And just as a soaking shower can cleanse a smoggy sky, so also can the presence of God's Spirit raining down on our dry and weary lives wash us clean and refresh us. Truth be told, it may seem that such a spiritual cloudburst is as rare as rain in the middle of a California summer. But God's showers of blessing and refreshing are not limited to weather patterns or seasonal variations. God's drenching presence falls on all those who will wait in His presence, confessing their sins and admitting their need for refreshment, cleansing, and revival.

Let it rain, Lord, let it rain!

Now turn from your sins and turn to God, so you can be cleansed of your sins.

—ACTS 3:19 NLT

Prayer

Find a favorite chair. Be still as the Holy Spirit reveals the "smog" of your life. Agree with what He says. Then call out to the Lord and ask that the refreshing rains of His forgiveness flood your heart.

WE FALL DOWN

Often we don't display our love for Jesus publicly by actually "falling down" on our faces before Him. Yet how about in the privacy of our homes, beside our beds, in our studies, alone with Him? When you seriously consider His love and sacrifice on your behalf, do you find yourself overwhelmed to the point that you fall down and worship before Him?

The Bible tells us that one day "at the name of Jesus every knee will bow, in heaven and on earth and under the earth, and every tongue will confess that Jesus Christ is Lord, to the glory of God the Father" (Philippians 2:10-11 NLT). One day, we will indeed fall before Him in glorious adoration. And one day, even those who have scorned Him in life will find themselves bowing in humiliation.

On that day, those who have believed will be rewarded with crowns for their service and their faith. And on that day, we will take those same crowns and lay them at the feet of Jesus, knowing that we had them only by His grace in the first place. They belong rightfully to Him.

On that day, with all of heaven joining in, we will sing holy, holy, holy is the Lamb. And we will sing that song forever.

The twenty-four elders fall down before him who sits on the throne, and worship him who lives for ever and ever. They lay their crowns before the throne.

—REVELATION 4:10

Prayer

Find a private place and lay prostrate before your
holy God. Think about what you can lay at His
feet in joyous response for all His gifts to you.

YOU ARE STILL HOLY

To be human is to experience change. We walk through times of joy and times of sorrow, times of glorious light and times of impenetrable darkness. We will inevitably find ourselves blinded by confusion at times, wondering about life, the world, even ourselves. We struggle with the "why" questions; we find ourselves facing doubt. In those difficult times, we look about for something to hold onto, something to keep us secure when everything seems uncertain.

That's where we find God—our holy, loving God who is not capable of change. He is constant and true. He is faithful and forgiving. He is not affected by circumstances or our capricious attitudes toward them. The darkness is light to Him; our confusion is crystal clear. He is the anchor, the rock, the foundation. We must hold fast to Him, remembering that even in our times of darkness and confusion, He is holy and sovereign. Our doubts do not affect Him. He is changeless, eternal, perfect.

So in your times of doubt, don't run away from God; instead, run to Him. Go to His chambers and be unafraid to dance, perhaps with slow and uncertain steps, but still, a dance. In your times of change, He does not change. He is and forever will be holy.

Jesus Christ is the same yesterday and today and forever.

—HEBREWS 13:8

Prayer

Hold on to God. No matter what your changing circumstances
may be today, thank God that He never changes. He is holy.
Ask Him to make you a pure reflection of His love.

YOU'RE WORTHY OF MY PRAISE

The word "all" is essential in defining the way God wants us to follow Him. When we are totally committed, it means we give Him all. As we come into His presence, we should come with a desire to offer Him everything within our hearts without reservation. Wholly and completely. He doesn't want us to hold anything back. When we praise, we praise with every ounce of our strength. The God who delights to be clothed in the tapestry of our praise longs for us to worship Him with every breath. The God who makes Himself known wants us to seek His face all of our days. He knows that we need to meet Him daily in order to follow all of His ways.

God is not content with some of our worship or part of our praise. He doesn't want our leftover time. He doesn't take well to being set aside while we complete our to-do lists. He knows it is not good for us to expend all of our energy on temporal pursuits, leaving nothing left for what is eternal. No, not God. He wants it all.

But do you know what? God doesn't demand it all without offering anything in return. In fact, when we give Him all, He will give us all—all of Himself.

He who did not spare his own Son, but gave him up for us all—how will he not also, along with him, graciously give us all things?

—ROMANS 8:32

Prayer

Be honest with your Heavenly Father. Open up all your heart to Him. Let Him know what areas of your life are difficult for you to surrender to His Lordship.

LOOK MY WAY

*L*ove and praise. The words go together like other famous couplets: salt and pepper, shoes and socks, dollars and cents. Imagine loving someone and never offering a word of praise or encouragement; imagine truly praising someone you didn't care about.

David expresses that the Lord is worthy of his love and his praise (Psalm 18:1,3). All of Psalm 18 expresses love and praise to God for delivering David from his enemies. He had thought that all was lost as "the cords of death entangled" him, but God "mounted the cherubim and flew," then "reached down from on high" and drew him "out of deep waters" (18:4, 10, 16).

What "cords of death" are entangling you? What "torrents of destruction" threaten to overwhelm you? Perhaps it is the pain of a child gone astray, a spouse seeking divorce, a relationship gone sour. Perhaps it is financial worries or a difficult illness. The last thing you want to do is praise God; you may not even feel like you love Him at the moment. But with the song writer, ask God to "look your way." Let Him know about your pain, but also tell Him that through this situation, you want to give glory and honor to His name, and you want to see His mighty power fall like rain.

I love you, O Lord, my strength...I call to the Lord, who is worthy of praise, and I am saved from my enemies.

—PSALM 18:1, 3

Prayer

Tell the Lord whatever is on your mind. If difficulties
are threatening your peace or your faith, express
your fears to God, but also express your desire
to love and praise Him no matter what.

ROCK OF AGES

*I*f you've traveled in Israel, you are well aware of the number of rocks that litter the landscape. Small stones and pebbles dot the roadways; big boulders burst out of the ground everywhere you look. Even the windswept plateaus in the Judean wilderness boast frequent rock formations. With that in mind, it is no wonder that Jesus made reference to rocky ground when He told the parable of the soils. Clearing the fields of rocks was a time-consuming but essential task for those who made their living planting seeds and cultivating crops.

Perhaps the stony ground of Israel explains why the people likened the Lord God to a rock. Such a metaphor may seem strange to our way of thinking, but in ancient times it was an image with which the people could relate. And so when poets and prophets looked for something familiar with which to compare God, they opted for an unchanging rock—a rock of all ages, a rock that stood for generations past and would continue to stand through the present and on into the future. The Lord was like a craggy rock fortress against which they could lean and find support or into which they could run and find refuge. He is the protection and the strength of those who look to Him. He is the unchanging One who delights in providing safe haven to all who draw near. Indeed there is no Rock, no God, like ours.

*From the ends of the earth I call to you, I call as my heart grows faint;
lead me to the rock that is higher than I.*

—PSALM 61:2

Prayer

Close your eyes and picture the rock of ages represented
by mountains. Thank the Lord for being the
Rock of ages—strong, dependable, secure.

FOR THE LORD IS GOOD

The situation appeared hopeless. A vast army was bearing down on Judah. Fortunately, King Jehoshaphat's first move was to inquire of the Lord. "We have no power to face this vast army that is attacking us. We do not know what to do, but our eyes are upon you," he prayed (2 Chronicles 20:12).

The Lord answered Jehoshaphat's pleas. "Do not be afraid or discouraged...For the battle is not yours, but God's." God gave the instruction for the army to go out to meet the invaders, but also promised that they would not have to fight. They would merely have to stand still and watch God work.

Well, this seemed a bit strange, but Jehoshaphat obeyed. The nation apparently needed some encouragement, and so "after consulting the people, Jehoshaphat appointed men to sing to the Lord and to praise him" (20:21). These singers went at the head of the army, singing to God, praising Him that His love endures forever. The battle was won, and Judah hadn't lifted a spear.

What enemy advances against you today? What impossible situation looms over you? Cry out to God that you have no power, that you don't know what to do. Then start singing as you move ahead. Sing that God is good; praise Him that His love endures forever. And watch Him bring the victory.

For the LORD is good and his love endures forever; his faithfulness continues through all generations.

—PSALM 100:5

Prayer

Reflect on this acronym for the word "good": God Only Offers Delights. Allow that to be your prayer focus as you count recent blessings. Trust Him to be with you today.

LET EVERYTHING THAT
HAS BREATH

Both of Wendy Steven's lungs had collapsed. A severe allergic reaction to tetracycline was to blame. The twenty-something teacher had gone into anaphylactic shock and was now on a ventilator. The doctors were pessimistic. They'd done everything to save Wendy's life, but her vital signs were not encouraging. As they sat with Wendy's parents in the waiting room of Western Medical Center, they did not hide their concern. Taking a deep breath, the lead physician suggested divine intervention might be their only hope. "If you believe in prayer," he said, "you'd better pray."

While a machine breathed for their daughter, Hugh and Norma Steven breathed their anxiety and hope to the Lord. It was as though they were exhaling their fears and doubts while inhaling the promises of God's faithfulness. As career missionaries with Wycliffe Bible Translators, they had experience in surviving in the atmosphere of faith. And so, there in a corner of the waiting room, they did their best to practice "spiritual breathing." Within a week, against all odds, it became clear that the Lord was going to spare Wendy's life. When their firstborn daughter was taken off the breathing machine, they realized that it hadn't been the breathing machine that had sustained her life. It was the One who gives breath to every living creature.

Let everything that has breath praise the LORD. Praise the LORD.

—PSALM 150:6

Prayer

Practice spiritual breathing. Exhale your confessions and concerns and then inhale God's forgiveness and promised protection from the traumas of life that would attempt to take your breath away.

FAITHFUL TO YOUR CALL

Their hearts belong to the Lord. Their journey to heaven has been prepaid. But except for where they spend two hours each Sunday morning, they act, look, and talk like those who never go to church. Quite honestly, you'd have difficulty telling them from Joe Pagan.

Who are they? "Undercover Christians," that's who. They are everywhere. Secret agents of sorts, they blend in wherever they are. They don't speak up when something is obviously wrong or unjust. They don't dare use the Bible as their standard of morality—at least in public. It's as if they are fearful of taking a stand.

Yet they have plenty of opinions about the latest television shows or movies, but they wouldn't be caught dead mentioning their pastor's sermon. While they are quite expressive over the hometown sports teams, they are mute when it comes to making reference to the spiritual things. You have to wonder what the Lord thinks of these "undercover Christians."

If we really do belong to Him, He desires that we be faithful to our call! After all, no treasure on this earth can equal what it will be like to spend even one day in His presence. We should desire to be His servants more than we desire anything else. And we should let everyone know it!

One thing I ask of the Lord, this is what I seek: that I may dwell in the house of the Lord all the days of my life, to gaze upon the beauty of the Lord and to seek him in his temple.

—PSALM 27:4

Prayer

Ask the Lord for courage to be faithful to your call.
Present yourself as an ambassador to speak on
His behalf whenever He should prompt you.

HOSANNA

Hosanna! Except for last Palm Sunday, when's the last time you remember hearing someone saying "Hosanna"? It's one of those words that we don't use much. Hosanna! It's an ancient Hebrew word that means "Lord, save us!"

Hmmm. Come to think of it, that expression of need is appropriate a whole lot more often than just one Sunday a year. For example, how many times this past week did you need the Lord's help? More than a few, right? It's normal to need Him. He created us that way. It's when we think we can save ourselves that we set ourselves up for disaster. Hosanna! Calling out to the Lord for His intervention is a declaration of our dependence on Him. Hosanna! Asking for His help is not a sign of weakness; it's a sign of maturity. Hosanna! It's proof that we have arrived at an accurate estimation of ourselves and as well as the role He desires to play in our lives.

Perhaps we should consider adding "Hosanna" to our list of everyday vocabulary words. It certainly is as appropriate as that other Hebrew word that finds our lips more than once a year. You know: "Hallelujah!"

The crowds that went ahead of him and those that followed shouted, "Hosanna to the Son of David! Blessed is he who comes in the name of the Lord! Hosanna in the highest!"

—MATTHEW 21:9

Prayer

Practice arrow prayers. Shoot up a "hosanna" throughout
the day whenever you feel yourself in need.

GREAT IS THE LORD
GOD ALMIGHTY

It was a miracle! The children of Israel crossed the Red Sea. Not in dugout canoes. They walked through on dry ground! Even though Pharaoh had them cornered, God's people were not caught and dragged back to slavery in Egypt. When the children of Israel came to the brink of the sea, God opened the waters for them. When Pharaoh's army tried to cross, however, the walls of water did not hold. Great is the Lord God Almighty.

The next generation of Israelites conquered the land, but not without miracles. They came upon the fortress city of Jericho. The walls were thick, strong, and impenetrable. But once again the mighty God intervened. By following His instructions, the walls collapsed, giving Israel a great victory. Great is the Lord God Almighty.

Every generation is dying and lost in sin. We need a miracle. We cannot defeat sin on our own for it is embedded in our very nature. So God did a miracle. He died for us and then rose again to save us. He took our blame so that we could be saved. Great is the Lord God Almighty!

We give thanks to you, Lord God Almighty, the One who is and who was, because you have taken your great power and have begun to reign.

—REVELATION 11:17

Prayer

Think about how the Lord delivered His people at the Red Sea. What challenges in your life right now seem just as impossible? Acknowledge your helplessness to the Lord. Thank Him for being your Lord God All-mighty!

YOU ARE ETERNAL

From the time that we are little, we learn that life lets us down. Parents divorce. Pets die. Best friends betray us. Dreams shatter.

And truth be told, pain is part of life. We experience great joys and terrible hurts. There's a time to rejoice and a time to grieve. We recognize that nothing lasts forever. Promises are broken; disappointment blindsides us.

Has it happened to you? You lose your job. You discover your teenager is experimenting with drugs. Your aging mother no longer recognizes you now that her Alzheimer's has advanced. The devaluation of your company's stock means your retirement is now a distant blur. What you thought you could count on changes—and it hurts.

And yet against that black backdrop of the reality of change is the stark contrast of God's changelessness. Our health may fail, but God remains the same. Beauty fades, but God is constant. We grow old, but He is eternal. No wonder when the Almighty encountered Moses at a flammable thicket, He introduced Himself as I Am. He is the same today as He was thousands of years ago. He is eternal, forever, unchanging.

Nothing lasts forever? Well, nothing but God. And when He is ours, we too will last forever. And that's a truth that will never change.

Every good and perfect gift is from above, coming down from the Father of the heavenly lights, who does not change like shifting shadows.

—JAMES 1:17

Prayer

As you finger the loose change in your coat pocket, thank the Lord for the reassuring reality that He is not capable of changing. Praise Him for the strength His constancy gives you.

BE STRONG AND TAKE COURAGE

Joshua's knees were knocking. As he held his staff (the same one that had belonged to Moses), his hand shook. Now that his mentor was dead, he knew what was up. God would be calling on him to finish guiding the Israelites to the Promised Land. It was a task much larger than he was capable of. Joshua knew that. He had never aspired to the level of leadership that now would be thrust on him. But as a faithful lieutenant under General Moses, the son of Nun had proven his dependability and willingness to trust God. He was the natural choice, but his ability to accomplish the job that yet remained would require supernatural assistance. With God's help, he would do it.

Although that scene is not mentioned in Scripture, you can assume something very similar to that took place. Why else would the Lord say to Joshua, "Be strong and very courageous" (or words to that effect) three times in the first nine verses of the Old Testament book that bears his name? That same God knows what it is that grips your heart with insecurity or fear. And it is that same God who would comfort you with the same words. Be strong and take courage, do not fear or be dismayed. The Lord will go before you, and His light will show the way.

Take courage.

Be strong and courageous, because you will lead these people to inherit the land I swore to their forefathers to give them.

—JOSHUA 1:6

Prayer

Candidly confess your fears to the Lord. Admit your
need of courage and confidence. Ask the Lord to
fill you with His power to the challenges of this day.

NO GREATER LOVE

*I*t was why He had come, but it didn't make the task any easier. He trudged the dusty highway, the heavy crossbeam grating against the raw wounds in His back. The crowd gawked. Some turned their faces away, unable to look at the horror. Others jeered. A few wept. Some went about their business as if the parade of Roman soldiers surrounding a condemned man were just another part of a typical day in Jerusalem.

This was no typical day, however. Other criminals had been crucified on cruel crosses, of course, but no man like this had ever faced this punishment—nor ever would again. For this was no ordinary man, and this was no ordinary crucifixion. In a matter of hours, however, the world—in fact, all of eternity—would be changed forever. Countless prophecies of old would be fulfilled, Satan would be dealt a blow from which he would never recover, death would be swallowed up in victory, sin would be completely paid for, and access to God would be given to all who sought to love and worship Him.

For that was why He had come. To love the unlovely, to seek the lost, to show how much He loves us by buying us at the highest cost. There truly is no greater love than this—that a man would lay down His life for His friends. That's what He did for you. That how much He loves you.

Greater love has no one than this, than to lay down one's life for his friends.

—JOHN 15:13

Prayer

Bask in God's great love for you. Praise Him that
He paid the price that your sins deserved so
that you can have a relationship with Him.

CROWN HIM KING OF KINGS

When Jesus first came to earth, the only crown that was placed on His head wasn't fit for a king. It wasn't shiny gold. It contained no jewels. Rather, it was fashioned from three-inch thorns. The crown the Roman soldiers shoved down on the Savior's head was nothing more than a crude facsimile. Hot red blood squirted from that innocent forehead and ran down Jesus' beard. He gasped in pain. A nearby guard mocked His Majesty by bowing low as the pretense continued. The whole clownish farce was the height of humiliation. The Son of God, stripped of all His clothing (and His dignity), wore nothing but a thorny crown while cursing soldiers stood around spitting and laughing. And as if that was not enough, the sinless Savior was nailed to a cross and hung to die.

He willingly submitted to the torture and He willingly took all of our sin upon Himself. It is because He subjected Himself to this unthinkable depth of human depravity that we will one day witness quite a different coronation. No shame this time. Just sheer celebration. And what a glorious celebration it will be! At long last the King of kings, clothed in purple and royal blue robes, will be gilded with the crown He deserves. On that day He shall reign forevermore!

Then the seventh angel sounded: And there were loud voices in heaven, saying, "The kingdoms of this world have become the kingdoms of our Lord and of His Christ, and He shall reign forever and ever!"

—REVELATION 11:15 NKJV

Prayer

Ponder the humiliation that the Lord Jesus endured
on your behalf at the hands of the Roman soldiers.
Then as you thank Him for His redemptive suffering,
picture Him upon His throne crowned with glory.

WE EXALT YOU

One night a man had a vision. He was standing in the midst of several thousand at the base of a majestic snowcapped mountain. The crowd was singing praise songs from memory. No one needed a hymnbook or projected words. The four-part harmony was glorious. "We exalt You, exalted King on high," they sang.

As the man looked around, he saw that every person's hands were raised in a symbolic offering of praise and surrender. Looking closer, he saw that the hands of the worshipers were gloved. As he looked toward the top of the mountain, he saw a figure clothed in brilliant white robes. The brilliance of the person prevented the man from looking at His face, but there was no doubt in his mind who it was. Jesus was receiving the homage that was due Him.

As he gazed toward the Savior, the man heard Jesus say, "I have called you from all the nations to be My priests, to demonstrate my grace. I intend your lives to be like the gloves you're wearing. Just as a glove is lifeless apart from the hand that indwells it, so is your life without Me. Although I inhabit the praises of My people, the ultimate expression of exaltation is allowing Me to live My life through you, reaching out to others and offering a hand to those in need."

To exalt the Lord your God, demonstrate His grace to everyone you meet—today and every day.

Exalt the LORD our God and worship at his holy mountain, for the LORD our God is holy.

—PSALM 99:9

Prayer

Ask the Lord that the way you go about speaking, thinking, and doing will be the means by which you exalt Him today. Ask Him to give you the ability to reflect His life in all you do.

HOLY, HOLY, HOLY

Even if you didn't appreciate his music, you couldn't deny Elvis Presley's ability to cast a spell on his audiences. With charm and poise, he would hypnotize fans as his mellow voice cranked out hit after hit. A lifestyle of promiscuity and personal dysfunction was somehow overlooked by those who called him "the king." Having attended a little country church in Tupelo, Mississippi, as a kid, Elvis's wide repertoire even included songs like "How Great Thou Art," "I Believe," or "Where No One Stands Alone." As he sang, it was obvious he had his audience in the palm of his hand. As each concert came to a close, the audience predictably demanded encore after encore. Elvis accommodated his subjects. But after two or three encores, the stage remained empty although the audience pled for more. From offstage an announcer's voice declared the concert was at last over. The repeated refrain became legendary, "Elvis has left the building!"

Unlike Elvis, the King we worship is worthy of all our praise. He is holy, perfect, and untouched by sin. He is worthy to receive glory and honor. His actions on our behalf do not contradict the words He speaks. Furthermore, He will never die or desert those who love Him. We can be confident as we come into His house to enjoy His presence that He will respond to our requests as long as we need Him. So praise His name forever.

For great is the LORD and most worthy of praise; he is to be feared above all gods.

—1 CHRONICLES 16:25

Prayer

What do you need the Lord to do for you today?
Verbalize the concerns that fill your mind.
Be specific. Thank the Lord that He is listening.

WE'VE COME TO PRAISE YOU

Perhaps you've heard of practical jokers who enter a crowded elevator, turn around to face the assembled group, and with a straight face say, "I suppose you're all wondering why I've called this meeting." Maybe not hilarious, but most people enjoy the person's attempt to lighten the monotony of riding an elevator to begin the routine of their day. A bit of laughter sure beats staring up at numbers that illuminate and ding.

Think about it. How many things do you routinely do—without a smile, without a hint of joy, without even thinking? Does church fall into that category? Has it become nothing more than routine? Why do you go?

If church has become a joyless routine, you don't need a jokester to distract you. What you need is a sense of purpose, a reason to be there, a goal to shoot for. Without a goal, there is no way you can know if you have accomplished what you set out for. To come into God's house without a sense of direction will most likely result in a lack of passion or meaning.

The next time you walk through the doors of your church, tell the Lord that you've come to praise Him. If you come determined that you are going to lavish your love on the living Lord, you can't help but leave feeling it has been worthwhile.

Enter his gates with thanksgiving and his courts with praise; give thanks to him and praise his name.

—PSALM 100:4

Prayer

Begin to prepare yourself for worship this Sunday.
Tell the Lord you have come to praise Him. In turn, ask Him
to speak to you through your pastor and the worship team.

I WAITED FOR THE LORD

The star-spangled sky on a clear summer night can be misleading. Astronomers tell us that some of the stars we see overhead have actually ceased to exist. Those stars are so far away from earth that by the time their light reaches us (traveling at 186,000 miles per second) what we see and what actually is are two different things. The light a dying star gives off takes untold years to eventually reach us. Such is the reality of distance and time.

Such is too often the Christian's perspective on prayer. When we wait for God to answer our prayers, it sometimes feels like we've been waiting for an eternity. But feeling is not fact. Our prayers are heard by our Father in heaven even before they fall from our lips. He hears our hearts. His response is just as immediate, although not always the response we want or expect. The waiting involved has more to do with understanding what God is about in the way He chooses to answer us. You see, waiting is just as much an activity related to relationship as it is to the passage of time. Waiting for the Lord reminds us that He is in control. It also helps us stay alert to ways He will surprise us with a sense of His presence. Needless to say, it is good to wait for the Lord.

Hear a just cause, O LORD, attend to my cry; give ear to my prayer which is not from deceitful lips.

—PSALM 17:1 NKJV

Prayer

Spend some extended moments in quiet.
Wait in silence with your hands open as if to receive a gift.
It is possible the Lord will chose to speak to your heart
while you listen. If He does, act on what He says.

CRY OF MY HEART

Novelist Jack London's life was short. He died at age forty. Some thought his political leanings shortsighted, but his insights on the wilderness have lasted a long time. This gifted author wrote books that reflected his love of adventure and personal experiences as a sailor and outdoorsman. Perhaps his most well-known volume is about the Yukon, the Alaskan gold rush, and the northern wilderness. In *The Call of the Wild*, London did more than tell a story of suspense and intrigue. He chronicled the mystery of nature and its undisturbed beauty that invites exploration. For him, the wilderness cries out to be explored and embraced.

In much the same way, the human heart calls out to God. It longs to be visited by the Creator. It desires to be in communion with Him. It is the cry of our hearts to know God and connect with Him. It is the cry of our hearts to follow Him and learn from Him what it takes to enjoy life the way He intended. The good news is that the Lord hears the call that originates deep within our soul and draws near to us. As a matter of fact, the message of the cross is that He's dying to spend time with us.

My soul yearns, even faints, for the courts of the LORD; my heart and my flesh cry out for the living God.

—PSALM 84:2

Prayer

Although the Holy Spirit is interceding on our behalf even if we aren't speaking words to God, the Father loves to hear the cry of hearts hungry for Him. Sing out a song of praise you especially love to sing.

I HAVE DECIDED TO
FOLLOW JESUS

When thirty-nine-year-old John Harper made the decision to follow Jesus, it was a decision that would cost the British pastor his life. Harper was en route to Chicago to speak at Moody Memorial Church. The date was April 14, 1912. The ship on which he traveled was the Titanic. Because he was a widowed father traveling with his young daughter and niece, the young cleric could have claimed a seat in one of the ship's twenty lifeboats. But Harper was determined to follow the example of the One who called us to take up a cross.

Harper made the decision. He kissed his girls goodbye and remained on the ship, witnessing to those who were about to perish. For him, following Jesus meant laying down his life so that others might have assurance of forgiveness and experience God's grace before they died. As a result of his courageous obedience, many of the 1,500 casualties were ready to meet the Lord. Although Hollywood's version of the Titanic story that won best picture in 1998 didn't make reference to John Harper, history does recall his Christ-like sacrifice.

For John Harper, the decision to follow Jesus was a decision from which he would not turn back. Neither should we.

But Jesus told him, "Anyone who puts a hand to the plow and then looks back is not fit for the Kingdom of God."

—LUKE 9:62 NLT

Prayer

Humbly come before the Lord and surrender your selfish desires to Him. Ask Him who it is that you could serve on His behalf today.

ALL HEAVEN DECLARES

From the time we were little, our parents reminded us that our actions speak louder than our words. And whereas some inappropriate behavior on our part prompted our parents' words, the principle applies just as much when it comes to acting the way we should. St. Francis is credited with having said, "Preach wherever you go. If necessary, use words!" Those famous words spoken several hundred years ago have been popularized in the following expression: "I'd rather see a sermon than hear one any day!" In other words, you don't have to recite Bible verses or defend your beliefs with a lengthy theological lecture in order to declare the goodness of the Lord.

Do you want to declare the glory of your risen Lord? Then take an example from creation. Sometimes words don't even need to be said. A winsome lifestyle that acts patiently and lovingly, actions that give evidence of genuine concern, and personal integrity can be the most powerful sermon of all. The psalmist gives us a picture of this principle when he writes about the eloquence of creation. In Psalm 19, he describes the movement of the sun, moon, and the stars as declaring the glory of God. For him, what people can see provides proof without need for human speech. And if nature can communicate so powerfully without words, perhaps we should put a little more stock in what we do instead of what we say.

The heavens tell of the glory of God. The skies display his marvelous craftsmanship.

—PSALM 19:1 NLT

Prayer

Review your behavior for the past week, being mindful
of the Lord's presence. What did you do that kept
others from seeing the Lord in you? Seek forgiveness.

HIS NAME IS WONDERFUL

The name of Jesus is wonderful. Yet "wonderful" doesn't even begin to capture all that His name suggests. The name of Jesus is music to the ears of all who have discovered the lyrics of the Father's love. The name of Jesus is far from just a man's name. It is a name that conjures up His divinity as well as His humanity. It speaks of His power and His gentleness as well as His purpose in coming to earth. It pictures a Mighty King who is Master of everything. Yet He is also personal—"my Lord."

The wonderful name of Jesus is the name of Almighty God. He is the Great Shepherd, patiently herding His skittish sheep down to green pastures and beside still waters. He is the Rock of all ages, providing the strong refuge of His protection against the tempests that rage around us.

The name Jesus means "Savior." No wonder we can't contemplate just how wonderful His name is without coming to terms with the fact that He has saved us from our sin. With the mere mention of the name of Jesus, the symphony of heaven fills the universe with harmony and joy. The One who has brought us into relationship with our Creator is the grace note with which the melody of the ages begins.

For unto us a Child is born, unto us a Son is given; and the government will be upon His shoulder. And His name will be called Wonderful, Counselor, Mighty God, Everlasting Father, Prince of Peace.

—ISAIAH 9:6 NKJV

Prayer

Take each letter of the word "JESUS" and meditate
on words that His wonderful name suggests.
For example: Joy, Eternal, Savior, Understanding, Shepherd.

GREAT IS THE LORD

Great is the Lord—sometimes this is a phrase so overused that it begins to lose its meaning. After all, we may have prayed this prayer from our youngest days, "God is great, God is good . . ." Yes, God is great, but are there other words we can use to describe His greatness? Look at a thesaurus and find that "great" can mean vast, enormous, and grand. It can also mean immense, noble, wonderful, and absolute. All of these words work in describing our great God—and we can enjoy the variety. Each word brings out a new facet of the greatness of our God.

But let's look beyond adjectives in order to replace the word "great." What about some verbs? The psalmist exclaims that so great is God's mercy that He has removed our sins as far as the east is from the west. Now there's a mind-blowing picture! Keep going east, and you'll never be going west. Turn around and go west and—well—same story. In other words, our sins are so far away from us that we can never meet them again. Now, that's a long way.

Good news? Absolutely! But then again, you might even say it's greater than good.

As far as the east is from the west, so far has He removed our transgressions from us.

—PSALM 103:12 NASB

Prayer

Make this a great day. Don't let it come to an end before you
jot down qualities of God's character that qualify as great.
Thank Him for the great ways He cares for you. Thank Him
for removing your sins as far as the east is from the west.

I WILL NEVER BE
THE SAME AGAIN

The title of this devotion calls attention to what is at the heart of the gospel. Just think about it. Being a Christian is all about being converted—changed, transformed, renewed, improved. It's about entering into a new level of living.

When Jesus was describing to Nicodemus what it meant to become a believer, He talked in terms of being "born again." He invited this truth-seeking Pharisee to a brand new start in his spiritual pilgrimage. He promised a disconnection from a disappointing past. Paul's platform was much the same. He talked of new persons, forgetting the past, and being transformed. But the most powerful illustration of Paul's belief in the transforming power of Christ is seen in a letter the aging apostle wrote to the Christians in Corinth. In 1 Corinthians 6, he rehearses the repugnance of their former lifestyles. Prior to a relationship with Jesus, their lives where characterized by adultery, promiscuity, homosexuality, abuse of alcohol, idol worship, and greed. But not any longer. That is what they were. Past tense. Paul wants them to know that the word "were" means lives changed forever.

For them and for us. Praise God! Thanks to Him, we will never be the same.

What this means is that those who become Christians become new persons. They are not the same anymore, for the old life is gone. A new life has begun!

—2 CORINTHIANS 5:17 NLT

Prayer

Finish the following sentence in your head: "Because of Your grace, Lord, I am no longer _____." Repeat this prayer exercise using different words to fill in the blank.

My Heart, Your Home

Robert Boyd Munger was a beloved pastor and professor. Although stricken with diabetes and other physical afflictions, he lived to nearly ninety. Early in his ministry at First Presbyterian Church in Berkeley, California, Dr. Bob (as he was affectionately called) gave a sermon based on Revelation 3:20. In this creative message, he compared the human heart to a home visited by Jesus. As the Lord was welcomed into the heart, He walked from room to room. For example, the kitchen was the place of appetites and desires, the closet was the place where unconfessed sin was locked. The library was a way of referring to the mind, where thoughts and ideas were digested. Although other rooms were described, the one that stands out was a room with a fireplace and overstuffed chairs where the Lord desired to spend time with the host of the home each day. Dr. Munger's message was published under the title, "My Heart, Christ's Home." A half-century after it was first preached, it continues to enrich Christians' lives with a graphic description of how our hearts can be rearranged and remodeled when Jesus is welcomed as a lifelong guest.

If you invited Jesus into your home, what would He find in the kitchen, the library, the closets, the attic, the computer room? Would you let Him search you through and through?

Here I am! I stand at the door and knock. If anyone hears my voice and opens the door, I will come in and eat with him, and he with me.

—Revelation 3:20

Prayer

Walk through the various rooms of your heart with the Lord
(your thought life, devotional life, entertainment, etc).
Ask what He thinks needs attention.
Give Him permission to begin the needed remodeling.

SONG OF JABEZ

Reading the genealogies in the Old Testament is a little like reading a telephone book. Endless lists of names you don't recognize or can't pronounce seem to have little redeeming value (except for maybe curing insomnia). The fourth chapter of 1 Chronicles is such a list. As you skim over names like Herzon and Shobal, your eyes start to cross. But like a vertical tombstone in a cemetery of inlaid grave markers, you unexpectedly find yourself tripping over verses 9 and 10. There before you is a headstone that boasts the name "Jabez." Unlike the names of those before and after, the biblical chronicler doesn't just chisel a name in marble. He immortalizes the life of this godly man by taking time to describe what set him apart from other family members. Jabez poured out his heart to the Lord. With courage and candor, he asked God to bless his life, maximize his effectiveness, and minimize his sorrow. And before the writer dives back into another lengthy list of names, he makes it clear that the Lord gave Jabez the desires of his heart. Here is a guy who distinguished himself from the pack by approaching God with confidence

We can do the same. And when we do, God is delighted to bless us.

Jabez was more honorable than his brothers. His mother had named him Jabez, saying, "I gave birth to him in pain." Jabez cried out to the God of Israel, "Oh, that you would bless me and enlarge my territory! Let your hand be with me, and keep me from harm so that I will be free from pain." And God granted his request.

—1 CHRONICLES 4:9–10

Prayer

Be bold as you fold your hands and close your eyes.
Let the Lord know what you need and then ask Him for the
faith to believe He will answer in His time and in His way.

MY REDEEMER LIVES

Downcast and despairing, a young woman made her way in the early morning darkness to a fresh grave. Her heart was breaking and her body was aching. And for good reason. Her best friend had been executed the day before and she had not slept all night. As Mary approached the place where the body had been buried, she trembled. So did the ground. It was the most powerful earthquake she'd ever experienced. But Mary refused to be detoured. She kept walking. The sight of the cemetery triggered all the emotions of the previous day. Sorrow, horror, fear. In her mind's eye, she could see Jesus looking at her with love. She also could see Him convulsing on the cross, bleeding and struggling for breath. She saw His limp body lowered to the ground. But her momentary replay of what she had witnessed was interrupted by a voice. "The one you are looking for is not here. He is risen!" As she looked up, she not only saw the glowing messenger who spoke these words, she saw that the once-sealed tomb was now wide open. It was a miracle! It was more than she could have imagined. As she ran back to tell her friends what he had seen and heard, she heard herself speaking three words over and over again. "My Redeemer lives!"

He is not here; he has risen, just as he said. Come and see the place where he lay.

—MATTHEW 28:6

Prayer

Allow the reality of Easter to motivate your
personal worship today. Ask the living Lord to
provide you with a tangible sense of His presence.

THINE IS THE KINGDOM

In Todd and Lisa Beamer's home fellowship, young couples had examined, phrase by phrase, the prayer Jesus had given His disciples. The prayer calls for God's kingdom to come, and then we all know the traditional ending: "For thine is the kingdom and the power and the glory forever. Amen."

Although it was a prayer Todd had learned when he was but a boy, he surely was amazed at how relevant it became on that fateful day. On Tuesday, September 11, 2001, Todd kissed his wife goodbye before heading to the Newark airport for a one-day business trip to San Francisco. His carryon luggage included a cell phone, a laptop, and a Tom Clancy novel containing a bookmark bearing the familiar words of the Lord's Prayer. As he boarded United Flight 93, Todd had no idea that this flight would carry him into the arms of his Father in heaven. But because of the amount of time he had recently spent contemplating the Lord's Prayer, he knew that, come what may, the Lord would provide for his daily needs and deliver him from evil. When Todd realized that terrorists had hijacked the plane and that his life was in jeopardy, it was only natural for him to pray the prayer that filled his heart. It reminded him that even in death, God's kingdom would prevail.

So He said to them, "When you pray, say: Our Father in heaven, hallowed be Your name. Your kingdom come. Your will be done on earth as it is in heaven."

—LUKE 11:2 NKJV

Prayer

Make the Lord's Prayer your personal prayer today. If it's a prayer you've known since childhood, pray it slowly and thoughtfully. Linger over each phrase. Make it your own.

THE NAME OF THE LORD

A name is a wonderful thing. It sets you apart from the mass of humanity. That's why when a baby is born, the very first thing parents do is give the child a name. And as that child grows and expresses his or her personality, his name comes to symbolize his character. It conjures up all that he is about: likes, dislikes, temperament, passions, and convictions.

Think about it. When you hear the name Abraham Lincoln, you can't help but think of a man of integrity who bravely led our nation through one of the most difficult periods in our history. When someone talks about Billy Graham or Mother Teresa, a picture emerges in your mind. You think of what set them apart from others and the wonderful things they accomplished.

For the psalmist, that same kind of name association took place. The mere mention of the Lord's name caused him to think of all that He had done for him. God's greatness towered above all of life. No wonder he likened the Lord's name to a strong tower. Just like a fortress rising high above all other structures in Jerusalem, the Lord's presence could never be overshadowed. We can run into His presence and be assured of safety.

The name of the LORD is a strong tower; the righteous run to it and are safe.

—PROVERBS 18:10

Prayer

Make a personal inventory of circumstances or individuals
that trigger fear in your heart. Surrender them to the Lord.
Ask Him to be your strong tower as you pray in His mighty name.

THE LORD REIGNS

If the Lord sat at a desk in a high-rise office building as He oversaw the universe, His nameplate would be solid gold (not brass). Chances are there would also be a paperweight engraved with the words, "The Buck Stops Here!" The reason is clear. The Lord is in control. He takes responsibility for what goes on in the world. Nothing catches Him by surprise and on His watch nothing falls between the cracks. Like an excellent CEO, He governs the organization with an eye on the big picture as well as the bottom line. Committed to the profitability of the corporation both for Himself and the shareholders, He moves heaven and earth to accomplish His strategic goals.

Now let's picture the Lord having a throne rather than a desk. As king, He is the supreme monarch. He reigns in accordance with His sovereign plans for our lives and His creation.

Or maybe He's the artistic director of the play being performed on the stage of the world. With all power and majesty, He choreographs the dance numbers. With precision and awesome creativity, He arranges our slips and falls into a divine dance that redeems the chaos.

No disinterested executive here. No figurehead ruler. No uninvolved director. The Lord reigns actively, powerfully, and with our best interests at heart. Now isn't that reason enough to rejoice?

The LORD reigns, let the earth be glad; let the distant shores rejoice.

—PSALM 97:1

Prayer

Bow down in the presence of His Majesty and make
yourself available for what He would have you do today.

WE'VE COME TO BLESS
YOUR NAME

The Jamaican melody that carries the lyrics of this song has a happy syncopated beat. Songwriter Don Moen would be the first to explain why the words he wrote call for a confident and joyful tune. As a matter of fact, Moen's lyrics give a rationale for why we should come before the Lord with voices, instruments, and hearts filled with praise. There's one little phrase in particular that says it all: "There is none like you, so faithful and so true." In a world in which we are routinely rejected or rebuffed by those who fail to keep their promises, God's reliable grace is a breath of fresh air.

Too often we feel like someone is kicking sand in our face. Minimized and undervalued in our homes, at work, at school, we begin to doubt our worth. But like the balmy Caribbean breezes, the warmth of God's unfailing presence provides us with a taste of paradise. When was the last time you really thought about that reality? Chances are pretty good that within the past week someone let you down or backed out of a commitment that you were counting on. But don't give in to the temptation to camp out on that beach. Celebrate the fact that God can be depended upon to do as He says. He honors the promises He's made. And He always will. Now, doesn't that make you want to kick up your feet and dance?

I will extol You, my God, O King; and I will bless Your name forever and ever.

—PSALM 145:1 NKJV

Prayer

Thank the Lord for His faithfulness.
Think of recent events when He has come through for you.
Go ahead and vocalize those blessings in His presence.

FIRM FOUNDATION

The word "hope" conjures up uncertainty. "I hope it doesn't rain today" expresses something we desire but have no control over. So what's the difference between a finger-crossed reliance on fate and a "living hope"? Just everything, that's all. When your only hope is making a wish without the certainty of getting what you long for, it's hardly any hope at all. Wishing is like fishing without a hook.

When the Bible refers to "hope," however, it's talking about certainty. We are hoping for something that God has promised; therefore, our hope rests secure. That's what the apostle Peter meant by believers being given a "living hope." The future Jesus promised is a certainty because death didn't defeat Him. His words are alive because He is alive. His promises are true because He is Truth. Our faith is grounded in a living Savior. And because He is alive and alert to our needs, He is a firm foundation on which we can confidently stand.

The only way to discover these promises, to stand on the firm foundation, is to put your hope is His Word. To do that, you need to read it. Pull out that Bible, blow off the dust, and dive in to riches untold!

Praise be to the God and Father of our Lord Jesus Christ! In his great mercy he has given us new birth into a living hope through the resurrection of Jesus Christ from the dead.

—1 PETER 1:3

Prayer

Bring your concerns about the future to the Lord in a season of extended silence. As you wait before Him in reverent surrender, give Him your anxious thoughts and fears.

CARES CHORUS

Back in the eighties, many a preschooler learned to praise Jesus by listening to audiotapes featuring Psalty, his wife Psaltina, and their three kids, Melody, Harmony, and Rhythm. Psalty introduced children to new worship music in fun and winsome ways. Songwriter Kelly Willard wrote a worship song known as "Cares Chorus" using simple lyrics even a child could learn—*I cast all my cares upon You.* Psalty repeatedly used this song to help kids understand that they can turn to the Lord when they are feeling afraid or worried.

Ironically, as parents drove their children to school, piano lessons, or sports practice, they often would find themselves singing along—with good reason. You see, Kelly Willard's words don't only apply to pintsize praisers. In fact, this song was written for grown-ups who know all too well about being overwhelmed with the cares of life. Concerns over choices our children make drive us to our knees. So too the anxieties that surround our jobs, marriages, physical maladies, and emotional health. In light of those given realities, isn't it good to know we can cast our cares on Someone who really does care for us? Isn't it good to know that when we don't know what to do, He does?

Cast your cares on the LORD and he will sustain you; he will never let the righteous fall.

—PSALM 55:22

Prayer

Picture Jesus speaking to you about coming to Him
to find rest. Lay down on the couch or on your
bed and spend five minutes "resting" in Him
while thinking of His promised care.

JESUS DRAW ME CLOSE

He hid among the tombstones at night. During the day, he dodged visitors by remaining in the shadows. Viewed as dangerous by those who knew of him, this mysterious man was bound by iron chains. But the links couldn't hold him. He tore them off just like he did his clothes. Although he managed to keep the manacles from his feet, he was hardly free. Demons held him hostage. That is, until the day Jesus walked into his cemetery and cemented his future.

When the pitiful man saw the Savior, however, he called out to Him to leave him alone. Jesus knew better. The words spoken from the man's lips were from the mouths of demons intent on destruction. So Jesus cast out the demons, who carried out the destructive intent on other victims instead—the herd of pigs. The next picture we have of the wild-eyed man is of him sitting quietly, clothed and sane, at the feet of his Savior.

Maybe you relate. Can you recall a time when your heart was far from free even though you boasted of an independent spirit? Can you remember the moment when you saw the emptiness of your life and called out to Jesus to draw you close? Do you need that today? Turn to Him. He promises to cleanse you and clothe you in His righteousness. Let Him draw you close in His loving arms.

A crowd soon gathered around Jesus, for they wanted to see for themselves what had happened. And they saw the man who had been possessed by demons sitting quietly at Jesus' feet, clothed and sane.

—LUKE 8:35 NLT

Prayer

Ask the Lord to disregard all the ways you attempt
to hold Him at arms length. Lift your arms
toward heaven and admit your need of Him today.

HEAR MY CRY

Talk about being in the pits. Joseph definitely was. His jealous brothers, tired of their father's preferential treatment of their younger sibling, first lowered him into a well shaft and then sold him into slavery. Upon reaching Egypt, Joseph was falsely accused and thrown in jail for years. Even though he was no longer in the slimy hole in which his brothers had tossed him, he was still "in the pits."

Psalm 40 is attributed to King David, but it could have as well been a page torn out of Joseph's journal. He was forced to wait. He continued to cry out to the Lord, who seemed to have abandoned him. But He hadn't. The account of Joseph's life in Genesis affirms the fact that God was "in the pits" with him. And in God's time, He lifted His man out of a premature "grave" and gave him life. Oh, yes—and an abundant life at that. Joseph became governor of Egypt with all the perks that position included. His jealous brothers ended up casting themselves upon his mercy. Joseph was the means by which God's people could resettle in Egypt. It was there they escaped the famine and grew strong in numbers.

Yes, God heard Joseph's cry just as He heard David's cry. He still hears His people when they pray. Do you feel like you're slogging through a swamp today? Are you stuck in a slimy pit? Cry out to the Lord, and then be willing to wait patiently. He promises that He will set your feet on a rock and give you a firm place to stand.

I waited patiently for the LORD; he turned to me and heard my cry. He lifted me out of the slimy pit, out of the mud and mire; he set my feet on a rock and gave me a firm place to stand.

—PSALM 40:1-2

Prayer

From the pit of your personal despair, cry out to God.
If words fail, simply express your need for help with
a deep sigh or open hands that symbolize your emptiness.

EL-SHADDAI

*I*t means "Almighty God." That's how El-Shaddai is translated in our Bibles. This Hebrew name for our Heavenly Father is a virtual word picture of His vast greatness and all-sufficiency. The word "Shaddai" occurs some forty-eight times in the Old Testament. In the King James Version, Shaddai is always translated "almighty." Similarly, the Hebrew root word "shad" is used twenty-four times. It is always translated "breast." The picture is this: In the same way that a mother's breast is "all-sufficient" for her newborn's nourishment, God is "all-sufficient" for His people.

When we combine El (almighty God) with Shaddai (all-sufficiency), we get a picture of the Almighty God who pours out sustenance and blessing. Just think about the implications this name suggests. El-Shaddai is a God who cares for us with the tenderness and compassion of a mother. But He is also a strong and powerful God who is not limited in His ability to protect or defend us. The images this song's lyrics project on the screens of our minds support that picture of God. He rewards the willingness of Abraham to offer his son. He delivers His people from bondage by making a path through the Red Sea. He guards the dignity of the outcast and adequately nourishes the hungry. He comes to do an awesome work in the frailty of a human body in order to die on our behalf.

He is our El-Shaddai, our almighty God, our Savior.

Can a mother forget the baby at her breast and have no compassion on the child she has borne? Though she may forget, I will not forget you!

—ISAIAH 49:15

Prayer

As a prayer focus, meditate on the picture of a loving, nourishing, tender God given in Isaiah 49:15. Think of such tender love combined with almighty power. Then thank God for loving you.

AND YOUR PRAISE GOES ON

"Now I lay me down to sleep. I pray Thee, Lord, my soul to keep. If I should die before I wake, I pray Thee, Lord, my soul to take." Perhaps your parents taught you that familiar prayer when you were little. And when you grew up and had kids of your own, you bequeathed them that same bedtime petition.

We say that little rhyming prayer because deep in our hearts we know it's true. God is trustworthy. Long after we have collapsed beneath our comforters, sick and tired of carrying the burdens of the day, He carries us. He is the ever-present Comforter. While we sleep, God is still at the switch. He maintains control over our lives and His universe. Our eyes close in slumber soon after our weary heads hit the pillow. But not the Master Craftsman. He never closes shop.

Indeed, he who watches over Israel will neither slumber nor sleep.

—PSALM 121:4

Prayer

Before dropping off to sleep tonight, recount the
events of the day and picture Jesus walking
beside you to bring closure to each one.

LET IT RISE

You don't have to be an expert in pyrotechnics to keep logs lit in a fireplace. You get a blaze started and add wood. Anybody knows that a log that comes in contact with those already ablaze will eventually ignite and burn. If for some reason a log rolls off the pile and is separated from the rest, it will not catch fire. The same is true of charcoal briquettes in a backyard grill. Those that glow with heat are those that are in touch with the rest.

This principle of combustibility applies to keeping a spiritual glow. Christians need to be in regular contact with other believers in order to fuel each other's faith. Like a log or a briquette, you can have all the properties needed to burn, but if you attempt to maintain your glow on your own, it won't be long till you've grown cold.

Back when the New Testament was being written, there was a tendency for followers of Jesus to go it alone. They found excuses not to meet regularly for fellowship and worship. They failed to realize the toll their choices would eventually make. Fortunately, the writer of Hebrews recognized the pattern of isolationism and challenged Christians to resist it. Because the same tendency is observable among believers today, passion for Jesus is growing cold in some. For the glory of the Lord to rise among us, we must make it a priority to be among His people.

Let us not give up meeting together, as some are in the habit of doing, but let us encourage one another—and all the more as you see the Day approaching.

—HEBREWS 10:25

Prayer

Thank the Lord for the privilege of Christian community.
Pray specifically for those who are part of
your small group or Bible study.

HE WILL COME AND SAVE YOU

Sometimes we can't help ourselves. We wonder if it's true. Is Jesus really coming back? After all, we reason, two hundred centuries have come and gone and the Lord hasn't kept His promise yet. What gives? Maybe Jesus was speaking figuratively and He's not really coming back at all.

If that sounds like you, cut yourself some slack. Even people of faith are prone to seasons of doubt. Questioning is normal. But take courage. The questions we pose are not new. Way back in the first century, people were wondering why Jesus hadn't returned to earth yet. Just a few decades after He ascended into heaven, His followers expected the Lord to make good on His promise to come back. When He didn't, those critical of Christianity began to say, "Where is this 'coming' he promised? Ever since our fathers died, everything goes on as it has since the beginning of creation" (2 Peter 3:4).

Those same voices would steal our hope and fuel our doubt today. When the pressures of daily routines or a doctor's diagnosis find us longing for Jesus to come and save us, the doubts can creep up. "Is God really faithful to His promises?" we ask fearfully. In those times of doubt and fear, we need to open the door of our hearts to the apostle Peter, who reminds us that the Lord has not forgotten about the second coming. His timing is perfect; His promises will prove true. The reason He is waiting has to do with His patient love that longs for more people to experience His grace. In the meantime, we can call on His name, for He will indeed come and save.

The Lord is not slow in keeping his promise, as some understand slowness. He is patient with you, not wanting anyone to perish, but everyone to come to repentance.

—2 PETER 3:9

Prayer

Confess your tendency to doubt some of the promises of Scripture. Ask Him for the ability to trust Him for what is still to play out in the future (including His return to earth).

NOT BY MIGHT NOR POWER

No Nike shoes required. People just do it. They leisurely stroll up and down the block on which they live, praying with their eyes wide open. As they walk, they talk to Jesus about their neighbors who need Him. It's called prayer-walking. It's the ultimate power walk. Although there is some aerobic benefit to this spiritual exercise, prayer-walking has more to do with evangelism than physical fitness.

If you are concerned about those who live in your neighborhood who don't know the Lord, it just might be the key to bringing about the change you desire. No strong-arm tactics. No power plays. No need for a knockout punch in a theological debate. Just walking and talking to the Lord. You ask Him for opportunities to get to know these neighbors more than you already do. You ask Him to give you courage to seize the opportunities He brings about. You ask Him for the willingness to be vulnerable and to acknowledge your own needs. You ask Him for the patience to allow genuine friendships to develop. You pray for needs in the lives of these people you may already know about. You ask the Lord for wisdom for ways you might be able to meet those needs.

Chances are you've long since come to the realization that you can't bring about spiritual change in the lives of your neighbors. It's not by might or by power. It's by God's Spirit—who longs to flow through you.

So he said to me, "This is the word of the LORD to Zerubbabel: 'Not by might nor by power, but by my Spirit,' says the LORD Almighty."

—ZECHARIAH 4:6

Prayer

Weather permitting, walk your street and pray for those neighbors with whom you have a relationship. For those you don't, ask the Lord to give you the desire to get to know them.

CHOSEN GENERATION MEDLEY

When Princess Diana and Prince Charles were married, many a young girl was mesmerized by the aura associated with royalty. The horse-drawn coaches that carried the wedding party to the cathedral seemed to bring the stuff of fairytales to life. Similar emotions were stirred less than twenty years later when we watched the royal family gather for Princess Diana's funeral. The pomp and circumstance of monarchs and castles call to something deep with all of us. We are impressed with the dignity and grace that defines the lives and traditions of royalty.

But wait! Do you know who you are? Are you aware of the fact that because you, by grace and election, have been adopted by the King of kings, you too are royalty? It's true. Within the kingdom of God, you are a son or a daughter of His Majesty. What is more, you are an ambassador serving on His behalf. Having been called out of the shadows into the brilliance of His throne room, it is our privilege to represent His interests in the world declaring His glory. Sound the trumpets. Hang the banners. We are a chosen generation, a royal priesthood, a holy nation. When we fail to celebrate our privileged identity or when we dishonor the King by our actions, we fail to live the life of royalty He intends.

But you are a chosen people, a royal priesthood, a holy nation, a people belonging to God, that you may declare the praises of him who called you out of darkness into his wonderful light.

—1 PETER 2:9

Prayer

Ponder in the Lord's presence the awesome privilege you've been given to be part of Christ's Church. Allow the Lord to suggest practical ways you might increase your level of involvement.

VICTORY IN JESUS / CHOSEN GENERATION REPRISE

Gary grew up in a Bible-centered congregation. He was in church Sunday mornings, Sunday nights, and Wednesday nights. After all, his daddy was the pastor. Through the influence of his father and his grandfather (also a pastor), the boy trusted Jesus as his personal Savior and was excited about his faith.

But by the time Gary entered college, he began to drift from his spiritual moorings. When he graduated college and began his career, he was an alcoholic and a practicing homosexual. While his family grieved the loss of a son with whom they had little contact, Gary wandered in a wasteland of unfulfilled passion and depression. For three decades, he drank to try and mask the guilt that gnawed at his leathery heart. And for three decades, those who knew him the best brought him in prayer before the One who loved him the most.

Amazingly, at the age of fifty, Gary returned to the faith of his childhood. Turning his back on a lifestyle that was anything but fun and free, he claimed victory over alcohol and sexual perversion. For Gary, it was a victory that could only occur through the power of Jesus. And it was that same power that allowed him to come into accountable relationships and grow in his rediscovered faith. Today, Gary travels the country sharing the story of how God broke the bondage in his life.

There is victory in Jesus. He sought you and bought you with His blood. He loved you before you even knew Him. Come out of the darkness and into His wonderful light.

No, in all these things we are more than conquerors through him who loved us.

—ROMANS 8:37

Prayer

Who do you know who is caged in the prison of sexual addiction or a homosexual lifestyle? Bring them before the Lord encouraged by Gary's story of deliverance.

GREAT AND MIGHTY IS HE

Jesus gave us permission to call the almighty God our Father. That was a breakthrough of major proportions. The Aramaic word He used when giving us the Lord's Prayer actually means "papa" or "daddy." It's a term of affection. Gratefully, those who come to terms with the intimate relationship God desires with us are freed from imprisoning images of a cosmic cop or some distant deity. He is not out to "get" them. He is their daddy; He loves them.

Sadly, however, that very familiarity has caused some Christians to overcompensate and treat the Lord of glory as if He were their best buddy. Many Christians throw a passing glance at the Savior, slap Him on the back, and say they'll see Him later—maybe. They show up on His doorstep only when they need something. They assume that He has nothing better to do than humor and spoil them. Such over-familiarity is presumptuous and inappropriate. The God who would not allow Moses to see His face is the same One who has made eternal life possible through grace. He has shown us the countenance of His love in Jesus, but this great and mighty God is still and always clothed in glory and arrayed in splendor. His awesome power, like electricity, illuminates and warms our lives. But it is nothing to take for granted.

To whom, then, will you compare God? What image will you compare him to?

—ISAIAH 40:18

---•---

Prayer

With humility and reverence fall on your face before the
Lord of lords and King of kings. Resist the temptation
to be flippant in His presence. Praise Him for being
great and mighty; thank Him for His love for you.

---•---

WONDERFUL, MERCIFUL SAVIOR

Who wants to be a millionaire? For a while, that was Regis Philbin's favorite question. He asked it over and over again on television. And then by asking a series of increasingly more difficult trivia questions, he gave contestants on the popular quiz show a chance to walk away with big money.

There wasn't anything trivial about His question when Jesus asked Peter, "Who do people say the Son of Man is?" (Matthew 16:13). Peter didn't need to phone a friend. Without hesitation he responded, "Some say John the Baptist; others say Elijah; and still others, Jeremiah or one of the prophets" (16:14). Jesus' next question was considerably more difficult. "But what about you? Who do you say I am?" (16:15).

Once again Peter stayed cool although the spotlight focused with intensity on him. "You are the Christ, the Son of the living God" (16:16).

Convinced that this was Peter's final answer, Jesus affirmed His friend. He also revealed that this was an answer Peter was not capable of coming up with on his own. It had been revealed to him by a lifeline—directly from heaven.

We all will be given the opportunity to answer that million-dollar question. Access to heaven depends on our answer. It all comes down to whether we can say this wonderful and merciful person is our personal Savior.

Simon Peter answered, "You are the Christ, the Son of the living God."

—MATTHEW 16:16

Prayer

In addition to Jesus being your personal Savior, spend some
time telling Him what other roles He consistently plays in
your life. Work at increasing your list of appropriate adjectives.

I WANT TO PRAISE YOU, LORD

As the first rays of the morning sun splash on the surrounding hills, Eddie Smith sits in his favorite chair with an open Bible and a hungry heart. Sipping a mug of coffee, he drinks in the goodness of the Lord. It's a routine that has marked Eddie's life for the past sixty years. Before he goes about embracing the demands of the day, this former Marine delights in pledging his allegiance to his Commander in Chief. It's obvious to his family and friends that Eddie wants to praise the Lord in personal worship and study. In spite of the fact that he will soon be eighty years old, he has no plans to alter his lifestyle. This successful businessman continues to oversee a family-owned company and is just as determined to maintain his walk with the Lord.

Does that sound unbelievable? Eddie recently admitted to a newspaper columnist inquiring of his spiritual disciplines that he is getting more out of his study of Scripture than at any other time in his life. "I wake up excited about what the Lord will show me. And when I recognize how much He's done in my life, I want to spend as much time with Him as I can."

Can you resonate with Eddie's desire? Do you want to praise, know, love, and serve the Lord much more than you do? Then make a daily appointment with God—and keep it.

In the morning, O LORD, you hear my voice; in the morning I lay my requests before you and wait in expectation.

—PSALM 5:3

Prayer

If your practice of personal Bible reading and prayer is
hit and miss, ask the Lord to help you find
the right time and place that works for you.

HUMBLE THYSELF IN THE SIGHT OF THE LORD (1)

Want an easy way to remember how to find joy? Consider this acronym for "joy": Jesus, others, you. If you seek to put Jesus first in your life and then intentionally place the needs of others ahead of your own, you will discover contentment and happiness you didn't know was possible.

Jesus taught much about self-denial. He made it clear that His mission in coming to earth was to serve, not to be served. And His actions lived up to His words. He humbled Himself when He chose to enter our world. He lived among us—experiencing pain, hunger, exhaustion. He washed the dirty feet of His disciples. He allowed Himself to be killed. Voluntarily giving up His rights and privileges, He blazed the trail to ultimate fulfillment in this life and provided a path for eternal life.

Similarly, He called us to take up our cross and follow Him. He said that in giving we receive. He said that the last shall be first. He told us that if we seek to save our lives, we'll lose them; but if we lose our lives for His sake, we'll find them. If Jesus had to humble Himself to make possible what God desired, we'd best follow His lead and humble ourselves in the sight of the Lord. And when we do, He promises to lift us up.

Humble yourselves in the sight of the Lord, and He will lift you up.

—JAMES 4:10 NKJV

Prayer

Admit your self-centered orientation to God (and yourself).
Think of the ways your willfulness distances you
from the Lord. Accept His forgiveness.

HUMBLE THYSELF IN THE SIGHT OF THE LORD (2)

Imagine what it must have been like for Abraham. God had promised that he would become the father of many nations. But years passed and Abraham and Sarah had no baby. How could there be descendants without first one child? Abraham began doubting God. Convincing himself that he'd misunderstood God's game plan, Abraham opted to father a child by his wife's attendant. Bad choice! The fruit of that union was a boy named Ishmael. His offspring (the Arab nations) would be in constant conflict with Israel.

When Abraham and Sarah waited for God's timing, God kept His promise. But then what happened? God told Abraham to take a knife to Isaac and sacrifice him as an offering. "No way, God! After making us wait so long, why take our child from us? What sense would that make? How can you possibly then fill your promise to give me many descendants?" Abraham must have pled. But Abraham found the faith to believe and the will to obey. He humbled himself and set out to do what God asked. Seeing Abraham's humility, the Lord did not require Isaac to be sacrificed. And the principle remains. When we say no to self and yes to God, He gives life!

For whoever wants to save his life will lose it, but whoever loses his life for me will find it.

—MATTHEW 16:25

Prayer

Acknowledge your tendency to doubt the demands
God places on your life. Ask Him for the faith
to obey what seems difficult to understand.

BEAUTIFUL

Perhaps it was one of those incredibly beautiful days. Brilliant sun, bright blue sky, and not too hot. But for Bartimaeus, one of Jericho's familiar beggars, "beautiful" was not a word he normally used to describe days. You see, Bartimaeus couldn't see. He'd been blind from birth. What others took for granted, Bartimaeus was oblivious to. But on this beautiful day all that would change. A caring man who redefined the meaning of beauty passed through the town. Based on Isaiah's prophecies of the Messiah, Jesus was not all that physically attractive, but His gentle eyes and contagious smile brightened every room He entered. Children felt safe with Him. They felt loved. So did wasted prostitutes and gouging tax gatherers. Not only that, the prophets had said that this man would make the blind see.

When Bartimaeus heard that Jesus was walking by, he called out, "Jesus, Son of David, have mercy on me!" (Luke 18:38). Struggling to his feet and slowly feeling his way toward the visiting rabbi, Bartimaeus felt warm hands on his weathered face. And the next thing he knew, he was healed. Seeing the eyes of Jesus and the smile that creased His bearded face was not only the first thing Bartimaeus ever saw. It would forever be the most beautiful thing he ever saw.

Jesus said to him, "Receive your sight; your faith has healed you."

—LUKE 18:42

Prayer

Contemplate the "beautiful" blessings you enjoy each day
(including nature, family, food and shelter).
Consider the ways Jesus is indeed a "beautiful" Savior.

GLORY TO THE LAMB

"Behold! The Lamb of God who takes away the sin of the world!" (John 1:29 NKJV). When John the Baptist confidently said those words while pointing to Jesus, a flock of sheep most likely was feeding nearby. The culture of the Bible was one of farming and livestock. Sheep, lambs, and goats were an economic necessity. They also were a theological necessity. According to God's laws for His people, the blood of a slaughtered lamb would be the only acceptable sacrifice for their sins. But no animal sacrifice was ever completely sufficient to expunge the guilt of all peoples. That's why the people had to bring sacrifices over and over. They brought the animal, placed their hands on its head, and killed it—a graphic demonstration of the animal dying in their place.

Jesus came as the once-for-all sacrifice. His perfect life qualified Him to bear the sin of the world. According to God's law, a sacrifice for sin had to be made—and He made it Himself. He died in our place so that we might live.

That's why He is called the Lamb of God. John the Baptist proclaimed it when he pointed out Jesus on the dusty road. John the apostle proclaimed it when he recorded the words of the angels in heaven. The Lamb of God, the perfect sacrifice, sits on the throne. And with countless millions of angels we will lift our voices in praise, singing glory to the Lamb!

> *Then I heard every creature in heaven and on earth and under the earth and on the sea, and all that is in them, singing: "To him who sits on the throne and to the Lamb be praise and honor and glory and power, for ever and ever!"*
>
> —REVELATION 5:13

Prayer

As you pray today, refer to Jesus as "the Lamb of God." Picture Him as the Lamb upon the throne. Since He died for you, thank Him that He is interested in what is on your mind today.

CHANGE MY HEART, O GOD

The work of a potter is serious business. If you've ever watched a potter at the wheel, you know the time it takes to create a clay jar, bowl, or pot. The clay must be prepared properly, first removing all impurities that would cause the vessel to crack under the heat of firing. The potter works the clay, cutting, pounding, and kneading in order to remove bubbles. Then he shapes the vessel, working deftly with his hands as the wheel spins. Finally, the vessel is fired to nearly twenty-four hundred degrees. All of this is done to produce a strong, usable, high-quality vessel.

How blessed we are to have the Master Potter molding us! He prepares us with His Word and removes all our impurities through His loving forgiveness. He makes us stronger as we endure the cutting, pounding, and kneading of trials and difficult circumstances.

Then a most remarkable change takes place. He takes us, ugly lumps of muddy clay that we are, and forms us into items of great beauty and usability. He shapes us into exactly what He wants us to be, then He burns His love into our souls.

Undergoing the process of being molded may not always be comfortable, but the end result is always worth it. Ask God to mold you and make you, for when He does, He makes you more like Himself.

Yet, O LORD, you are our Father. We are the clay, you are the potter; we are all the work of your hand.

—ISAIAH 64:8

Prayer

Repeat aloud the first four lines of the song.
With a willingness to change, pray that God will
change your heart and make it ever true to Him.

HOW GREAT, HOW GLORIOUS

Why do we praise? What causes us to lift our voices and worship God? From the beginning of time, all of humanity has had reasons to praise almighty God—from the creation of the heavens and the earth to the promise of new heavens and a new earth, from the gift of the Promised Land to the gift of salvation through the promised Emmanuel. Indeed, God is great and greatly to be praised!

How should we praise the Lord? How can we lift Him high upon our praise? We do that when we live to glorify Him, when we thank Him, when we use our gifts to serve Him. How many ways can we praise God? As many ways as we can imagine! David played his harp; Solomon ruled with wisdom; Paul wrote letters to churches; C. S. Lewis wrote great literary works; Charles Colson ministered in prison; Fanny Crosby composed hymns; Billy Graham preached to hundreds of thousands. But most important, we praise God when we enthrone Him in our lives—making everything we do a sacrifice of praise to Him.

God is great, glorious, and excellent. May our lives reflect His power and glory. May His praise be ever on our lips, for He is greatly to be praised!

Through Jesus, therefore, let us continually offer to God a sacrifice of praise—the fruit of lips that confess his name.

—HEBREWS 13:15

Prayer

Thank God for the great and glorious things He has done in your life. Praise Him for His daily blessings and guidance.

JEHOVAH-JIREH

Do we truly believe that Jehovah-Jireh (which means "God our provider") cares for us? We may say that we trust Him, but do we really?

So we work hard to save the money to buy a car, a house, and a quality education for our children. While such planning is not bad, it can become a problem if having our needs met is not enough and we feel that we must assuage all our desires as well.

God our Provider promises to supply all our needs. What are our needs? Food, clothing, and shelter are life's most basic needs. Does God provide these? We would probably have to answer that yes, indeed, we have food, clothing, and shelter—that God has provided for us. While He may not have met all our desires, He has indeed met all our needs.

But even more important than Jehovah-Jireh's provision for our physical needs is His provision for our spiritual need. He has provided grace that is sufficient to fill the longing in our hearts for God. It is by His grace alone that we can come to Him.

Unlike the trendy clothes, gourmet food, and fancy house, grace is free and it is eternal. We don't have to earn it. We can't purchase it. It is offered as a gift. And it is ours—forever.

But he said to me, "My grace is sufficient for you, for my power is made perfect in weakness."

—2 CORINTHIANS 12:9

Prayer

Thank the Lord for His gift of grace and ask Him to help you share your faith and your abundance with others.

SEND IT ON DOWN

Imagine how the disciples must have felt at the day of Pentecost when the Holy Spirit literally came down upon them! Picture that powerful scene: God made His presence known with the blowing of a violent wind and tongues of fire (Acts 2:2-3). Those who had been touched began to speak in other languages, proclaiming the wonders of God.

The disciples had been on a roller coaster of emotions. They had seen Jesus heal the sick, raise the dead, die on a cross, rise from the dead, and ascend to heaven—only to leave them to carry on His work. Now they were expected to go into all the world, preaching the gospel. How were they to accomplish this task? How could God have left such a responsibility in their inexperienced hands? He could do it because He knew, when the Holy Spirit came down upon them, they could change the world. So God sent the Spirit down—and the world has never been the same.

Do you feel weak? Incapable of running the race set before you? You already have the Holy Spirit, but sometimes you need to be reignited with fresh fire; sometimes you need to be refreshed with power sent down like rain into your soul. Ask God to send it on down! At your request, He will pour down His power and refreshment to help you do whatever He has called you to do, no matter how weak you feel.

But you will receive power when the Holy Spirit comes upon you.

—ACTS 1:8

Prayer

God promises extraordinary results when we ask for
His power. Ask Him to reignite your fire and to refresh
your spirit so that you can do His work in your world.

THE SOLID ROCK

If you have ever stood on a sandy beach as the waves lapped at your feet, you know that the longer you remain, the further your feet sink into the shifting sands. Eventually, you'll be up to your ankles! On a rocky coastline in Maine, however, you can stand on the shore with wave after wave rushing over your feet and you won't sink at all. You stand firm on the strength of the boulders beneath you.

Shifting sands don't make a very good foundation—for our feet or for our faith. We need solid rock—strong and unchanging. Like the wise man who built his house upon a rock (Luke 6:48), we can rest secure in building our faith upon the firm foundation of Jesus Christ. When the winds of change blow and the waves of uncertainty rush over us, we can cling to the immovable, unchanging love of Jesus.

For this we have reason to praise. Christ is the solid rock on which we stand. We can depend upon His words, trust in His tender mercies, and praise Him day after day for the grace that has saved us. Praise the risen Lamb and in everything be glad. Our foundation is firm; our salvation is sure. Praise His name!

Consequently, you are no longer foreigners and aliens, but fellow citizens with God's people and members of God's household, built on the foundation of the apostles and prophets, with Christ Jesus himself as the chief cornerstone.

—EPHESIANS 2:19-20

Prayer

Thank the Lord for His strength, support, mercy, and unchanging love. Thank Him for the gift of His Son, Jesus, the solid rock on which you can stand secure, no matter what the waves of circumstance bring your way.

AS FOR ME AND MY HOUSE

What better example to your family than proclaiming and living the words, "As for me and my house, we will serve the Lord"? Most people, especially children, learn by example. When you take a stand for God, not only proclaiming His lordship over your life but also living it to the fullest, others will learn to do the same.

However, sometimes we run into trouble. Many daily activities tend to take priority over our lives: the quest for a promotion at work, striving to be a top athlete, or pursuing excellence in academics. While all are noble causes, when we slip into seeking to control our lives in order to reach our goals, we rebel against the lordship of Jesus Christ and we are serving other gods.

God knows the desires of our hearts. He knows our needs and our wants. He wants us to be happy, but He also knows what is best for us. When we decide to serve the Lord, we open ourselves to His blessings. When we surrender ourselves to His will, we choose to let Him be Lord of our lives—every part of them.

Have you made the choice? Whom will you and your family serve? Can you say with confidence, "As for me and my house, we will serve the Lord"? How will you make that a reality in your home today?

And if it seems evil to you to serve the LORD, choose for yourselves this day whom you will serve...But as for me and my house, we will serve the LORD.

—JOSHUA 24:15 NKJV

Prayer

As a family, pray that God will guide you and
bless you as you choose to serve Him together.

THE FAMILY PRAYER SONG

Try this experiment: Go outside and pick up a twig. Grasping each end, bend the twig. It bends easily, doesn't it? It may even break. Now, pick up four or five twigs. Holding them together in a bunch, try to bend them. Not as easy, is it?

The same principle holds true for families. When all in a family are united in harmony—staying together, praying together—the storms of life may shake us, but they won't break us.

How much more powerful, then, the family who stands together in the Lord! In Matthew 18:20, Jesus promised, "Where two or three come together in my name, there am I with them." When we invite Jesus to fill our home with His presence, we will be blessed to find harmony and love which could never exist without Him.

We need one another in every way—praying before meals, doing devotions daily, attending church services as a family, working in the yard, and watching TV together. The family that is unified, that vows to live according to God's Word, will weather the storms of life and be stronger for the journey.

How good and pleasant it is when brothers live together in unity!

—PSALM 133:1

Prayer

Make a commitment that your family will live in unity,
working together that you may be a positive example
in the world. Ask the Lord to help you as
you work toward this goal each day.

PURIFY MY HEART

As gold is heated to a temperature of nearly two thousand degrees, impurities rise to the surface, making them easy to remove. When the remaining gold is cooled, the result is a refined, pure, high-quality gold; it is precious and valuable.

We are precious to God and valuable enough for Him to have sent His Son to earth to suffer death on a cross. His death served as a payment for us to spend eternity in heaven with Him. As Christians, we know we have been cleansed of our sins, yet we constantly face the struggle with our sin natures. What can we do? We can continually ask for His cleansing fire. Each day, we can ask Him to purify us.

There is no need to fear the Refiner's fire. Isaiah submitted to the cleansing fire of a burning coal upon his lips (Isaiah 6:5-8). A cleansing process was necessary before Isaiah could fulfill his purpose as a prophet of God. God's method of purification may not be comfortable. It may force us to wrestle with issues buried deep within our hearts. It may even be painful. But submission to the cleansing fire of God will allow us to be made pure in His sight.

And that is all we could ever desire.

These trials are only to test your faith, to show that it is strong and pure. It is being tested as fire tests and purifies gold—and your faith is far more precious to God than mere gold.

—1 PETER 1:7 NLT

Prayer

Pray that the Lord will reveal your weaknesses, forgive your sins, and purify your heart as you lean on His everlasting love.

HE KNOWS MY NAME

On a transcontinental flight, cruising along at thirty thousand feet, everything on the ground looks miniscule. Mountains appear as bumps in the landscape, roads are thin ribbons, and houses and people are indistinguishable.

How awesome it is to know that God, looking down from His lofty throne, knows your name. He sees your struggles and pain; He hears every prayer and longing of your heart. He sees each tear that falls. You aren't just a tiny dot in the landscape on planet earth. You have a Maker and Redeemer. You have worth. You are loved.

Not only does He know you, He has a purpose for your life. He calls you His own. He never leaves you; He walks with you wherever you go. Each day, you interact with dozens of people who don't know you and may never interact with you again—from the telemarketer to the cashier at the grocery store. How you respond to others is a witness to your relationship with God. When your life displays the fruit of the Spirit (love, joy, peace, patience, goodness, faithfulness, gentleness, and self-control), you show to whom you belong.

Does how you live bring your Father pleasure?

I knew you before I formed you in your mother's womb. Before you were born I set you apart and appointed you as my spokesman to the world.

—JEREMIAH 1:5 NLT

Prayer

Thank the Lord for being the One who knows you better than you know yourself, and for recognizing you by name when you come to His throne in prayer.

I WAS GLAD

Jesus Christ is your Savior and Friend, but He is also your sovereign Lord. When you approach Him, whether in a house of worship or on your knees at your bedside, you must show reverence and respect.

When you step into your church, how do you feel? What do you see? What brings you to the realization that you are in His house, His courts? Do you ever contemplate the fact that you are there by His grace alone? When you praise with a pure and contrite heart, reverently stepping into God's presence, you can meet Him anywhere, transforming an elevator, your backyard, or even your car into a place where you are in His awesome presence.

When you come to God in worship, you come knowing that you are worthy of His blessings only because of His undeserved grace. In Psalm 28, David calls out, "Hear my cry for mercy as I call to you for help, as I lift my hands toward your Most Holy Place." You can receive all God has to offer when you reverently approach the throne of grace with heart and hands open to the blessings of the Most Holy Lord.

I was glad when they said unto me,
Let us go into the house of the Lord.

—PSALM 122:1

Prayer

Approach the Lord in prayer with respect and reverence,
knowing that wherever you meet Him is holy ground.
Ask Him to remind you each day of His holiness.

YOU ALONE ARE HOLY

God alone is holy! The only being in the universe worthy of our praise is our Lord Jesus Christ. If we are silent, the whole of creation will rise and shout praises to the Creator, Most Holy God. In Jerusalem, the Pharisees told Jesus to tell the crowds to be quiet, to cease their praises. Jesus replied, "If they keep quiet, the stones will cry out" (Luke 19:40).

In the book of Revelation, John is blessed to see the holiness of Jesus revealed to him in a dream. The heavenly beings never cease in saying, "Holy, holy, holy is the Lord God Almighty, who was, and is, and is to come" (Revelation 4:8). How wonderful to know that we will someday join with the angels in proclaiming the holiness of God face to face with our Savior!

Until then, we can live life in His presence, worshiping and offering our hearts to Him. He loves us so much! Loving Him in return is what He desires; as the song says, "it's the least we can do." And when we live in praise, we find great blessings. He will keep us safe in the shadow of His wings (Psalm 17:8), watching over us as a mother hen would protect her young by spreading her wings over them. He allows us to drink from the "fountain of life" (Psalm 36:9).

Offer yourself to the Holy One. You will not be disappointed.

Let them praise the name of the LORD, for His name alone is exalted; His glory is above the earth and heaven.

—PSALM 148:13 NKJV

Prayer

Fall on your knees and worship the Lord.
Thank Him for His mercy and protection.
Proclaim His holiness for He is worthy to be praised!

NO EYE HAS SEEN

Even in your wildest daydreams you could never imagine what eternity with Jesus will be like. The inkling John gives us in Revelation 21 only serves to heighten the mystery and our anticipation. John describes a city made of precious and rare jewels, with gold so pure it is transparent.

Because we are all unique in our perception of written descriptions, each one of us will picture something different in our mind's eye. You may have a detailed image in your mind of what you think heaven will be like. When you finally arrive there, no matter what your preconceived ideas, you will not be disappointed.

Until then, live each day seeking to know what God has planned for you right here, right now. He has much in store for your life. When you pray daily for His guidance, the Holy Spirit will lead you. The Old Testament prophet Jeremiah encouraged God's people by telling them God's promise: "I know the plans I have for you...plans to prosper you and not to harm you, plans to give you a hope and a future" (Jeremiah 29:11). Just as God was with the ancient peoples, He is with you today, leading you all the way. His plans are good, bringing hope for the future in this life and beyond. God has prepared something wonderful just for you!

No eye has seen, no ear has heard, no mind has conceived what God has prepared for those who love him.

—1 CORINTHIANS 2:9

Prayer

Think about heaven—the place God has prepared for you.
Thank Him for the plans He has for you, for giving
you hope for this life and life with Him for eternity.

I BELONG TO JESUS

We all want to feel like we belong. We are conditioned from birth to need to belong to someone. We experience belonging in our families, with our friends, with a spouse, in our church. And although each of these relationships fills that need to a certain extent, we can never feel truly satisfied, we can never truly belong, until we belong to Jesus.

The reason is simple. Life changes. We grow up and move out of our parents' home. Some of our friends move away. We may lose our spouse to divorce or death. There is only one person to whom we can belong forever—in this life and beyond. If we've made the choice to belong to Him, He will never leave us.

In fact, His life and death were meant for the purpose of giving all people a chance to belong to the family of God. He took your sin upon Himself as He was nailed to the cross. He bought your freedom with His blood. This is an intense, all-encompassing freedom—freedom from Satan's power, from sin and destruction, freedom to live your life in the joy of belonging to Christ the King. Rejoice that you can proclaim "I belong to Jesus!" now and forever.

He destined us for adoption as his children through Jesus Christ...In him we have redemption through his blood, the forgiveness of our trespasses, according to the riches of his grace .

—EPHESIANS 1:5, 7 NRSV

Prayer

Recognize how good it feels when you repeat "I belong to Jesus" again and again. Thank the Lord for setting you free and allowing you to belong to Him. Ask Him to help you share your joy and freedom with others.

I LOVE YOUR GRACE

Why do you love Jesus? What causes you to rely on Him and trust Him enough to give your heart and soul to Him?

Those trying, stressful days when everything seems to be closing in on you sometimes feel like more than you can handle. You fall into bed at night wondering how you made it through. Then you remember that you spent time with God at the start of the day. You recall how, when the pressure was on, you called out to God for strength and serenity. And in the quiet of your heart, it hits you: He was there with you all day long!

That's why you love Jesus. All you had to do was ask, and His mercy was poured out upon you; grace was freely given. Now His presence surrounds you day by day. He is there, listening to your prayers and answering when you call. He is there, lending His strength. He is there, providing a place of refuge from the stormy day. Praise Him, for He is there.

Have mercy on me, O God, have mercy on me, for in you my soul takes refuge. I will take refuge in the shadow of your wings until the disaster has passed.

—PSALM 57:1

Prayer

Think about the times when you felt overwhelmed.
Now think of the ways in which God made His
presence known to you through those stressful periods.
Tell Him that all you want is what He wants for you.

WHERE DO I GO?

While working at a small, non-religious private school, a Christian teacher handled the stresses of the environment with a positive attitude and a calmness not exhibited by his co-workers. Because of the way he responded to volatile situations, he was respected by his students. They went to him with their problems and concerns, and listened intently to his advice.

One day, another faculty member asked him, "How do you do it? How do you maintain your positive outlook with everything we go through each day?"

His answer was simple: "Jesus." He told of his daily quiet time in which he asked God for strength and wisdom for what lay ahead. He told of the peace he receives when, in his uncertainty, he relies on Jesus. And he told his co-worker how she could also find this peace and the strength to handle the day.

Where do you go when you need shelter, help, and a friend? How do you face each day with all of its uncertainty? When you go to Jesus in prayer, He will answer your call. He will not leave you to go it alone—He can, and will, carry it all.

When I pray, you answer me; you encourage me by giving me the strength I need.

—PSALM 138:3 NLT

Prayer

Go to the Lord and ask for His peace and wisdom.
Ask Him to help you live in a way that, by your
example, others will want to know Him too.

HEAVEN IS IN MY HEART / GOD IS SO GOOD / AMAZING GRACE

Heaven: a most spectacular and beautiful place where there will be no night nor need for sun to light the day (Revelation 21:23, 22:5). The reason for this phenomenon? The presence of Jesus!

When you invited Jesus to live in your heart, you invited an everlasting light. The presence of His majesty drove out the darkness of fear and doubt and replaced it with joy. His holy light, residing on the throne of your heart, becomes a symbol of heaven within you. God is so good to you that He gave His only Son as a sacrifice for your sins. That sacrifice cleansed your heart and made it a suitable place for God to dwell. Now heaven is indeed in your heart.

Yes, Christ saved your soul when you accepted His gift of grace. You probably know the words by heart, but read them once again: "Amazing grace, how sweet the sound, that saved a wretch like me." Your heart was once in darkness, but God, in His goodness, gave you a second chance. When you asked Him to enter your life and make your heart His temple, your blindness was removed and you saw the light of His presence. Hallelujah for His great love!

But because of his great love for us, God, who is rich in mercy, made us alive with Christ even when we were dead in transgressions—it is by grace you have been saved.

—EPHESIANS 2:4-5

Prayer

Thank the Lord for His goodness, His willingness to bring His everlasting light into the darkness of your heart and, most of all, for His sacrifice that cleansed you from sin.

BLESSED BE THE ROCK

When Jesus entered the city of Jerusalem riding on a donkey, the people shouted their praises, "Blessed is the king who comes in the name of the Lord!" (Luke 19:38). They were praising God for giving them someone whom, they thought, would be their king—a man who would become ruler of Israel. They had the wrong idea.

Jesus came not to overthrow the government, but to overthrow the powers of hell and their ruler. He came to rule in people's hearts. He came to be a cornerstone on which the church would build its faith—He came to be the rock of our salvation.

Blessed be the rock of our salvation! This mighty rock provides a solid place on which to build our faith as we read the Scriptures and learn more about Him every day. His great love saved us—giving us victory over anger, doubt, fear, and death because He is on our side. For that, He is worthy of our praise.

Blessed be the rock!

The LORD is my rock, my fortress and my deliverer; my God is my rock, in whom I take refuge, my shield and the horn of my salvation. He is my stronghold, my refuge and my savior.

—2 Samuel 22:2-3

Prayer

Ask God to remind you every day to cling to the rock, to stand firm in your faith, and be an example for others to follow.

HE IS THE KING

In the Old Testament, you'll find that the Israelites were often engaged in battle—most of the time for land or for freedom from oppressors. They gave credit to the Lord for their victories, for delivering them from the hand of their enemies. In Psalm 24, the priests inside the temple would ask, "Who is this King of glory?" The people outside would respond, "The LORD strong and mighty, the LORD mighty in battle." Then the gates to the temple would be opened and the people would enter to worship and offer their thanksgiving to God.

Today, you can give credit to the Lord for your victories. The battles may be large (your triumph over an unhealthy or self-destructive habit) or small (you didn't lose your temper during the traffic jam). He is the one who delivers you in every situation. He provides patience or self-control when you need it the most. He hears and answers every time you call. He is the King, He is the Lord. Praise His name, the name of Jesus, the strong and mighty ruler of the kingdoms of this world—and of the kingdom of your heart.

Who is this King of glory? The LORD strong and mighty, the LORD mighty in battle.

—PSALM 24:8

Prayer

Praise the Lord for His victory in your heart.
Thank Him for providing the strength needed
to help you overcome your personal battles.

October 15

YES, LORD, YES

Obedience. Now there's a word that meets with resistance! Due to our nature, we often balk at authority, at the very thought of doing what we're told.

Jesus, in the Garden of Gethsemane, faced the question of obedience. He knew what lay ahead if He followed God's plan for Him. He would be mocked, His friends would desert Him, He would be whipped and nailed to a cross, die by suffocation, and endure total separation from God. He even asked God if He could get out of the whole situation, saying, "Father, if you are willing, take this cup from me." But in the same breath, He reaffirmed His commitment to obedience, "Yet not my will, but yours be done" (Luke 22:42).

Jesus obeyed God's plan—He answered with a "yes" that resulted in salvation for all who believe. After all He's done for you, how then could you tell God "no" when He asks you for your obedience?

You can't always know or even predict the outcome of your obedience to God. But when you respond with a "Yes, Lord, yes," you can be assured He will use you for His glory. And you also can be assured that your life will be richer and fuller than you could ever have imagined.

Those who obey his commands live in him, and he in them. And this is how we know that he lives in us: We know it by the Spirit he gave us.

—1 JOHN 3:24

Prayer

Think about some areas in your life in which you need to be obedient to God. Commit yourself to obedience to God's Word, and reaffirm this by saying "Yes, Lord, yes" to each area in need.

JESUS IS THE ANSWER

The world today has many religions to offer those who are searching for answers. You could choose to believe whatever makes you comfortable—from reincarnation here on earth to populating your own planet in the afterlife.

But no matter where you look, there is one truth to Christianity that no other religion can claim: God sent His Son Jesus to die for the sins of all mankind, and three days later, Jesus rose from the dead. Jesus provided the way for a sinful humanity to find God. Because of the cross, you can have a loving, personal relationship with God. Jesus is alive today, listening to the desires of your heart and answering when you call out to Him.

Yes, Jesus is the answer. Do you have a question about the meaning of life? Jesus is the answer. Do you wonder about your future? Jesus is the answer. Are your skies dark? Are you facing a mountain you don't think you can climb? Jesus is the answer. He knows your discouragement and fear, and He will help you find peace. He brings light to your darkest night.

The risen Savior is your answer, and the answer for anyone in the world who chooses to believe!

Jesus said to him, "I am the way, the truth, and the life. No one comes to the Father except through Me."

—JOHN 14:6 NKJV

Prayer

Write down some questions you have about God.
Ask Him to help you find the answers as you
spend time each day in prayer and Bible study.

JESUS LOVES ME / O HOW HE LOVES YOU AND ME

When you listen to this song, do you recall when you were a child, innocently singing the words in Sunday school? You believed the words without question. "Of course Jesus loves me. The Bible tells me so!" Then you grew up, and the childlike innocence evaporated.

At a Christian college, a student sat in her Biblical Literature class and asked, "How do we know Jesus loves us? How do we know the Bible is true?"

The professor replied, "You tell me. How do you know?"

The young co-ed responded that she didn't know. Her belief was based on what she had been taught as a child by her parents and her church. The wise professor explained that, like a nice house that needs a new foundation, she should keep in her heart everything she had been taught—she just needed to "jack up" the house and build a new foundation formed from the cement of her own prayer and study of God's Word. She did just that and, as a result, her faith was made stronger.

In your heart you know the truth—that Jesus loves you so much that He gave His life for you. Continue to strengthen the foundation and build the house of faith by learning more about Jesus and sharing your faith with others.

Does Jesus love you? Of course He does. The Bible tells you so!

For God so loved the world that he gave his one and only Son, that whoever believes in him shall not perish but have eternal life.

—JOHN 3:16

Prayer

Think about how much God loves you. Thank Him for sending His Son to save you, providing you with a firm foundation for your faith.

I SEE THE LORD

What a marvelous vision! Can you picture the image in your mind? Jesus on the throne, the train of His robe covering the whole floor of the temple. Such a sight of splendor and majesty would bring anyone to his knees, bowing before the King.

Such a vision came to the prophet Isaiah in the Old Testament, who saw the Lord seated on His throne, high and exalted. The apostle John in the New Testament also was invited to see God's throne in heaven and experience the worship there. "Day and night they never stop saying, 'Holy, holy, holy is the Lord God Almighty, who was, and is, and is to come'" (Revelation 4:8). They fall on their knees and lay their crowns before Him.

When you come before the Lord in prayer, begin by worshiping His holiness, His majesty, and His glory. Picture Him as your King, seated high and exalted on a throne with all the powers of heaven giving Him praise and adoration. Allow yourself to be in awe of this great and awesome Creator of the universe who made Himself approachable by sending His Son to become human and die for your sins. Then do as the Bible says: "Come boldly to the throne of our gracious God. There we will receive his mercy, and we will find grace to help us when we need it" (Hebrews 4:16 NLT).

In the year that King Uzziah died, I saw the Lord seated on a throne, high and exalted, and the train of his robe filled the temple.

—ISAIAH 6:1

Prayer

Out loud, repeat, "Holy, holy, holy, holy. Holy is the Lord." Praise God for His holiness and thank Him for His mercy.

HEAR OUR PRAISES

With our finite human minds, we cannot begin to imagine the celebration that takes place in the kingdom of heaven every time a sinner surrenders to Jesus. And greater still will be the rejoicing when each sinner saved by grace enters the gates of heaven, welcomed by those who have gone before.

But for now, we can pray as Jesus taught us to pray—"Your kingdom come" (Matthew 6:10). But how is that possible? How could His kingdom come? What exactly are we praying for when we say that? We're praying both for revival and for His return. Our prayers are answered when Christians all over the world unite their hearts and voices in praise! When His people pray—alone by their bedside or as thousands of believers at a gathering—He will be there. When we praise, our voices join the chorus of millions, rising to heaven. As a result, the glory of God will fill the earth and His people will dance for joy. The nations will hear the praise of God's people; we can be a light shining in the darkness.

You can make a difference for God right where you are—in your home, at work, on vacation. Lift praises to God and be a true example of joy.

Shout for joy to the LORD, all the earth. Worship the LORD with gladness; come before him with joyful songs.

—PSALM 100:1-2

Prayer

Worship the Lord with thanksgiving and praise. Let your
heart rejoice and thank Him for the joy He has given to you.
Ask Him to let your joy overflow to others today.

I WALK BY FAITH

Can you tell the future? Sure, there are lots of people who claim they can tell you what job you will have, whom you will marry, how long you will live—some even claim to know the day and the hour that Jesus will return. One thing is certain: The future is in God's hands and only He knows what is in store for you.

This doesn't mean you can just sit back and not think about what is ahead. Plans should be made for your well-being and security. Goals should be set. You do need to look ahead to the coming years. What it does mean is that when you place your faith in God's leading, you don't have to worry about what lies ahead. God will give you the ability to gain what you need; He will provide you with strength to survive in times of trouble; He will give you a heart big enough to hold the joys He has in store for you.

"Trust in the LORD with all your heart, and lean not on your own understanding; in all your ways acknowledge Him, and He shall direct your paths" (Proverbs 3:5–6 NKJV). When you walk by faith and live by faith, you can trust in God to guide you through your future and on into eternity.

For we walk by faith, not by sight.

—2 CORINTHIANS 5:7 NKJV

Prayer

Ask the Lord to strengthen your faith and to
help you to rely upon His leading in your life.

YOUR EVERLASTING LOVE

The dictionary defines everlasting as "never coming to an end; lasting forever; eternal." What kind of love could be described in such a way? Only the love God has poured out upon those who believe in Him.

It is difficult to imagine a love that will never end. Human beings are certainly capable of great love, but the wonder of a love that will never end is beyond our comprehension. God loves you so much, He knew you in your mother's womb—He knows everything about you from your thoughts to the desires of your heart, even to the number of hairs on your head! He knows your past, and He has forgiven you.

"Greater love has no one than this, that he lay down his life for his friends" (John 15:13). Jesus loved us enough to die for us; as Christians, we need to show the same sacrificial love toward others. His wonderful love is higher than the sky and deeper than the sea. He holds us close and reaches out to us when we stray. He is always there to give us more and more—and the well of His love will never run dry! Praise Him for His everlasting love!

I have loved you with an everlasting love; I have drawn you with loving-kindness.

—JEREMIAH 31:3

Prayer

Think of someone to whom you can show love.
Thank the Lord that His love reached out to you,
then reach out to others with His wonderful love.

MY GOD REIGNS

"Blessed are those who have learned to acclaim you, who walk in the light of your presence, O LORD. They rejoice in your name all day long; they exult in your righteousness" (Psalm 89:15-16). There is no place more amazing than the presence of the Lord. In His presence we can become fully involved in praise, dancing and singing as He sings over us.

Just as a proud father exults in the triumphs and joys of his children, our Father in heaven celebrates over us. When we hit bumps in the road, when we struggle, just like a loving dad, He is there to pick us up, dust us off, and fortify our spirits with His strength. He reigns supreme forevermore—yet even in His glory, He still has the desire to be our Friend.

So rejoice and be glad in the Lord. Worship without shame. Release your heart and soul as the Lord sings over you! Dance, shout, rejoice. Your God reigns!

The LORD your God is with you, he is mighty to save. He will take great delight in you, he will quiet you with his love, he will rejoice over you with singing.

—ZEPHANIAH 3:17

Prayer

Pray aloud and thank God for His presence in your life.

I WILL CELEBRATE

Celebrate and praise God! Sometimes we aren't sure how to go about doing that. One way to praise is with our voices. The song declares, "I will celebrate, sing unto the Lord." Through our sincere desire to praise God, we can lift our voices and sing.

Jesus came to save all people from sin and, one day, He will return to this world to gather His children unto Himself. Someday, we will see our Jesus, our Savior, face to face—and we will sing praises with the heavenly host! What an astounding reason to celebrate!

We believe God is great and we should not keep our joy to ourselves. What He has done for us is overwhelming and we must share our appreciation for His victory—over sin, over death, over our lives. Knowing what He did for us should strengthen our commitment to Him—and to sharing our joy.

Sing your praise to God that others might hear the celebration and be drawn to know the truth: that Jesus is the Savior! Celebrate His triumph and victory. Sing a new song to the Lord!

I will praise you, O Lord, among the nations; I will sing of you among the peoples. For great is your love, reaching to the heavens; your faithfulness reaches to the skies.

—PSALM 57:9-10

Prayer

Praise the Lord for giving you a song in your heart
and a voice to lift in celebration of His great love.

THAT'S WHY WE PRAISE HIM

We praise Jesus for everything His life on earth meant for us, and we praise Him for all He continues to do in our lives.

Our lives without Jesus were no better than slavery—to the ways of the world, to our own desires, and to the power of Satan. When we knelt down at the feet of Jesus and allowed Him to conquer our hearts, we were set free.

Jesus heals the lost and transforms those dead in their transgressions to be made alive in Him. Where we were once subject to evil, we are now raised up in glory, free to live in the joy of His mercy and truth. We had been separated from God, but now we can be called His children. We are shown mercy instead of wrath, joy instead of sorrow, eternal life instead of eternal separation and death. He continues to be our King and our Friend. He is preparing a place for us in heaven, where we will have the blessing of praising Him forever.

That's why we praise Him; that's why we sing. He gave Himself up for our salvation—that's why we offer Him our everything.

I have come as a light to shine in this dark world, so that all who put their trust in me will no longer remain in the darkness.

—JOHN 12:46 NLT

Prayer

Thank Jesus for dying for your sins that you
might be reconciled to God. Offer Him all that
you are that He may use you for His glory.

JESUS, JESUS

She had been under the care of many doctors, but instead of getting better, she only became worse. When she heard about Jesus, she sought Him out and found Him in the midst of a crowd. Because her illness caused her to be considered "unclean," she assumed Jesus would not want to touch her. So she came up behind Him in the crowd and touched His cloak, thinking, "If I just touch His clothes, I will be healed." She was right. Immediately, she was freed from her suffering.

Jesus felt the power go from Him, so He asked who touched His clothes. The woman, trembling in fear, admitted what she had done. To her surprise, Jesus replied, "Daughter, your faith has healed you. Go in peace" (Mark 5:25-34).

In times of desperation and pain, we can reach out to Him and He will respond to our faith and bless us beyond measure. When we look to Him to heal our brokenness and sorrow, we understand the real Jesus—the One who came not only to help us in this life, but to make a place for us in eternity.

So put your faith into action. Reach up to God. One touch of His hand brings healing to your hurting soul. One touch of His life brings glory so that your life will overflow.

And we, who with unveiled faces all reflect the Lord's glory, are being transformed into his likeness with ever-increasing glory, which comes from the Lord, who is the Spirit.

—2 CORINTHIANS 3:18

Prayer

Ask the Lord to touch your life—offer Him your hurt
and your pain and trust in the power of His love.

JESUS, YOUR NAME

Jesus has many names. He called Himself the Son of Man, emphasizing His humanity (John 3:13). He called Himself the bread of life. Bread, giving sustenance and energy, refers to His role as a giver of life—eternal life (John 6:35). He referred to Himself as the gate for the sheep; He also called Himself the good shepherd (John 10:7, 11). Those names focused on His love and guidance, affirming that He is the only way to God's kingdom.

The most powerful of His names is "the resurrection and the life" (John 11:25), for this embodies all of the healing, power, light, might, and holiness that cause us to bow down in praise. Powerful things can happen when we call upon the name of Jesus—the disciples healed the sick in the name of Jesus, and the dead were raised in the name of Jesus!

Think about the names you have for Jesus: faithful Friend, Deliverer, Healer, Master, Savior, precious Lord, King of kings. Each name is an accurate description of Him. What is He to you today? Do you need power and might to face a battle ahead? Call on His name. Do you need to break strongholds in your life or experience healing? Call on His name. Call on the name of Jesus, for His name is above every other.

Therefore God exalted him to the highest place and gave him the name that is above every name, that at the name of Jesus every knee should bow, in heaven and on earth and under the earth.

—PHILIPPIANS 2:9-10

Prayer

Call Jesus by the name that means the most to you today.
Thank Him that His name brings healing and life.

TIMES OF REFRESHING

*T*here is no greater joy than to be with the Lord. Have you found that to be true in your own life? Do you anxiously sit down to open your Bible? Do you hurry with other tasks in order to have time to talk with God?

That's what Jesus did. The Bible tells us of many times when Jesus went off alone to be with His Father. Mark wrote that "very early in the morning, while it was still dark, Jesus got up, left the house and went off to a solitary place, where he prayed" (Mark 1:35). The life of Christ is our example. If Jesus needed to meet with His Heavenly Father, how much more do we! Only by communicating with Him will we learn to walk in His ways and be able to follow Him step by step. When we follow where He leads, He promises to make our paths straight (Proverbs 3:5-6). He longs for us to follow Him because He knows what good and wonderful things He has in store just down the road.

Seek God in the morning and all day long. Experience His refreshment, enjoy His blessings. Let your soul be restored and your mind renewed. Experience the great joy of being with your Lord.

Repent, then, and turn to God, so that your sins may be wiped out, that times of refreshing may come from the Lord, and that He may send the Christ, who has been appointed for you—even Jesus.

—ACTS 3:19-20

Prayer

Find time alone to focus on God.
Experience His refreshment. Ask Him to restore
your soul and renew your mind. Enjoy Him!

I NEED YOU MORE

When we truly love someone, that love grows deeper day by day. We come to realize that we indeed love that person more than yesterday, and our love will continue to grow deeper on into the future.

The same holds true with our love for Jesus. As time goes by, the more we know Him, the more we love Him. We needed Him to cleanse us and make our lives whole, and He met that need! Now we find that we continue to need Him more and more every day because we are learning to trust Him more and more each day.

His grace is sufficient for us and His love is never-ending. What a blessing to know that the old life is gone for good. Because we have been freed from a life of brokenness and have entered the presence of the Lord, we will never be alone again.

More than a breath of fresh air, more than a heartbeat, we need the Lord. Without Him, life would be lonely, sad and empty—and death would mean eternal separation from Him. We were meant to be filled with His Spirit. We belong in His presence.

Don't be ashamed to tell Jesus, "I need You more—more even than I needed You yesterday!" It's not a sign of weakness; it's a sign of coming home where you belong.

The LORD is good, a refuge in times of trouble. He cares for those who trust in him.

—NAHUM 1:7

Prayer

Tell the Lord how much you need Him. Praise Him for healing your broken heart and staying by your side.

I Need You /
Strength of My Life

Even the strongest people will, at some point, need to slow down and rest. They have need of the power of Christ just as much as the weak.

Those who are strong often have difficulty admitting their need for mercy, for forgiveness. But Jesus didn't die just for those who are weak—He died for all of us! He knows everything about us, from the way we go about our day to our deepest needs; He even knows the number of our days on this earth! He created us, He will sustain us, and He will always be there to help us when we call.

Unlike us, He will never grow tired or weary. He is the strength that keeps us going day after day. We all have twenty-four hours in a day, seven days in a week, and fifty-two weeks in a year—we must use the days given to us to honor Him.

No one can fathom His mercy and understanding or His willingness to meet all of our needs. When you feel the crushing weight of life on this earth, admit your need and call upon God to renew your strength. He will answer. Be strong and take heart, all you who hope in the Lord (Psalm 31:24)!

The LORD is my strength and my shield; my heart trusts in him, and I am helped. My heart leaps for joy and I will give thanks to him in song.

—Psalm 28:7

Prayer

Praise Him for being the strength of your life,
and for knowing everything about you and
still loving and forgiving you.

I WANT TO BE MORE LIKE YOU

I"I want to be more like You" is a prayer we should pray continuously. As Paul told the Philippians, "Your attitude should be the same as that of Christ Jesus" (Philippians 2:5).

Being like Jesus is not an easy task. Jesus was a living sacrifice. In His humility, He was willing to give up His life in order to do the will of His Father and provide salvation for us all. For us to imitate that would require sacrificing our selfishness and pride; it would require dying to ourselves and accepting His lordship over us. The tough thing about a living sacrifice is, it wants to crawl off the altar and run away—it doesn't want to die!

So how can we be more like Jesus? It seems impossible. Fortunately, we don't have to do it on our own. The Holy Spirit within us teaches us humility and obedience. We can indeed be transformed; we can indeed be more like Him. The Bible says, "Those who become Christians become new persons. They are not the same anymore, for the old life is gone. A new life has begun!" (2 Corinthians 5:17 NLT).

Allow Jesus to change you, to transform your heart and mind, that you may be a vessel for His use. Cry out to Him today and every day, "Jesus, I want to be more like You!"

Dear friends, now we are children of God, and what we will be has not yet been made known. But we know that when he appears, we shall be like him, for we shall see him as he is.

—1 JOHN 3:2

Prayer

Repeat the words, "I want to be more like You,"
with sincerity and commitment. Pray that Jesus
will help you be more like Him day by day.

GOD IS IN THE HOUSE

*I*s God at home in your home? In other words, does His presence permeate the atmosphere of your home? Does your family find a sanctuary of God's presence and peace when they walk through the front door? Do guests find a joyful welcome?

Too many homes are like war zones. There is anger, piercing words, painful hurts, even heavy silence. Even Christian homes are seldom sanctuaries of peace. We run from activity to activity, job to job, commitment to commitment. Lost is the art of conversation by a family around the dinner table. Seldom do guests come our way. Few and far between are the conversations with the neighbors next door or down the block.

God would not have it that way. He wants to lift us up above the world we know and set us in a higher place. He wants us to look from His perspective. He would have us invite Him into our homes as a permanent guest. He desires that our home be little oases of peace, joy, and love in an all too often unpeaceful, joyless, unloving world.

What happens when you open your front door? Is God there? Begin today to make your home a place where God dwells, a place that invites your family and friends to come and experience Him.

And now, O Israel, what does the LORD your God ask of you but to fear the LORD your God, to walk in all his ways, to love him, to serve the LORD your God with all your heart and with all your soul.

—DEUTERONOMY 10:12

Prayer

Close your eyes and think about the atmosphere in your home.
Ask God to dwell there constantly.

ABOVE ALL ELSE

Who is Jesus Christ to you? Is He just a prophet or great teacher, or is He the mighty warrior who has conquered the darkness of sin in your life?

As Christians, we know Jesus Christ is the Son of God sent down from heaven. Because of what He has done for us, we must place Him at the highest place in our lives—the throne of our hearts. Right now where we stand and everywhere we go, we must place Him front and center so that the world may know who He is and what He has done for us. When other people or things, take priority in our lives, we must step back and take a look at what is most important. The psalmist said, "For you, O LORD, are the Most High over all the earth; you are exalted far above all gods" (Psalm 97:9). Therefore, the only place fit for Him is to be first and foremost in all we do.

Maybe you know who Jesus is to you, but where is He in your life? Have you put Him on the throne or locked Him in a closet? Today, talk to Him about placing Him in the highest place, central to all you do. When you do, you'll find victory—in this life and in the next.

The one who comes from above is above all; the one who is from the earth belongs to the earth, and speaks as one from the earth. The one who comes from heaven is above all.

—JOHN 3:31

Prayer

Ask the Lord to take the throne of your life
that you may hold Him above all else.

O MOST HIGH

Change can be very threatening. We don't like to see changes in the world—war looming and terrorists lurking. We don't like to see our friends' marriages dissolve, or watch them self-destruct in other ways. We don't like the way the arrival of a new boss changes a job we so enjoyed. We don't like the change in our church when things don't go as planned. Changes for the worse can be extremely painful. How we long for a change for the better.

Thankfully, we have a stronghold in this changing world. Our Lord is unchanging. He is the same loving and just Lord who created the heavens and the earth. He will be the same God when we see Him face to face in glory. He is our stronghold when we are besieged by the enemy. He is our hiding place when we need a refuge. And He will never forsake us when we seek Him.

Give thanks to the Lord with all your heart! He never changes—what an amazing comfort for us! The God who kept His promises to Abraham, guided Moses, gave strength to Joshua, loved David, forgave Peter, and empowered Paul is the same God who is at work in your life today. He has no need to change because He is perfect. His love, His sacrifice, and His grace have paved the way for your salvation. He can take care of the sins of your yesterdays, the struggles of your todays, and the worries about your tomorrows. So move forward with confidence, for the Lord Most High goes with you!

Jesus Christ is the same yesterday and today and forever.

—HEBREWS 13:8

---•---

Prayer

Are you facing a difficult change today? Talk to the
unchanging God about your frustrations and fears.
Be thankful that you can always count on Him.

---•---

LORD MOST HIGH

Stories of God's love and understanding are passed down from parent to child, from generation to generation. When we hear stories of God touching the lives of our parents and grandparents, our hearts are warmed and our spirit rejoices. If we are the ones to begin the song for future generations, then we have a story to tell and plenty of praising to do!

We praise our Lord Most High for all He has done in our lives. We praise Him for the promises of the future, when every nation will bow and acknowledge that He is the rightful King of all. We praise Him for the earth itself that knows its Creator and blazes with color and sound in an effort to praise the living God.

Do you want to pass your faith along to your children or others in your sphere of influence? Then join in the chorus of praise that is echoing across all of creation. There is no place on earth where you could go that God will not be with you. If you climb the highest mountain peak, praise Him from there. If you dive to the depths of the sea, praise Him from there. If you're feeling weak, praise Him even with what little strength you have. When you do, God will be glorified and you will be a living example of the power of your Lord Most High.

Let them know that you, whose name is the LORD—that you alone are the Most High over all the earth.

—PSALM 83:18

Prayer

Pray that God will make Himself known in your life that others may see your example and join the song of praise.

BE MAGNIFIED

It's so easy for us to try to go it alone, isn't it? We forge ahead, working on sheer emotion or will. We dash headlong into a situation thinking we can handle it all on our own. This is a little problem, why bother God with it?

Or, on the flip side, we don't go it alone; we just run away. The problem seems as big as an enemy army and so we hide in the castle, pulling up the drawbridge behind us. This is a big problem, maybe even too big for God. Or because it's a problem of our own making, we think God doesn't care.

In both cases, we've developed an out-of-focus view of God. We think He's too big to deal with our little problems, or He's too small to deal with our big problems. When we see God as smaller and less powerful than He is, we miss out on the blessings of His strength to help us. When we set aside His promises to be with us through everything we face—small or big, our own fault or not—we miss out on experiencing His mercy and grace to help us in our time of need.

Is your God too small? Then He needs to be magnified. Ask God to fix your vision and bring His power into clear sight for whatever situation you face today.

Oh, magnify the LORD with me, and let us exalt His name together.

—PSALM 34:3 NKJV

Prayer

Seek the Lord's forgiveness for the times when you have
lost faith. Ask Him to open your eyes to His strength
and glory that He may be magnified through you.

REDEEMER, SAVIOR, FRIEND

The hill was Golgotha, located on a roadway outside of Jerusalem. The stripes on His back came from a leather whip studded at the ends with pieces of bone—designed to rip and tear flesh. The thorns had made a "crown," fashioned of branches from a thorn bush, then pressed down upon His head. The nails pounded into His hands and feet secured Him to the wooden cross, guaranteeing a slow and agonizing death.

Why?

Because with His "eternal eyes," God had designed a way to bring sinful humanity to Himself. The blood sacrifices of the Old Testament became one perfect sacrificial Lamb hung on a cross, killed to take away sin. And when it was over, death and sin had been forever defeated and access provided for sinful humanity to the throne of God.

Jesus was devoted to the end. Every thorn that pierced His brow, every nail that went through His guiltless hands told how His love has no end.

He did this just for you. When He went to the cross, you were on His mind. If you had been the only person on the planet, He'd have done the same. He is your Redeemer, your Savior, and your Friend. What can you do for such a Friend? Thank Him, praise Him, love Him, live for Him.

Greater love has no one than this, that he lay down his life for his friends.

—JOHN 15:13

Prayer

Dwell upon what Christ went through for you. Thank Him for His sacrifice and praise Him for giving you life eternal through His name.

HALLOWED BE THY NAME

Hallowed means holy, sacred. Above all that Jesus is to us, He is holy. He is set apart, perfect, untouched by sin, clean, pure. It was that very holiness that allowed Him to be the perfect sacrifice for our sins. Perfect God, perfect man united to take the punishment for sin that we deserved. And because He is holy—hallowed—He is the only one worthy of our praise.

The song goes on to give us more names of Jesus, all found in the Bible. He is love (1 John 4:8), He is life (John 1:4), He is Lord over everything (Deuteronomy 10:17). He's the Alpha and Omega (Revelation 1:8) and the King of kings (1 Timothy 6:15). He makes a way for us (Isaiah 43:19).

We can go to Him with our problems and He will help us solve them (Psalm 34:19). In His grace and goodness, He will supply all our needs (Philippians 4:19). When difficult times threaten to close in upon us, He is a fortress into which we can run (Psalm 18:2); because He loves us, we are more than conquerors in all situations (Romans 8:37).

He is God—the one and only holy Lord, and He alone is worthy of your praise. The Bible overflows with His promises to you. Do you want your soul set on fire for God? Then meditate on all He has done for you, praise Him for His promises, and honor His holy name.

In this manner, therefore, pray: Our Father in heaven, hallowed be Your name.

—MATTHEW 6:9 NKJV

Prayer

Think about the holiness of Jesus, about how His name is sacred above all other names. Pray to Him with that in mind—that you are approaching the holy God who is worthy of your praise.

JESUS IS MINE

The idea that we belong to Jesus is at once both a comforting and a convicting thought. How wonderful to know that Jesus is ours! He is with us all the time. In the morning and in the evening, all day long, with us wherever we go...

So where did your feet take you today? Were you aware of Jesus' presence? Did your knowledge of His proximity make a difference in what you said and how you acted? Do you think the people with whom you interacted might have been surprised to know that you claim the name of Jesus?

King David asked, "Where can I go from your Spirit?...If I go up to the heavens, you are there; if I make my bed in the depths, you are there...If I settle on the far side of the sea, even there your hand will guide me" (Psalm 139:7-10). The apostle Paul exulted that nothing "in all creation, will be able to separate us from the love of God" (Romans 8:39). If Jesus is yours—your Savior and your Lord—rejoice in the fact of His presence!

But realize that this is also an awesome responsibility. You represent Christ wherever you go. By your actions and attitudes, you either draw people one step closer to Christ or you turn them off to Him. Everywhere you go, Jesus goes with you. Morning, evening, all day long!

Praise the LORD. Praise the LORD, O my soul. I will praise the LORD all my life; I will sing praise to my God as long as I live.

—PSALM 146:1-2

Prayer

Praise the Lord for His constant presence in your life—for being with you through every day of your life, and for all of eternity.

HOW GREAT ARE YOU LORD

How great are You, Lord! Considering all that God has done for us, an outburst of praise is only natural. We have so much to praise Him for!

Think of His mercy, His undeserved favor. We did nothing to cause Him to love us. We did not deserve His love, but He loved us anyway. Mercy alone caused Him to reach out to a dying world and give His life so that we might live.

Think of all that He has done for us. He redeemed us, saved us, called us to be His own, and sent us His Spirit to strengthen and guide us all the days of our lives.

Think of His kindness, that He lovingly reaches down to protect us when we are in danger, encourage us when we are downtrodden, comfort us when we are hurting.

Think of such love that would seek us and rescue us. Such love is unfathomable, such love is unimaginable, such love is drenched upon us from our great Lord.

Great is the LORD and most worthy of praise; his greatness no one can fathom.

—PSALM 145:3

Prayer

Remember that Jesus sought you in your sin
and rescued you from it. Thank Him and
praise Him for His greatness in your life.

LEAD ME, OH LEAD ME

Most of us are not content to follow—we like to lead! As human beings, we automatically want to go our own way, sure of ourselves that our way is the right way.

When we put aside our selfishness and pride, we can then admit that we don't know the way. We can acknowledge that we need to follow someone greater than ourselves—that we need to be led in the right direction.

God knows the direction our lives will take long before we are even capable of choosing what crayon to use in a coloring book. When we are willing to be led by the Spirit, He will bring us to Himself. He will show us the path of the cross and bring us to our knees. When we pour out our heart and soul to Him, He will listen. He is always present, always listening for our call, always waiting for us to ask for His leading in our lives.

What questions do you have today? What guidance do you need? Ask Jesus to meet you at the cross. Why there? Because when you look upon the cross, you cannot help but set aside all your pride, get down on your knees, and feel the very breath of God.

I will lead the blind by ways they have not known, along unfamiliar paths I will guide them; I will turn the darkness into light before them and make the rough places smooth. These are the things I will do; I will not forsake them.

—ISAIAH 42:16

Prayer

Pour out your heart to God and ask for
His leading in every situation in your life.

AH, LORD GOD

He desperately wanted a child, but both he and his wife were old. God had made a promise, but He certainly seemed to be in no hurry to keep it. Didn't God understand that there would be a certain age beyond which childbearing would be impossible?

Then God came once again, repeating the promise and asking, "Is anything too hard for the Lord?" (Genesis 18:14).

The prophet Jeremiah had warned the nation of Judah that God would punish them. Yet God had also promised to return His people to their land. To prove the reliability of that promise, God told His prophet to buy a plot of land—now in enemy hands. Not seemingly a very good investment.

Yet Jeremiah trusted God. "Nothing is too hard for you," he said (Jeremiah 32:17).

Fast forward. Jesus has explained that it is difficult for the rich to enter the kingdom. The astonished disciples ask, "Who then can be saved?"

Jesus answered, "With man this is impossible, but with God all things are possible" (Matthew 19:26).

Our God is the God of the impossible. When the situation looks bleak, when all hope is gone, "with God all things are possible." When the problem is too big, ask yourself, "Is anything too hard for the Lord?" And then answer yourself, "Nothing is too difficult for Him!"

Ah Lord GOD! Behold, Thou hast made the heavens and the earth by Thy great power and by Thine outstretched arm! Nothing is too difficult for Thee.

—JEREMIAH 32:17 NASB

Prayer

Come to God with the knowledge that nothing is too difficult for Him—His counsel is perfect and His power is overwhelming.

JESUS, WE CELEBRATE
YOUR VICTORY

We celebrate His victory because His victory means we also have victory! Satan had his major victories in the Garden of Eden and at the cross (or so he thought). But God turned Satan's victory into utter and devastating defeat when Jesus rose from the dead.

Death no longer brings fear to our hearts. "Where, O death, is your victory? Where, O death, is your sting?" (1 Corinthians 15:55). Jesus defeated death when He broke through its grasp and rose from the grave. We now have hope that extends beyond the grave and into eternity!

Jesus has set us free from the bondage of sin, from the stronghold of death, and from the power of Satan. His Spirit releases us from fear. Jesus opened the door from death to life and gave us the victory.

With the door now open, we can enter the presence of the Lord. We can draw near to Him and respond to His love. He will flood our hearts with peace and our problems will disappear in the presence of His greatness. "For everyone born of God overcomes the world. This is the victory that has overcome the world, even our faith" (1 John 5:4).

We can celebrate our victory in Jesus, because He is victorious over all!

Death has been swallowed up in victory.

—1 CORINTHIANS 15:54

Prayer

Thank the Lord for His victory over sin and death,
and for passing on that victory to you.

THIS KINGDOM

The Pharisees asked Jesus when the kingdom of God would come. They were looking for a kingdom on earth in which God would vanquish all enemies and become a ruler. Jesus responded to their question by telling them that the kingdom of God "is within you" (Luke 17:20-21). The kingdom of God is the work of the Holy Spirit within the hearts of those who trust in Jesus.

The kingdom of God is here—it is now. If we have given our hearts to Jesus, if we have committed ourselves to His power, His kingdom is within us! The grace of God, His word, and His holiness are displayed for all to see as His will is done in us and as we live to honor Him.

But make no mistake. There will indeed be a physical kingdom—a time when Christ shall reign on this earth. We are awaiting that kingdom, anticipating its arrival with joy. In that kingdom, "the dwelling of God is with men, and he will live with them...He will wipe every tear from their eyes. There will be no more death or mourning or crying or pain, for the old order of things has passed away" (Revelation 21:3-4).

This kingdom will know no end. Its glory will know no bounds. This kingdom is ours because of Christ Jesus. "Amen. Come, Lord Jesus."

Your kingdom is an everlasting kingdom, and your dominion endures through all generations. The LORD is faithful to all his promises and loving toward all he has made.

—PSALM 145:13

Prayer

Pray the Lord's Prayer, knowing that His kingdom has come in your heart because you have placed your faith in Him.

THE HAPPY SONG

Nehemiah's task had not been easy. Called by God to return to Jerusalem and encourage the rebuilding of the city's wall, Nehemiah had faced numerous setbacks and frustrations—enough to make most of us mount our donkeys and be gone. But not Nehemiah. No matter what new opposition surfaced, Nehemiah constantly prayed for God's guidance and encouraged the people. Under his leadership, the people finished the wall in fifty-two days.

The next step was to remind the people of the law of God. When Ezra read the law, the people realized how far they had strayed, and they wept. But Nehemiah told them to focus on the future, to commit to serving God. "This day is sacred to the LORD your God. Do not grieve, for the joy of the Lord is your strength" (Nehemiah 8:10).

Perhaps you feel convicted by God's Word. Sin seems to overwhelm you. Take courage from Nehemiah's example. Begin rebuilding your relationship with God. Mourn for your past sins, but then commit to obedience in the future. Let this be a day of rejoicing. Let your voice sing and your feet dance! Tell others how He saved you and how He changed your life.

Shout it out—sing from the rooftops! Let your joy be heard far beyond the confines of your heart. Everybody sing, everybody dance—joy is in this place!

And on that day they offered great sacrifices, rejoicing because God had given them great joy. The women and children also rejoiced. The sound of rejoicing in Jerusalem could be heard far away.

—NEHEMIAH 12:43

Prayer

Rejoice that the Lord has wiped away the past and saved your soul. Praise Him with all of your being.

DAYS OF ELIJAH

In the Old Testament, the Year of Jubilee was meant to be celebrated every fifty years. This would have been a time of great rejoicing among the Israelites. As dictated in Leviticus 25, all debts were to be cancelled, all land returned to its original owners, and all slaves set free.

Unfortunately, there is no record of this celebration ever being carried out. But when Jesus came, He gave every one of us a Year of Jubilee, not just once every fifty years, but every day! Thanks to His sacrifice, our debts of sin are cancelled whenever we ask, we are promised a place in eternity, and we are made free by the power of His love.

Such good news must be shared! We may feel like voices in the desert, but we need to call out this wonderful message to all who will hear, just as the prophets Elijah, Moses, and Ezekiel did so many years ago.

The fields are ready to be harvested. Will you join the prophets of old in sharing the message of forgiveness, freedom, and a fantastic future?

Oh, that salvation for Israel would come out of Zion!...Look, he is coming with the clouds, and every eye will see him.

—PSALM 53:6; REVELATION 1:7

Prayer

Ask the Lord to help you share the joy of your salvation
so others may know the freedom of jubilee.

I SEE THE LORD

*I*n our daily lives, filled with pressure and frustration, we often don't see God as He really is. We tend to push Him aside, too busy to focus on His holiness.

When we recognize how great God is, we realize how we could never enter His presence if not for what Jesus did for us. We who were unclean and impure have received forgiveness. We have been given the ability to see the Lord in all of His holiness and power. We have been given the honor of being called heirs of the King, able to be in His presence forever and evermore.

The Lord, the Lamb upon the throne, is surrounded by praise. The Book of Revelation gives us a snapshot: "Each of the four living creatures had six wings and was covered with eyes all around, even under his wings. Day and night they never stop saying: 'Holy, holy, holy is the Lord God Almighty, who was, and is, and is to come'" (Revelation 4:8).

We can cry out in fellowship with all believers that Jesus Christ is holy—He is the Lamb and He alone is worthy of our praise. So join with the heavenly worshipers and proclaim the holiness and glory of the Lord!

They will see his face, and his name will be on their foreheads. There will be no more night. They will not need the light of a lamp or the light of the sun, for the Lord God will give them light. And they will reign for ever and ever.

—REVELATION 22:4-5

Prayer

Ask the Lord to help you to see Him high and exalted.
Praise Him for His power and glory.

SING, SHOUT, CLAP

The book of Psalms is a collection of songs and prayers to the Lord. The writers chose to sing their praises to God and record their songs so that others, ourselves included, would someday join them in praise. The words they sang are timeless, applying to our lives even today.

Just as in days long past, we who believe in God demonstrate our joy when we sing, shout, and clap our hands. We can make a joyful noise unto the Lord!

Our reasons for praise are many, and the depth of our gratitude may sometimes leave us speechless. But when we sing songs exalting His holiness, shout for the joy of our salvation, and clap our hands in gratitude for all He has done for us, He responds with unmeasured blessings.

The songs we sing give praise to our Maker. The shout of the righteous has the power to tear down walls. Our hands rejoice that the Lord our God is our Deliverer. So, sing, shout, and clap your hands for this is the day to rejoice!

Come, let us sing for joy to the LORD; let us shout aloud to the Rock of our salvation.

—PSALM 95:1

Prayer

Sing for joy to the Lord; shout aloud to the
Rock of your salvation; clap your hands in
gratitude for all He has done for you.

YOU ARE CROWNED WITH MANY CROWNS

Jesus first came to earth as a helpless baby. He was born of the Virgin Mary, grew up learning the family business (carpentry), and didn't begin His ministry until He was thirty years old. As a human being, He suffered at the hands of other human beings. He became like a Lamb, sacrificed for the sins of everyone. He came first to redeem us.

When Jesus comes again, He will come as the ultimate conqueror and King of all kings. He will wear the crowns of all nations. He will rule with power. He will bring judgment to the people of the earth. He will rule in power and reign in glory. He will separate those who know and obey Him from those who do not (2 Thessalonians 1:7–10). Those who have accepted His forgiveness will stand before Him without fear for He will claim them as His own children. Those who have rejected Him will, in turn, be rejected.

Which group will you be in? If you know Him and love Him, you will join with the multitude, rejoicing and giving Him the glory. He is returning, He is Lord of heaven and earth. Your acceptance or denial of these facts does not change them, but it does change you—both for now and for eternity.

His eyes are like blazing fire, and on his head are many crowns. He has a name written on him that no one knows but he himself.

—REVELATION 19:12

Prayer

If you have accepted Christ as your Lord, rejoice that you will someday stand before God and be recognized as His child. If not, what is keeping you from taking that step?

IN HIM WE LIVE

When we awake each morning, some of us hop out of bed and greet the day with a smile; some of us hit the snooze button and groan as we pull the covers over our head. Eventually, we face the day—we "live and move and have our being."

No matter how we greet the dawn, we should be thankful for each day we are given. Whether you've jumped out of bed in joyous anticipation or are still hiding under the covers, you can take a few moments to pray, asking God's guidance for every step of your day. In Him you live and move and have your being—so ask Him to make you a good example for Him throughout your day, at work, at school, in the store, on the road. Ask Him to keep you keenly aware of His presence to guide, help, and comfort each step of the way.

Then get out of bed and, if you can do it, sing unto the Lord! If you can't sing that early, then just tell Him of your love—He is the reason you live. Need some early morning exercise? Dance before Him—He is the reason you move. If your voice leaves something to be desired, then just make a joyful noise—He is the reason you have your being!

"For in him we live and move and have our being." As some of your own poets have said, "We are his offspring."

—ACTS 17:28

Prayer

Thank the Lord for giving you a reason to live.
Ask Him to teach you what it means to live,
move, and have your being in Him.

I LOVE TO PRAISE HIM

*T*he Bible is full of people praising God! They loved to praise Him then just as we love to praise Him today—and probably for many of the same reasons. Here are some examples:

"You will have plenty to eat, until you are full, and you will praise the name of the LORD your God, who has worked wonders for you" (Joel 2:26).

"Seven times a day I praise you for your righteous laws" (Psalm 119:164).

"I thank and praise you, O God of my fathers: You have given me wisdom and power" (Daniel 2:23)

"He jumped to his feet and began to walk. Then he went with them into the temple courts, walking and jumping, and praising God" (Acts 3:8).

"Jehoshaphat appointed men to sing to the LORD and to praise him for the splendor of his holiness as they went out at the head of the army, saying: 'Give thanks to the LORD, for his love endures forever'" (2 Chronicles 20:21).

Now, just as in biblical times, we praise God for providing our basic needs, for teaching us rules to live by, for giving us wisdom and power, for healing our brokenness, and most importantly, for His holiness and His love which endure forever.

Sing hallelujah and lift up His holy name. Praise and exalt the Lord on high for He has done great things!

But you are a chosen people, a royal priesthood, a holy nation, a people belonging to God, that you may declare the praises of him who called you out of darkness into his wonderful light.

—1 PETER 2:9

Prayer

What can you praise God for today? For meeting your needs? For providing you with His Word? For giving you wisdom and power to handle a certain situation? For healing and help? For His holiness and love? Be specific as you praise Him.

CHANGE MY HEART, O GOD

A true desire to change comes from a heart that trusts in Jesus. Before we put our faith in Him, we could not understand spiritual things. We couldn't comprehend God or how He could possibly work in our lives.

While no one, believer or non-believer, can ever fully comprehend God, by the help of His Spirit we can be led to obey and grow. The Spirit will whisper in our hearts and fill us with the desire to follow the Lord.

In 1 Corinthians 2:14, the apostle Paul tells us that those without the Spirit of God cannot understand or accept the things that come from the Spirit. Why? Because the lines of communication were never established. Because they were not willing to change, to grow, or to obey the Spirit of the Lord.

Praise the Lord that He provided His Spirit to those who trust in Him. He has taken away the desires that drive us from Him and has replaced them with the desire to follow Christ. No matter where He leads, we will follow. We will trust and obey.

We have not received the spirit of the world but the Spirit who is from God, that we may understand what God has freely given us.

—1 CORINTHIANS 2:12

Prayer

Make the words of this song your prayer. Ask God to change your heart, take away desires that drive you from Him, and fill you with a desire to follow and obey.

BLESSED BE THE NAME
OF THE LORD

Blessed be the name of the Lord, for that name brings life and power to all who call. His name is many different things to many people, and each name describes His attributes.

He is the Lord of Glory, Lord Almighty, and the King of kings—strength, power and majesty pour down from His throne. He is the Eternal Father—we can run to Him with our problems and He will lovingly guide us. He is the Bread of Life—He sustains us and provides for our most basic human needs. He is Yahweh, Redeemer, Deliverer—He purchased our freedom with His own blood as the payment for our sins. He is Messiah, Jehovah—the anointed one who delivers us. He is the Prince of Peace—no one else could bring peace to our hearts, minds, and souls. He is the soon and coming King—those who know Him will meet Him in the air.

Every aspect of our lives is enveloped by the many names of the Lord. He brings light to the darkness and healing to the broken spirit. When we seek Him in all of His righteousness and glory, we find exactly what we need, for He is everything to everyone in every situation. All we need to do is call on Him. Blessed be the name of the Lord!

And everyone who calls on the name of the Lord will be saved.

—ACTS 2:21

Prayer

Call upon the name of the Lord and He will answer. Call upon
Him with the name that most matches your need today—
Father, Bread of Life, Redeemer, Deliverer.

NO HIGHER CALLING

Kneeling humbly at the feet of Jesus is the highest place we could be. Two women who were contemporaries of Jesus found this out for themselves.

Mary, the sister of Lazarus and Martha, welcomed Jesus into her home. While her sister was preparing the meal, Mary chose to sit at the feet of Jesus listening to what He said. Jesus praised her, saying she had chosen what was better—spending time with Him. Her devotion was more important than anything else (Luke 10:38-42).

At another time, Mary again sat at Jesus' feet, this time pouring expensive perfume on Jesus' feet and wiping them with her hair. Her sacrifice provided a lesson for the disciples about the divinity of Jesus (John 12:1-11).

In a separate, yet similar incident, a woman referred to only as having "lived a sinful life" entered the house where Jesus was a guest and knelt at His feet. She too poured perfume on His feet and it mingled with her tears. Jesus extended the ultimate gift to her for her love and devotion when He said to her, "Your sins are forgiven" (Luke 7:38-50). She was embraced by His mercy.

We, too, will find our highest glory and our highest calling when we humbly kneel at His feet.

Come, let us bow down in worship, let us kneel before the LORD our Maker.

—PSALM 95:6

Prayer

Kneel as you come into the presence of the Lord. Pray that He will embrace you with His power, His glory, and His mercy.

MORE OF YOU

When we come to the end of a long and tiring day, when our strength and energy are depleted, we need something to revive us. As a long, cool drink of water quenches our thirst on a sizzling day, so we need something to quench our thirst for meaning behind all of the endless activity of life. The world offers only empty platitudes, leaving us dry and unfulfilled.

When we let Jesus quench our thirst, however, we find that He fills us up to overflowing. As the psalmist said, "My cup overflows" (Psalm 23:5). And He fills us with living water. As He told the woman at the well, "The water I give them takes away thirst altogether. It becomes a perpetual spring within them, giving them eternal life" (John 4:13-14 NLT).

So Jesus says to you, "If you are thirsty, come to me!" (John 7:37 NLT). When you thirst for meaning, purpose, revival, or restoration, you need only to seek the Lord and ask for more of the living water. All you could ever need or desire can be found in Him, and He is faithful to satisfy.

All you want is more—that's not asking much when you know that the source is unending, that the river will never run dry. Say to Him, "All I want is more of You!"

If you are thirsty, come to me! If you believe in me, come and drink! For the Scriptures declare that rivers of living water will flow out from within.

—JOHN 7:37-38 NLT

Prayer

Ask the Lord for more—more of His mercy, His love, and His presence in your life. Ask Him to fill you to overflowing that you may be an example of His love.

PREPARE THE WAY

If you're like most people, the occasion of guests coming to your home requires preparation, perhaps scooping up piles of stuff and tossing it into the back reaches of your house, carefully closing the door on the mess. A quick swipe at piles of dust makes your home presentable. Why do we go through this ritual? Because we want to present our best selves.

Jesus is coming—He announced it long ago. The only problem is that He didn't say when He would arrive. To make our hearts and our homes ready for Jesus requires something more than stashing extraneous material behind closed doors, however. It means we need to keep our lives free of the clutter of useless thoughts or harmful activities. It means not allowing the dust to collect on our obedience and faithfulness. It means we are constantly watching, always ready for His arrival.

John the Baptist prepared the people to meet Jesus. They came to him confessing their sins. As Christians today preparing the way for Jesus, we should follow the example of those early converts. The apostle Paul later wrote, "So be careful how you live, not as fools but as those who are wise. Make the most of every opportunity for doing good in these evil days" (Ephesians 5:15-16 NLT).

Is your heart ready for Jesus' return? Is your life helping to prepare the way for others to meet Him as well?

It is written in Isaiah the prophet: "I will send my messenger ahead of you, who will prepare your way"—"a voice of one calling in the desert, 'Prepare the way for the Lord, make straight paths for him.'"

—MARK 1:2-3

Prayer

Ask the Lord to show you where you might need to do some cleanup work in your heart. Ask Him to help you prepare others for Him to make His way into their hearts and lives.

NEW SONG ARISIN'

Sometimes we wonder if God hears our prayers. We pray and plead, and then we wait. Sometimes the waiting is the hardest part. But we can rest assured that God does hear us when we call—He will answer our prayers and give us a new song, a hymn of praise to sing of our joy!

Take Abraham for example. He prayed and asked God for a son; twenty-four years later, God granted his request and Isaac was born. "Is anything too hard for the LORD?" the angels asked Abraham in Genesis 18:14. In the heart of Abraham was a song of hope, a song of peace—God had blessed him with a child.

We can have that same joy when we put our trust in the Lord! We can sing a new song, one of hope and peace, liberation and victory. "The music He gives sets the nations free." As His children, we know He hears our prayers as well as our praises. His song sets us free!

What are the needs in your life? Take them to the Lord in prayer and trust that He will answer. Put your hope in the One who gives you a new song to sing, for the music He gives is unlike any other in the world. Sing with a joyful heart! Hallelujah!

He put a new song in my mouth, a hymn of praise to our God. Many will see and fear and put their trust in the LORD.

—PSALM 40:3

Prayer

Ask the Lord for peace in all aspects of your life.
Tell Him your needs and your hopes and ask Him to
put a new song in your heart as you put your trust in Him.

STAND UP AND GIVE HIM THE PRAISE

Many have attempted to set themselves up as "gods." Confucius and Buddha were men of great wisdom. Hare Krishna spoke of peace. The Dalai Lama tells others how to show kindness and compassion. Movements, cults, and full-fledged religions surround these men, but they all have one thing in common—they were and are just human beings. Confucius, Buddha, and Krishna are dead and they never rose from the grave. Someday, the Dalai Lama will meet the same fate.

Like those self-made gods, Jesus spoke of peace and love and showed compassion to those who needed it the most. Unlike them, however, He was capable of more: He healed the sick and even raised the dead. He walked on water and calmed the raging storm. He offered Himself to God as a payment for our sins that we might not face the judgment of God. And He did something else that no one else has done—He rose from the dead and ascended into heaven, never to die again! Now, He sits at the right hand of God interceding for us and forgiving our sins.

So stand up and give Him the praise! The Lord strong and mighty, He is the only one worthy. There never was and never shall be anyone like Him. No one in heaven, on earth, or under the earth is like our Lord and Savior, Jesus Christ.

Who among the gods is like you, O LORD? Who is like you—majestic in holiness, awesome in glory, working wonders?

—EXODUS 15:11

Prayer

Praise Him for being the one and only true God, working wonders in your life and forgiving your sins. Give Him the glory He deserves.

BREATHE ON ME

Our God is all-powerful. When He wants our attention, He will get it! Sometimes He does it in the most unexpected ways.

Elijah was frightened. He'd experienced great victory against the prophets of Baal—proving that God alone was to be worshiped. But that hadn't stopped the contract put out on his life by wicked Queen Jezebel. Elijah ran away, afraid for his life and certain that he was the only one left who truly believed in God.

When God wanted to speak to His discouraged servant Elijah, He took him up on the mountain and told him that He Himself would pass by. Then came a wind powerful enough to shatter rocks, an earthquake, and a fire—but the Lord was not in any of those things. Instead, His voice came to Elijah in a quiet whisper (1 Kings 19:9-13).

When Elijah heard the voice, he went out and talked to God. Elijah told the Lord his fears and worries. The quiet and soothing voice of God responded with comfort and with a further assignment, getting Elijah back on track.

When you are weighed down by fear, doubt, and worry, you may need to sit quietly and simply ask God to breathe on you. He will restore your weary soul and speak to your heart with His gentle whisper.

Can you hear it?

And behold, the LORD passed by, and a great and strong wind tore into the mountains and broke the rocks in pieces before the LORD, but the LORD was not in the wind; and after the wind an earthquake, but the LORD was not in the earthquake; and after the earthquake a fire, but the LORD was not in the fire; and after the fire a still small voice.

—1 KINGS 19:11-12 NKJV

Prayer

Quiet yourself before the Lord. Listen with your heart and He will comfort and restore; listen for the still small voice that will lead you.

FEAR NOT

When I tuck my daughters into their beds at night, they inevitably ask that I leave on the night-light. I know their fears are unfounded, but they still need the comfort of a softly glowing light. So I leave the little light shining.

After all, I know what it's like to feel afraid. Even when I know my fears are irrational—like being afraid of the dark—I can't help but feel afraid. Sometimes, however, my fears are well founded indeed, such as when a loved one faced a difficult medical diagnosis or a tough situation at work made the future look bleak.

Unfounded or not, God has an answer for our fears. His answer is that we "fear not." Easy for Him to say, perhaps, but He also tells us why we can do that: "For I am with you." He has promised to always be with us, His children, whom He has called by name. The darkness may be terrifying, but He will be there, shining a light to guide us on our way. The diagnosis may be grim, but He will strengthen and help us. He will be there with us through it all.

Fear not! He has redeemed us from the grave and has promised us everlasting life. When we come to the end of our rope, He will catch us. And when we come to the end of our lives, He will greet us and welcome us into glory and say, "Child, you are Mine."

Fear not, for I am with you; be not dismayed, for I am your God. I will strengthen you, yes, I will help you, I will uphold you with My righteous right hand.

—ISAIAH 41:10 NKJV

Prayer

Cast your fears before Him. Pray that He will give you the courage to face the circumstances of your life and thank Him for being by your side, for promising to be with you always.

HIGH AND EXALTED

Who is in charge of your life? As Christians, we should allow the most high and exalted God to rule our hearts and guide our thoughts and desires. When we attempt to control our lives, we remove God from the highest place—the throne of our hearts.

Yet it can be so difficult to give God control. We want to see results; we want to step in and affect our destiny; we want to make sure that our needs are met. We're not quite sure this invisible God is concerned about every aspect of our lives. We don't want to bother Him with our needs—especially since we think we're perfectly capable of figuring things out on our own.

While God has given us brains to use, we should always keep in those brains the reality of God's rule in our lives. When we give God His rightful place—high and exalted—the Bible promises that we will "lack nothing" (Psalm 34:9). This is not to say we will get whatever we want whenever we want it. On the contrary, God knows that what we want may be detrimental to us, or that right now isn't the best time for us to have it. Instead, we will never lack what we need.

So exalt God in your life. Place Him at the very center of every activity, every decision, every joy, every sorrow, and every need. After all, that's right where He wants to be.

The LORD is exalted, for he dwells on high.

—ISAIAH 33:5

Prayer

Ask the Lord to take charge of your life.
Give Him the throne of your heart and exalt Him on high.

GOD IS THE STRENGTH
OF MY HEART

Go get your Bible and take the time to read Psalm 73 all the way through. Many people have found the words there to be very comforting—describing exactly how they have felt at one time or another.

The psalmist tells of the struggles within his heart and mind. He can't understand why those who are wicked are also prosperous. He asks if God knows what is going on down here! In verse 13, he wonders if he's been wasting his time, living a life of purity. Indeed, it is hard to understand (or accept!) the prosperity of those who hate the Lord.

But then one day the answer comes to him when he is at prayer. The riches those evil people have exist in this life only. What the psalmist has—what we as Christians have—are riches that will last for eternity. Because we love the Lord, He will guide us all our lives, and afterwards, He will welcome us into the glories of heaven (73:23-24).

Our health may fail, our spirits may droop, and our bank account may be slim, but God remains with us through everything. God is the strength of our hearts. Get as close to Him as you can! It is good to be near the One who remains forever.

My flesh and my heart may fail, but God is the strength of my heart and my portion forever.

—PSALM 73:26

Prayer

Thank the Lord for loving you, for holding your hand,
and for giving you strength. Praise Him
for His presence in your life forever.

IN YOUR PRESENCE, O GOD

In Your presence, O God, that's where we want to be. Yet how do we get into the presence of God? How do we know if we're there?

The fact is, because we are His children and because He loves us, we could not get out of His presence even if we tried. He is with us always.

However, when we run into trouble, we often think that God has left us. We forget that we are constantly in His presence and can trust in His help. When we are weak or scared, we can run to the Rock. When we go through deep waters, we will not drown. When we try to keep our balance in the currents of difficulty, we will not be swept away! When we walk through the fires of oppression, we will not be consumed by the flames.

God is our firm foundation. Even if all of the powers of darkness swirl around us, we are safe. In His presence we are secure. He has called us His own children, and like a loving parent, He is there to comfort and to guide us.

Call upon Him. Enter His presence with joy! In His presence find strength, comfort, joy, safety, and a song that will fill your heart with praise. In His presence is where you belong!

Fear not, for I have redeemed you; I have summoned you by name; you are mine. When you pass through the waters, I will be with you; and when you pass through the rivers, they will not sweep over you. When you walk through the fire, you will not be burned; the flames will not set you ablaze.

—ISAIAH 43:1-2

Prayer

Ask the Lord to help you with the problems that seem
to overwhelm you. Seek His strength, His wisdom,
and His power, and then rest in His presence.

I AM THE GOD THAT HEALETH THEE

She sat in a wheelchair and prayed with all her might. Someone had told her that if she just had "enough faith," she would be able to get up and walk. But try as she might, she remained seated. What of God's promise to heal? The Bible is full of accounts of the healing power of God. When Jesus walked the earth, people were healed by His touch. Why wouldn't He touch her?

The young woman's name is Joni Eareckson Tada, whose story is well known to many. A quadriplegic since a diving accident as a teenager, she became a believer and prayed to be healed. But God had other plans for this marvelous young woman. He began to use her—wheelchair and all—in a worldwide ministry.

When we pray for healing, for ourselves or for those we love, we must remember to pray that God's will be done. Sometimes physical or mental pain will remain no matter how much we ask God to remove it. Living with afflictions often puts believers in the path of others who deal with the same struggles, providing the opportunity to be witnesses for Him.

And what of the promise? Healing has come—for we have been spiritually healed by His death on our behalf. And physical healing will indeed come. When we enter the gates of heaven, we will all be completely healed. Praise the Lord for His healing power!

Praise the LORD, O my soul, and forget not all his benefits—who forgives all your sins and heals all your diseases...He himself bore our sins in his body on the tree, so that we might die to sins and live for righteousness; by his wounds you have been healed.

—PSALM 103:2-3, 1 PETER 2:24

Prayer

If you're praying for healing today—for yourself or for someone you love—humbly ask God to do His will. Ask Him to give you the courage to accept His plans—whether that includes immediate healing or not.

OUR HEART

If our desire really is to see the nations—every race upon the earth—worship the Lord, then we must put that desire into action.

Before Jesus ascended into heaven, He told His disciples to go into all the world and teach others about Himself. Because of the faithfulness of the disciples and those whom they taught and baptized, we know about Jesus today. If the story had not been written down and passed on from one person to the next, from generation to generation, those alive today would not know of the Son of God who came to save us.

Therefore, we must continue to spread the good news. Let us rise in honest worship and declare His matchless worth! Let us share with our family, friends, neighbors, and co-workers the goodness of God—that He came to save us from our sin and break the chains of death. Let us be bold as we intercede for others, claiming His promise.

No power can withstand the greatness of God. When we share His glory, our desire to bring others into the family of God will become active. We will reach all nations and His name will be praised among all peoples of the world.

Send your heart, your prayers, your treasure, and even your very own feet out into the lost world. The Bible asks, "How can they hear without someone preaching to them?" (Romans 10:14). Is that "someone" you?

Therefore go and make disciples of all nations, baptizing them in the name of the Father and of the Son and of the Holy Spirit, and teaching them to obey everything I have commanded you. And surely I am with you always, to the very end of the age.

—MATTHEW 28:19-20

Prayer

Pray that the Lord will make you bold—that your desire to share the good news of His salvation will become action so that others may be led into the family of God.

CAN'T STOP TALKING

There's nothing like an excited new Christian! Someone who has just experienced the joy of being set free from sin has an infectious spirit—he just can't stop talking about what Jesus has done for him.

The Bible tells us the story of a man who was so thankful for what Jesus had done for him that he immediately went out and told people about his experience. The man is not named in Scripture, but he could represent any one of us. He was beyond all human help, yet Jesus set him free. The man was so thankful, he begged Jesus to be allowed to join Him. But Jesus sent the man back to his own hometown and to share what had happened to him. So the man told everyone about the great things Jesus had done for him, and people were awestruck by his story (Mark 5:1-20).

What is your salvation story? Can you boil it down to three minutes and have it ready to tell at a moment's notice? The apostle Peter advises, "Always be prepared to give an answer to everyone who asks you to give the reason for the hope that you have" (1 Peter 3:15).

If someone asked you about your faith, what would you say about the hope that you have?

Jesus did not let him, but said, "Go home to your family and tell them how much the Lord has done for you, and how he has had mercy on you."

—MARK 5:19

Prayer

Think about your story. Write it down. Say it to yourself.
Then ask the Lord to give you opportunities
to share the joy of your faith with others.

CAN YOU BELIEVE

Sometimes joy surprises us—it catches us off guard. When we think about what the Lord has done for us, it's hard to grasp. We get a "can you believe this?" feeling inside.

What God did to save our souls is beyond our ability to comprehend. God, the Creator of the heavens and the earth, loved us so much that He sent His one and only Son to earth. While here, Jesus taught the multitudes about repentance, forgiveness, and love. Then Jesus allowed Himself to be sacrificed for our sins and died a horrible death. He did this willingly. "God demonstrates his own love for us in this: While we were still sinners, Christ died for us" (Romans 5:8).

Not only has He done great things for us, but He also does great things in us. He cleanses us from sin and forgives every wrongdoing in our past. He turns our lives around so we understand how to live a new life and not repeat the mistakes of the past. He lifts us out of the shifting sands of fear, doubt, and worry and sets our feet upon the solid rock of faith.

Sometimes it's hard to believe what He did for us and in us, but we only need to take a look in the mirror and know it is real. Praise the Lord for surprising us with the joy of His salvation!

But if we are living in the light of God's presence, just as Christ is, then we have fellowship with each other, and the blood of Jesus, his Son, cleanses us from every sin.

—1 JOHN 1:7 NLT

Prayer

Thank the Lord for all He has done for you, and for giving you the joy of His salvation. Take a moment to consider what a privilege it is to have been saved by Him.

THOU ART WORTHY, GREAT JEHOVAH

To be "worthy" means to be of great value. When we look at what we hold dear, we need to keep Jesus at the top of that list.

He is worthy of praise (2 Samuel 22:4)—praise that comes from those who value Him above all that this world holds dear. He is worthy to receive all glory, honor, and power (Revelation 4:11) because He is the Creator and Sustainer of everything. He is worthy to break the seals and open the scroll that contains God's plan for the world (Revelation 5:5). He is the only one worthy to do this because He is the only person to ever live a perfect, sinless life. He died for the sins of the world and then showed His power over sin and death by rising from the grave!

Because of His sacrifice, those who love Him are also worthy! He makes us worthy to enter the kingdom of heaven by presenting us with the gift of salvation. "For He has rescued us from the dominion of darkness and brought us into the kingdom of the Son He loves, in whom we have redemption, the forgiveness of sin" (Colossians 1:13-14). And Paul encourages us, "Live a life worthy of the calling you have received" (Ephesians 4:1).

Because He is worthy, we as His heirs are also worthy. Abba, Father, You are worthy!

Worthy is the Lamb, who was slain, to receive power and wealth and wisdom and strength and honor and glory and praise!

—REVELATION 5:12

Prayer

Thank God for the worthiness you have received in Christ. Ask Him to help you to hold Him up in the most valuable and honored place in your life.

TAKE ME IN

In the Old Testament, the most holy place of the temple, the holy of holies, was to be entered only by the high priest, and only once a year in order to sacrifice and atone for the sins of the people (Leviticus 16). God Himself was present there.

God had given very strict rules regarding entrance into the holy of holies. The high priest was to throw handfuls of incense onto a fire, producing a cloud that would obscure any view of God. If anyone looked into the holy of holies, he would die.

But the death of Jesus changed the rules. In fact, at the very moment when His life ended on the cross, the curtain separating the holy of holies from the rest of the temple was torn in two from top to bottom (Matthew 27:51). From that moment on, the barrier between sinful humanity and the holy God was removed.

Where the high priests had to spend hours preparing to enter the presence of the Lord, we can meet God any time, any place. Whenever we desire to see His face, whenever we hunger and thirst for His righteousness, we need only to call out to Him. The blood was shed by the Lamb of God and we are now welcomed into the holy of holies—the presence of the Lord.

Blessed are those who hunger and thirst for righteousness, for they will be filled.

—MATTHEW 5:6

Prayer

Draw near to the holy of holies in prayer.
Ask the Lord to lead you as you seek His righteousness.

EAGLE'S WINGS

Much has been written about the legendary "fountain of youth"—a place where one could sip luscious water and stay young, healthy, and vibrant even into old age.

Who doesn't want to stay young? As we age, we bemoan our aching muscles, our wrinkles, our health issues, our waning strength. We long for the days when we thought we could take on the world. Now we only hope to stay healthy through the long winter.

You know, there's nothing wrong with aging. In fact, the Bible sees it as a great blessing. Proverbs 16:31 says, "Gray hair is a crown of splendor." Psalm 71:18 records the prayer of one who is old and gray as he desires to declare God's power to the next generation. The Bible acknowledges the changes of old age but honors the wisdom and experience that replace the strength and vigor of youth.

If you're among the aged today, honor God with your experience and your wisdom. Pass along your faith to the next generation. Despite the aches and pains of your aging body, you can have your youth renewed by continuing to do the work God still calls you to do.

If you're still among the youthful, thank God for your health. Serve Him with your vigor. In addition, honor the wise older believers in your family and at your church. Ask them about their faith; encourage them to share what God has done for them. Then be ready to listen!

Praise the Lord, O my soul...who satisfies your desires with good things so that your youth is renewed like the eagle's.

—PSALM 103:2, 5

Prayer

Talk to the Lord about your age. Ask Him to teach you how to be His servant no matter how old or young you are.

IN YOUR PRESENCE

Exceeding—to go beyond the limits. Abundance—a plentiful or overflowing supply.

In His presence, we find an exceeding abundance of joy. So much that we cannot begin to take it in. He surrounds us with limitless love, mercy, and forgiveness. The earth is plentiful and supplies all of our needs. In His goodness and love, He created all that we enjoy from the earth.

What more could we ask for? He has provided for us exceedingly and abundantly. And then, on top of that, He tells us to enjoy His provision.

So enjoy! Take in the sunset. Feel the wind whipping through your hair. Marvel at the smile of your child. Revel in the sweetness of a blueberry pie. Let your feet sink into the sand and let the waves lap at your legs. Smell the luscious aroma of a rose. Hug your friends. Laugh at the good jokes. Thank the Lord for all in life that He has given you to enjoy—and enjoy!

Now to Him who is able to do exceedingly abundantly above all that we ask or think, according to the power that works in us, to Him be glory in the church by Christ Jesus to all generations, forever and ever. Amen.

—EPHESIANS 3:20-21 NKJV

Prayer

Thank the Lord for filling you with joy and surrounding
you with His goodness exceedingly and abundantly.

SUCH JOY

Sometimes we just wish we could control everything around us. Control our spouse, control our kids, control our boss, control our physical bodies, control our church, control the world! If we could just be put in charge, we could make everything just right. But give us that much control and we'd soon find ourselves in a big mess—out of control.

Without Christ in our lives, however, we are left with way too much to try to control. Imagine having to make the big decisions of life without any recourse except the advice of friends and our own limited understanding and knowledge. Contrast that with our being able to talk to the God of the universe who knows the future, who loves us, and promises to guide us. Suddenly being in control doesn't seem quite so important.

What we need, instead, is Spirit-control. And as the song says, "There's a peace that floods my soul when the Spirit of the Lord is in control." Like a stuffy room in which the windows are thrown open to let in the spring air, the Spirit blows a fresh wind through our souls. When we open our hands and release control of our lives, He brings His unspeakable joy, everlasting peace, and pure and holy love.

So don't seek to be in control; seek to have "Spirit-control." You'll find your greatest peace when you let go and let God.

Though you have not seen him, you love him; and even though you do not see him now, you believe in him and are filled with an inexpressible and glorious joy.

—1 PETER 1:8

Prayer

Ask the Lord to help you identify the areas of your life where you feel the need to control. Then let go of them—give them over to Him.

HE IS THE KING OF KINGS

Jesus is often referred to as our Friend, our Brother, and our Savior. While He is all of these, He is also a King—the King—and we must not forget the importance of that title.

The word "king" brings many visions to the mind's eye. A king is responsible for his nation. A king sits in judgment over the deeds of others. A king protects his people from invaders. A king solves the problems of his people. A king is powerful and mighty.

Where many kings on earth, in the past and today, failed miserably at one or more of their responsibilities, we know that there is one King who will live up to all of the expectations we can place upon kingship. That is why He is called "King of kings."

Our King will never let us down. He is always there to guard our hearts, protecting us from attempted invasions by the armies of Satan. He judges us by the law, but is always willing to forgive us when we ask. Our King exudes power and might. No one is powerful enough to stand against Him.

Praise the Lord that we can approach the throne of the King and know that He will always forgive our sins and protect us from evil. He is the King of kings!

God, the blessed and only Ruler, the King of kings and Lord of lords, who alone is immortal and who lives in unapproachable light, whom no one has seen or can see. To him be honor and might forever. Amen.

—1 TIMOTHY 6:15-16

Prayer

Thank Jesus for being more than a brother, more than a friend—thank Him for being your Savior and King.

REJOICE FOR THE STEPS

Imagine taking a long journey without a map. We wouldn't dream of just getting on the road, driving aimlessly, and hoping to get to our destination. Instead, we follow the map and watch for the right crossroads. If we get lost, we can search the map and get back on track.

As Christians, we're all on the road of life taking our different paths. Some of us will take a more scenic route, some of us will find ourselves driving through deserts, others are in the mountains. But we all have the same destination—we're seeking to obey God and become more like Christ. So we need to follow a map— and that map is God's Word. The Bible contains directions for the journey of life. Sometimes we're too proud to ask for directions or we decide we want to go our own way. Then, when we are hopelessly lost, miles from the nearest paved road, and the rain begins, suddenly we realize that if we had just consulted the map, we wouldn't be in such a jam.

Are you lost today? Not sure where you're going? The steps of righteous people are ordered of God. Check out the map and follow the directions daily. When you do, you're sure to reach your destination.

The steps of the godly are directed by the LORD. He delights in every detail of their lives.

—PSALM 37:23 NLT

Prayer

Ask the Lord for His guidance. Pray that He
will uphold, preserve, and sustain you as
you follow His direction for your life.

THE NAME OF THE LORD

Different towers are built for different purposes. Some are for keeping watch, such as the fire towers that stand throughout America's national forests. Other towers are for providing a point of reference on a landscape, such as the lighthouses that dot the shores of our oceans and the Great Lakes.

These towers are necessary for the safety of many people. Without them, fires would go unnoticed until they burn uncontrollably; ships would be lost or would run aground without the light to guide them.

It is no coincidence, then, that the Lord is compared to a tower. In ancient times, towers were placed on the corners of walled cities. Lookouts could see great distances and warn the people inside the city when an unfriendly army was approaching. Those outside the city would have time to find safety within the walls, even as the army of that city could be assembled for battle.

The Lord is our tower—the place to which we run when we need protection, the light that guides us through the darkness. Then, when we've seen the advancing enemy, we can burst forth from the tower and claim victory, as only the army of the Lord can do!

The name of the LORD is a strong tower; the righteous run to it and are safe.

—PROVERBS 18:10

Prayer

Thank the Lord for being your place of refuge, the strong
tower to which you can run and prepare to do battle.
Ask Him to guide you to victory.

FROM THE RISING OF THE SUN

Our days are hectic—full of appointments, tasks, and deadlines—from the rising of the sun to the going down of the same. From the moment we roll out of bed in the morning until we roll back in at night, we are on the go. How in the world are we to find time to praise?

Yet the author of this psalm reminds us that we must praise God all day long. Now and then won't suffice. From the rising of the sun to when it sets—that's all day long—the Lord's name is to be praised. When we keep our minds focused on Him, the day will go more smoothly. When we remember to praise Him for the things He has done for us and for what He has given us, complaining and griping don't have a chance!

Begin the day with praise. Thank the Lord for another day in which to live and work, to spend time with family and friends, to share His love. Praise Him all the day long for everything from the minute (an empty parking space near the front door) to the grand (a loved one recovering from an illness). Let His praises permeate your thoughts, words, and actions.

Praise the Lord from this time forth, and forevermore!

Blessed be the name of the LORD from this time forth and for evermore. From the rising of the sun unto the going down of the same the LORD'S name is to be praised.

—PSALM 113:2-3 KJV

Prayer

Ask the Lord to make Himself evident to you
throughout the day that you may begin to
build a habit of praising Him all day long.

I SEE THE LORD

There is so much about God that we don't know. The Bible gives us an amazing account of everything He has done, from the creation of the world to the life, death, and resurrection of Jesus. We even have a glimpse into the future. The Bible gives us so much, and yet our view of God is still hazy and blurred. Our human minds cannot comprehend His glory.

How awesome, then, is the thought that someday we will see Him face to face. He will be seated on the throne of heaven and will appear in all His majesty and power. Revelation 4 describes how beautiful, and yet how terrifying, the throne room of God will be. His throne is made of precious gems and from it come flashes of lightning and the rumble of thunder.

The train of His robe fills the heavens. His eyes are full of fire, He shines like the sun. His voice is like the waters. Can you picture it? Can you hear it? Even the greatest artist could not do this scene justice. For now, we are bound by human experience. Then, we will see heaven with new eyes and everything will be made clear.

Join with the thousands in singing, "Holy, holy, holy is the Lord God Almighty." His splendor is magnificent beyond imagination. But, praise be to God, someday we will see Him face to face.

In the same way, we can see and understand only a little about God now, as if we were peering at His reflection in a poor mirror, but someday we are going to see Him in his completeness, face to face. Now all that I know is hazy and blurred, but then I will see everything clearly, just as clearly as God sees into my heart right now.

—1 CORINTHIANS 13:12 TLB

Prayer

Meditate on God's holiness. Think about His beauty and power. Try to picture in your mind what it will one day be like to stand face to face with your Savior and Lord.

LET GOD ARISE

Sometimes we become so wrapped up in what we don't have that we forget all of the blessings we do have. When a job is hard to find or we don't have the money for the little extras that we think will make us happy, we become unhappy, maybe even angry or jealous of those who have more.

Discontent, anger, and jealousy—these are the enemies of joy. It is difficult to be happy—to rejoice in the Lord—when those enemies invade our hearts. We need to be content and thankful with what we have been blessed with. The high-profile job might not be ours, but we will be able to pay the bills and provide for our family's basic needs by waiting tables. We might not be able to pay for summer camp, but we can spend time with our family at the local park. Others may have more things than us, but are things really that important?

Let God arise in your heart and mind and remove the enemies that drive away your joy. Be thankful for all He has given you—His love, forgiveness, and eternal life. You may not have all of the physical things you desire, but those things will pass away. The love of family, friends, and your Savior is eternal.

May God arise, may his enemies be scattered; may his foes flee before him...Sing to God, sing praise to his name, extol him who rides on the clouds—his name is the LORD—and rejoice before him.

—PSALM 68:1, 4

Prayer

Think about the many blessings you have received
from God. Thank Him and ask Him to help
you to be content with all you have been given.

GOD IS MY REFUGE

The future. What will happen tomorrow, next week, or a decade down the road is anybody's guess. But not knowing shouldn't upset Christians. God knows our fears, but more importantly, God knows our future.

God will never give you more than you can handle. Therefore, you can trust that God will give you a future that will be fit for you. The future may not be easy or pleasant, but God will give you the strength to endure any trial.

The Living Bible puts it this way: "We need not fear even if the world blows up and the mountains crumble into the sea...The Commander of the heavenly armies is among us. He, the God of Jacob, has come to rescue us!" (Psalm 46:2, 11). What a promise! We need not fear even the utter destruction of the earth. God is our refuge! God is our strength!

Whatever the future may hold—a new job, moving to a new town, the loss of people or things you hold dear—never forget that God is your refuge and strength. When you are in trouble, when you begin to fear what lies ahead, trust in His unfailing love for you. His blessings and promises run deeper than any trial.

God is our refuge and strength, an ever-present help in trouble. Therefore we will not fear, though the earth give way and the mountains fall into the heart of the sea.

—PSALM 46:1-2

Prayer

Come before the Lord with your fears about the future.
Ask Him to remind you to run to the refuge of
His love whenever you face doubt or uncertainty.
He is your ever-present help in troubled times.

MAKE A JOYFUL NOISE

When my three daughters are playing together—at least in those moments when they're all getting along—the cacophony brings laughter to my heart. It is indeed a joyful noise! In fact, I worry most when it is quiet. That surely means trouble is afoot. When my oldest daughter (then age six) used her daddy's beard trimmer to cut her sister's (age four) hair, it was indeed very quiet—at least until I discovered what had happened!

God loves our joyful noise! He loves it when we sing and clap our hands. Of course the times of quiet are good for our souls, but so are the times when rejoicing bubbles to the top of our spirits and we can't help but declare the goodness of God and the attributes of His character.

Sure, we can sing along with the worship leader on Sunday morning or with the CD in the car stereo. But when the song of praise reaches into our souls and lifts us to the Rock that is higher, we can enter into fellowship with God. We worship not just with our mouths, but with our whole beings. The joyful noise coming from the hearts of His people is evidence of our gratefulness for all He has done for us. Don't stay quiet. Make a joyful noise unto the Lord!

Sing to the LORD, all the earth; proclaim his salvation day after day. Declare his glory among the nations, his marvelous deeds among all peoples. For great is the LORD and most worthy of praise; he is to be feared above all gods.

—1 CHRONICLES 16:23-25

Prayer

Give thanks to God for bringing joy to your life. Praise Him with your whole heart and ask for His blessing upon you.

HALLELUJAH TO THE LAMB

I don't generally like crowds. Living on Long Island gives us ample opportunity to visit the wonders and excitement of New York City, but besides the annual anniversary celebration, my husband and I don't often make the trip. Some people are energized by crowds; we prefer the quiet and solitude of the seashore.

There is one crowd I'm looking forward to joining, however, and this song sings about it. I look forward to standing in the midst of the multitude of believers from all over the world as we bow before our Savior!

We are His people, redeemed by His blood. We will stand with the multitude, with Christians from every tribe and every nation, praising God in every language. We who were rescued from death will lift our voices in thanks to our Lord and Savior. What an awesome chorus that will be! I love to sing—and I can hardly wait to sing with that multitude and all the angels of heaven, giving praise to Jesus Christ, the Lamb of God.

Hallelujah to the Lamb! He is worthy to be praised, our Lamb of God, our Rescuer, our Redeemer. Give Him the praise forever and ever!

After this I looked and there before me was a great multitude that no one could count, from every nation, tribe, people and language, standing before the throne and in front of the Lamb. They were wearing white robes and were holding palm branches in their hands. And they cried out in a loud voice: "Salvation belongs to our God, who sits on the throne, and to the Lamb."

—REVELATION 7:9-10

Prayer

If you have not done so before now, bow before Him and confess your sins. Thank Him for being your sacrifice and accept His gift of grace and Lordship of your life. Then you can join that glorious multitude in heaven!

JESUS, YOU ARE WELCOME

There are certain things we do—and don't do—when we are expecting guests. Most of us try to tidy up our home, maybe even dust the furniture and sweep the floors. If the guests are staying for an extended period, we give them a room in our home with fresh linens on the bed. But most importantly, we make them feel welcome.

When we attend church, we attempt to make each other feel welcome; we extend a greeting to visitors; we catch up with our friends. The church is like a home to us with a big extended family. We feel welcome, and we in turn seek to make others feel welcome.

But does Jesus feel welcome there? Have we noted His presence with us? Have we entered His place of worship and invited Him to join us there? After all, we have gathered to worship Him. He is the special guest who sits in every pew, speaks to every heart, and listens to the praises of each one of us.

Enter your church service with an open heart, inviting Jesus to fill you with His presence. Remember to welcome Him into your heart and into your worship. Give Him the honor of a special guest and tell Him that you welcome His presence. Then join with the rest of your family and friends as you bless His holy name!

As God has said: "I will live with them and walk among them, and I will be their God, and they will be my people."

—2 CORINTHIANS 6:16

Prayer

Invite Jesus to be your honored guest in your heart—
tell Him He is welcome there.

EVERY MOVE I MAKE

My husband is an avid runner. Not your run-of-the-mill type runner. No, he's the every day, on the road, marathon-training sort of runner. He also teaches about physical training. He'll be the first to tell you that you need to have a plan. You won't be able to do a few stretches at the starting line of a marathon and think that, without training, you can finish it. You need to learn the mechanics of running, training different muscles, eating right, wearing the right clothing and shoes, and even breathing correctly. In fact, if you're going to be really good, you have to take running and competing to the level of an art form. You must be committed to the running "lifestyle."

You see, our bodies are amazing. The more I learn, the more I'm amazed at what intricate creatures we are. We have been created by a loving God—we are not accidents of evolution. When God breathed the breath of life into the first man, the Bible tells us he "became a living being" (Genesis 1:7). We owe our very existence to our Creator. Every move we make, every breath we take is ours because of His loving breath on our lives.

Maybe you won't run a marathon—but you probably have a busy schedule that will keep you running today. Thank the Lord for breath and life. Ask Him to be with you every step of the way. Ask Him to show you how to make that dependence upon Him your lifestyle.

It is God who arms me with strength and makes my way perfect. He makes my feet like the feet of a deer; he enables me to stand on the heights...You broaden the path beneath me, so that my ankles do not turn.

—PSALM 18:32-33, 36

Prayer

Ask the Lord to help you to walk in His way.
Commit to learning what it takes to be dependent upon
Him every moment of every day, for every breath you take.

WE WILL RIDE

*I*n the book of Revelation, Jesus is often referred to as the Lamb—the One who was sacrificed for the sins of all. But when the end draws near, Jesus appears not as a Lamb, but as a warrior on a white horse. He is coming back as a conqueror and King!

Where will your heart be when He returns? Will your heart be His that you may join with the armies of heaven? Will you be taking part in the marriage feast when Jesus calls His bride (the Church) to join Him? If your sins were forgiven by the Lamb of God, then your heart belongs to the King of kings, the rider on the white horse.

Christians can look forward to the return of the King because we are His people! But until then, we must take up the sword of truth and be bold in telling others about Jesus. We must be willing to share His love and the way of salvation. We are soldiers in the army of God; we can't afford to go through life acting as if we are not! Those whose lives we touch each day must be given the chance to know Him too. Some will be willing to join with the army of heaven; some will not. But they must be given the choice.

As for us, we can sing out, "Yes, Lord, yes!" We will ride with Him and we will fight the final battle in which all evil will be defeated forever. Hallelujah to the Lamb! Hallelujah to the King!

I saw heaven standing open and there before me was a white horse, whose rider is called Faithful and True. With justice he judges and makes war...The armies of heaven were following him, riding on white horses and dressed in fine linen, white and clean.

—REVELATION 19:11, 14

Prayer

Pray that the Lord will make you a true warrior of faith.
Ask that He will make you strong in sharing His salvation
with others. Tell Him "yes," you'll ride with Him.

COME INTO THE HOLY OF HOLIES

The holy of holies (also called the Most Holy Place) was a room in the tabernacle, and later in the temple, separated by a curtain. Behind this curtain was the Ark of the Covenant where God Himself dwelt. This room was to be entered only by the high priest, and then only once a year on the Day of Atonement when he would offer a sacrifice for the sins of the entire nation.

When Jesus became the sacrifice for all, there was no longer the need for a high priest to sacrifice for us. The curtain that had separated the holy of holies was torn in half on the day Jesus died (Matthew 27:51). His shed blood allows all who believe to come into the presence of God at any time—not just once a year.

As believers, we are privileged to have immediate personal access to God through His Son, Jesus. No one can come to the Father except through Jesus. The blood of the Lamb has cleansed us and given us the blessing of worshiping before the throne of God. We can now boldly enter the holy of holies and go right into God's presence.

Praise the Creator, Redeemer, King of kings. He has made a way for us and has given us access to God. Join with the redeemed and come into the holy of holies. The blood of the Lamb has made it possible—for you!

And so, dear brothers and sisters, we can boldly enter heaven's Most Holy Place because of the blood of Jesus...Let us go right into the presence of God, with true hearts fully trusting him.

—HEBREWS 10:19, 22 NLT

Prayer

Thank God for giving you a way to reach Him through His Son, Jesus Christ. Praise Him for giving you entrance into the holy of holies by covering your sins with the blood of the Lamb.

LET YOUR GLORY FALL

Worship time in church means different things to different people. For some, the singing of beloved hymns accompanied by a pipe organ and a choir is true worship. For others, singing choruses accompanied by a band of musicians with a trumpet, electric guitar, and drum set is the epitome of worship.

Whatever music style you may choose, when your congregation comes together praising the Lord in song, God is there. When we come together in one voice to thank the Lord for what He has done, the glory of the Lord will fill the place, just as it did when Solomon dedicated the temple.

So get involved in your worship time. You are entering a great tradition stretching back through the centuries. Listen carefully to the words. Even if you personally don't like the old hymns or if you can't quite get used to the drumbeat, open your heart to God. Thank Him for songwriters and musicians who put into words praise for God's goodness, love, mercy, forgiveness, and strength.

No matter how you worship, whatever your method of praise, the Lord accepts it all—from the a cappella choir to the orchestra. When we unite in thanking and glorifying God, His glory will fall upon us!

The trumpeters and singers joined in unison, as with one voice, to give praise and thanks to the LORD. Accompanied by trumpets, cymbals and other instruments, they raised their voices in praise to the LORD and sang: "He is good; his love endures forever."...Then the temple of the LORD was filled with a cloud, and the priests could not perform their service because of the cloud, for the glory of the LORD filled the temple of God.

—2 CHRONICLES 5:13-14

Prayer

Begin your prayer by thanking God, by worshiping
His holiness. Then the way will be clear for you
to bring your needs and concerns before Him.

WE WILL WAIT

History is filled with the names of people who, even after failing again and again, achieved great successes. Abraham Lincoln, Orville and Wilbur Wright, Albert Einstein, Benjamin Franklin, and Thomas Edison are just the tip of the iceberg. What they all had in common was that they never gave up. They pressed on toward their goals. Their discoveries and inventions are widely known—their failures are largely forgotten.

For Christians, our ultimate goal is life in heaven. While still here on earth, we sometimes become weary. When we see injustices or face persecution, we become weak. It's not always easy to be a Christian.

But God has made us a promise. Our troubles are not hidden from Him. He understands the human condition far deeper than we can comprehend. He is the Creator, the everlasting God, and He never grows tired or weary. No matter how many times we fail, stumble, or fall, if our hope is in the Lord, He will renew our strength. That is His promise to us.

Wait upon the Lord. He will give the strength to be witnesses for Him and to face the harsh words of those who don't believe. He will forgive our failures and renew our ability to serve Him. We can accomplish much for Him in the time we have been given. He is faithful to remember our successes and forget our failures. Thanks to Him, we can mount up with wings like eagles, soaring into His presence with joy.

But they that wait upon the Lord shall renew their strength. They shall mount up with wings like eagles; they shall run and not be weary; they shall walk and not faint.

—ISAIAH 40:31 TLB

Prayer

Thank the Lord for His promise to renew your strength when you are weary, and for loving you enough to forgive you when you fail.

THINK ABOUT HIS LOVE

In a live-in discipleship program in downtown Los Angeles, the disciples meet in a large square room for worship each day. One by one, they step up to the front of the room and lead the rest of the group in a single worship song—no music, no instruments, just voices raised in praise.

Some of the voices are weary—they're in the process of leaving addictions behind. Some are tough—years on the street have hardened them. Sometimes the words and rhythms are modified to fit the surroundings a little better: "Think about His goodness— *yeah.*" But what is heard above the voices and the words is the powerful message of God's amazing, transforming love.

As we reflect on God's goodness, on the many things His grace has brought us through, we know that His love has the power to transform lives. We know that our weary souls can find healing, and that we can receive strength to care for a weary world.

Great is the measure of our Father's healing, life-altering love.

And may you have the power to understand, as all God's people should, how wide, how long, how high, and how deep his love really is. May you experience the love of Christ, though it is so great you will never fully understand it. Then you will be filled with the fullness of life and power that comes from God.

—EPHESIANS 3:18-19 NLT

Prayer

Take a minute to remember the ways God's love has changed you. Then spend a few minutes thanking Him, and another few minutes asking Him to give You opportunities to share His love with others.

EAGLE'S WINGS

On lots of occasions, we find ourselves waiting for something—a test result, a tax return, a family member who's taking her time at the grocery store. Waiting is something we all have to do from time to time.

That doesn't mean waiting is easy, especially when we're waiting for something we desperately need, those times when we're waiting for God to intervene and rescue us. And in every long wait, we reach a frightening point when we start to wonder if what we're waiting for will ever really happen. Will this relationship ever be repaired? Will that financial need ever be met?

But no matter how long we've been waiting, we can rest assured that God's promises will come to pass. When we pray for provision and for relief from anxiety, He promises to meet our needs and give us peace. When we pray for wisdom, He promises to provide it.

Best of all, while we're waiting, He promises us His presence, that He will indeed come live within us each day of our lives.

Those who hope in the Lord will renew their strength.
They will soar on wings like eagles;
they will run and not grow weary,
they will walk and not be faint.

—ISAIAH 40:31

Prayer

What are you waiting on the Lord for today? As you remember
His past goodness to you, pray a prayer of surrender,
inviting Him to fill you and be in charge in your life.

ALL THINGS ARE POSSIBLE

When the rich young ruler came to Jesus, he was looking for something—urgently. He wanted eternal life, and he ran to Jesus and fell at His feet in pursuit of it.

"You know the commandments," Jesus replied, and the rich young replied that he had done all those things. Jesus, moved with compassion, told him to sell everything he had and give it to the poor, and then come and follow Him. And the young man turned away.

Then Jesus delivered His famous "eye of a needle" analogy: It was easier, He said, for a camel to squeeze its way through the eye of a needle than for a rich man to enter the kingdom of God. Practically impossible.

The disciples were shocked—if the rich, who were traditionally considered blessed by God, couldn't enter the kingdom, who stood a chance?

"With man this is impossible," He said, "but not with God; all things are possible with God" (10:27).

Nothing is impossible for God. Someone who seems impossibly beyond hope is well within His reach. When we come to Him desperately seeking something, we can know that He is more than able to meet our need. And when what we need is a heart change like the rich young ruler, we can know that He is more than able to accomplish that too.

Ah, Lord GOD! Behold, You have made the heavens and the earth by Your great power and outstretched arm. There is nothing too hard for You.

—JEREMIAH 32:17 NKJV

Prayer

What are you waiting on the Lord for today? As you remember His past goodness to you, pray a prayer of surrender, inviting Him to fill you and be in charge in your life.

GIVE YOU MY HEART

When thirteen-year-old Daniel met Jonathan, he met a man who had been through a lot. Jonathan had overcome drug addiction, dealt with the grief of losing his brother, and daily battled the mirror since losing his eye as a teenager. Daniel desperately wanted to lighten Jonathan's burden—how could he make a difference in his life?

Daniel gave Jonathan every penny he had in savings, about two hundred dollars—and then raised the rest of the money Jonathan would need to get a glass eye.

What made Daniel's gift so special was that he gave everything he could, and then gave more. He gave *deeply*. He gave from his heart.

When we set out to follow Jesus, He calls us to give no less sacrificially. He even makes the hard statement that "Anyone who loves his father or mother more than me is not worthy of me; anyone who loves his son or daughter more than me is not worth of me; and anyone who does not take his cross and follow me is not worthy of me" (Matthew 10:37-38).

But Jesus also promises us that "whoever loses his life for my sake will find it" (10:39). What's more, when we give our whole heart to Jesus, we experience the awesome privilege of knowing Him, of having Him take on our burdens. His yoke is easy; His burden is light.

What a sweet thing it is to say to Jesus, "Have Your way in me."

Whoever finds his life will lose it, and whoever loses his life for my sake will find it.

—MATTHEW 10:39

Prayer

As you prepare to pray, "Lord, I give You my heart," think
about all the things that make Jesus worthy of receiving
your heart, and praise Him for those things.

GREAT IS THE LORD

"Great" can be a somewhat vague word. The Grand Canyon is great in its expansive and rugged beauty. An A-plus paper might have "Great!" scrawled across the top in red ink. Sometimes we say "great" when we don't mean it at all: "Another flat tire? *Great.*"

So when we say that the Lord is great, it's easy to forget what that means. The psalmist declares that God's mercy is great (Psalm 4:7), that His compassion is great (51:1), and that His strength is great (66:3). God is great in His power over the world He created: "O LORD my God, you are very great...He makes the clouds his chariot and rides on the wings of the wind" (Psalm 104:1, 3).

In Isaiah, we find that the people of Israel are encouraged to praise God's greatness when He forgives and saves and comforts them (12:6). And in Luke, the angel tells Mary that her Son "will be great and will be called the Son of the Most High" (1:32).

When we sing songs about His greatness, we'll truly understand the words we're singing when we remember all the things about Him that make Him great—His great love, His great compassion, the greatness of His saving work. Our Lord is truly great and worthy of praise.

Great are the works of the LORD;
they are pondered by all who delight in them.
Glorious and majestic are his deeds,
and his righteousness endures forever.

—PSALM 111:2-3

Prayer

How is God great in your life today? How do you need Him
to reveal His greatness? Praise His great qualities today.

BE GLORIFIED

We all know the feeling of desire, of anticipating something so much that it's all we can think about. A job promotion. The birth of our first child. A double tall caramel latte.

Jesus desired something too: He lived and breathed to establish God's kingdom. When He predicted His death—the very event which would bring about the kingdom—He expressed sorrow. But then He said, "What shall I say? 'Father, save me from this hour'? No, it was for this very reason I came to this hour. Father, glorify your name!"

Jesus' desire was to glorify the Father. He was single-minded in that pursuit. And if He is our model, we must adopt that goal as well. So how do we get our hearts to beat in time with His—how do we cultivate a desire to glorify the Father that's so strong it's all we can think about?

It may not happen overnight. The longer we follow Jesus, the more we become caught up in His agenda. The more time we spend reflecting on His works and words, the more we find ourselves looking for things to do for the Kingdom, for ways to glorify the Father—in our lives and in our songs of praise.

I will praise God's name in song
and glorify him with thanksgiving.

—PSALM 69:30

Prayer

Ask God to fill you with a desire to glorify
Him in every aspect of your life.

Index

More Devotionals Available from Integrity Publishers

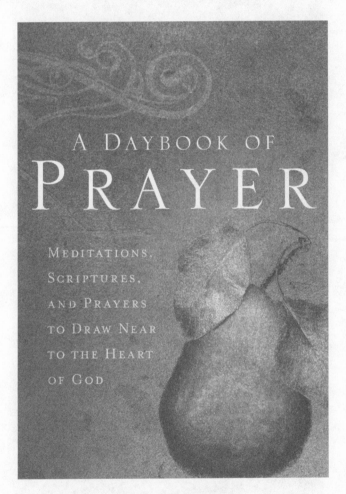

A DAYBOOK OF
PRAYER

MEDITATIONS,
SCRIPTURES,
AND PRAYERS
TO DRAW NEAR
TO THE HEART
OF GOD

A Daybook of Prayer
ISBN: 1-59145-476-X

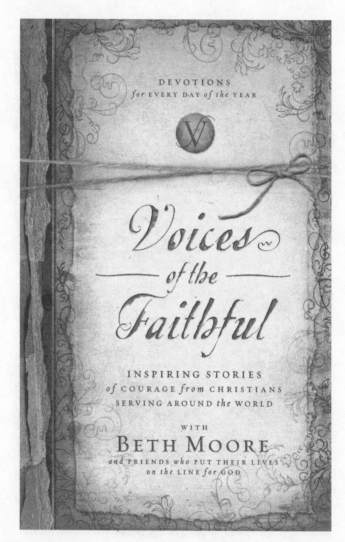

DEVOTIONS
for EVERY DAY *of the* YEAR

V

Voices
— *of the* —
Faithful

INSPIRING STORIES
of COURAGE *from* CHRISTIANS
SERVING AROUND *the* WORLD

WITH
BETH MOORE
and FRIENDS *who* PUT THEIR LIVES
on the LINE *for* GOD

Voices of the Faithful
ISBN: 1-59145-364-X